# Russia's Last
# Capitalists

# Russia's Last Capitalists:

*The Nepmen, 1921–1929*

Alan M. Ball

UNIVERSITY OF CALIFORNIA PRESS
*Berkeley • Los Angeles • London*

University of California Press
Berkeley and Los Angeles, California

University of California Press, Ltd.
London, England

**Library of Congress Cataloging-in-Publication Data**
Ball, Alan M.
  Russia's last capitalists.

  Bibliography: p.
  Includes index.
  1. Soviet Union—Economic policy—1917–1928.
I. Title.
HC335.2.B33 / 1987      338.947      86.14662
ISBN 0–520–07174–3 (alk. paper)

Printed in the United States of America

1  2  3  4  5  6  7  8  9

The paper used in this publication meets the minimum requirements of the
American National Standard for Information Services—Permanence of Paper
for Printed Library Materials, ANSI Z39.48–1984.

# Contents

# List of Tables

# Preface to the Paperback Edition

On March 6, 1990, the Supreme Soviet repudiated a long-standing taboo and voted 350 to 3 to grant citizens the right to own "means of production." The legislators also approved private ownership of small-scale commercial enterprises, prompting some in the hall to describe their work as a return to the New Economic Policy (NEP) of the 1920s. The parallels with NEP may be more numerous, and less encouraging, than they realized. Apart from the obvious similarity—enlisting private economic endeavor to help revive a moribund economy—the new law contains hints of the same sentiments that proved fatal to NEP sixty years ago. A majority of delegates, for example, still found the term "private property" ideologically offensive and substituted the less objectionable "citizen's property" in their legislation. Similarly, while the law provides new protection against confiscation of entrepreneurial property, it also bans in sweeping terms "the exploitation of man by man"—a formula brandished at the end of the 1920s in the drive to "liquidate the new bourgeoisie." As some deputies noted, it remains to be seen which of the bill's features, if any, officials throughout the country will decide to promote.

The Supreme Soviet's handiwork is by no means the only step taken by Mikhail Gorbachev to revitalize the nation's economy by harnessing private initiative. Three years ago he encouraged citizens to form "cooperatives." Institutions of this name, familiar in the 1920s as units in a state-dominated network, are today essentially private operations—the label "cooperative" an ideological fig leaf like the term "citizen's property." From 1987 to early 1990, cooperatives mushroomed to the point where, according to *Izvestiia,* they now employ 5.5 million people. Moscow alone contains approximately 15,000 cooperatives, and they have branched into areas far removed from the customary sale of food and clothing. There are cooperative banks, insurance agencies, excursion bureaus, lawyers' associations, hotels, software designers, scrap metal processors, lavatories, and taxis, to name just a few of the diverse ventures. Though most are small, some employ hundreds of people. These cooperatives are widely and correctly regarded as private concerns by citizens and officials alike. Their fortunes over the past few years thus anticipate the prospects and problems facing the Supreme Soviet's new legislation.

The proliferation of cooperatives in turn echoes the legalization and flourishing of private trade during NEP. While the two eras have significant differences—including the state's much larger share of the economy today—the cooperatives' recent experience and behavior bear striking similarities to the events described in this book. Just as in the 1920s, for example, mixed signals from Moscow indicate that the central government is not certain how far and how rapidly to encourge private enterprise. A draft law bestowed on cooperatives "social significance equal to that of factory and office workers," and Gorbachev called them "an equal component part of the single national-economic complex of the country." But before the draft law had graduated to a page in the statute volumes, the Ministry of Finance announced in the spring of 1988 a severe new income tax on cooperatives. An outcry from reformers forced a reduction of the tax, and subsequent decrees have failed to strike a consistent note. New ventures receive official permission at the same time that ministries ban or restrict other activities—notably medical, film, publishing, and video establishments—previously tolerated.

By 1989 the central government had given local authorities a freer hand to regulate cooperatives, and in many regions the hand formed a fist. Provincial officials often bristled at the new enterprises, which they claimed (as did their counterparts in the 1920s) corrupted government employees with bribes, drove up prices, and disrupted agricultural deliveries to the state. Thus in numerous cities and towns, even before 1989, Party chairmen sought to throttle cooperatives without casting themselves too prominently as foes of *perestroika*. They dragged out the registration of new businesses, subjected those in existence to withering regulatory scrutiny, withheld supplies, froze bank accounts, and raised taxes. Whatever the provisions in the Law on Cooperatives, a public prosecutor explained, "We must look further and deeper. Why should we blindly abide by a law which is not in people's interests?" In 1989, over one thousand cooperatives were liquidated in Krasnodar Territory during a campaign promoted by the chairman of the region's executive committee: "Enough empty talk! We are on the offensive. My people have the right to know who is robbing them. As long as I live I will have no mercy on speculators and grabbers."

Along with frequent policy shifts in Moscow and harassment at the local level, cooperatives face a decidedly ambivalent public. So did the Nepmen, and for much the same reasons. Ever since the 1920s, no one could deny that private traders offered many goods and services superior to those available (or unavailable) in the state sector. At the same time, many resented (and still resent) the higher prices commonly charged by private/cooperative merchants. Cooperatives are often regarded as speculative parasites, reselling scarce products with large markups rather than producing anything themselves—in the process aggravating shortages of inexpensive goods in state stores. The large incomes of some cooperatives, widely reported in the press, inflame hostility toward those whose ambition has taken them above the general population's living standard, a reaction whose roots in Russian society stretch back centuries.

Animosity finds expression in numerous channels, including the indifference of many citizens (and police) to organized crime preying on cooperatives. In Chita an officer of the local garrison became something of a folk hero after he shot two people associated with a cooperative. Public opinion polls, more numerous and comprehensive than in the 1920s, leave no doubt as to the strength of popular distaste. Questions phrased most broadly—"Do you agree that individuals should be able to set up their own enterprises in the Soviet Union?"—tend to receive a more positive response than queries focused on existing private undertakings. But even the general propositions on personal enterprise commonly find a third or more of the respondents opposed. Regarding cooperatives specifically, a nationwide survey conducted in the autumn of 1989 recorded approximately half the sample in disapproval. Only a quarter supported the ventures, and the rest offered no opinion.

In the years since 1987, with the economy deteriorating and shortages growing ever more pervasive, aversion to cooperatives appears to have intensified. A Soviet legislator sensed the tide: "Shouts are heard from all sides: 'Life is becoming worse! Do something!' . . . One needs an 'enemy image' as a scapegoat. Now there is such an enemy [the cooperatives]." At the Supreme Soviet's session late in 1989, more than one speaker punctuated his attack on cooperatives with a leading observation that earlier, when stores still contained essential products, the cooperatives did not exist. This presentation of cooperatives as a central cause of hard times has been promoted vigorously by some local officials, perhaps from conviction, but in any case attempting to discredit *perestroika*. Cooperatives, after all, are linked clearly—and accurately—in the popular mind with Gorbachev's reforms rather than with the stagnation or abuses of earlier decades. Nowhere is enmity toward the ventures more virulent than among the numerous Russian nationalist groups that have sprouted up around the country, sometimes with the winking approval of Party conservatives. The nationalists base their criticism of private enterprise on the alleged threat to "native Russian" values posed by this conduit of "Western materialism, individualism, and capitalist exploitation." And they are often inclined to lace the attack with anti-Semitism, recalling the stereotypical blending of Nepman and Jew in the 1920s.

All of this has produced a business environment unpredictable at best and at worst, in some locales, openly malignant. Voicing sentiments similar to those heard from Nepmen, a cooperative member wondered in the pages of the *Moscow News* whether he was regarded as a productive citizen or a villain. "We haven't produced plenty and prosperity in a short time, but we've felt, in full measure, the population's anger and the pressure of [the] state apparatus. Right now, I'm not the only person asking myself: 'I'm a cooperator, but who am I?'" The fluctuation of government policy and the severe treatment often encountered at the local level have left many entrepreneurs, like their brethren in the 1920s, uncertain about the future. "Are we building," asked the head of a Moscow cooperative. "just so that they can take what we've built away from us?" The experience of NEP offers him little encouragement.

Cooperatives have turned in a variety of directions to cope with the difficulties they face. High taxes are countered with higher prices and concealed incomes—and occasionally re-registration in a different region, such as the Baltic Republics, where taxes are lower. Denial of supplies begets bribes to government employees. In other words, as always, official pressure tends to drive surviving businesses toward the surreptitious shadow economy. Some cooperatives, rather than vanish into the black market, have sought to counter their unsavory reputation by contributing millions of rubles to such projects as Armenian earthquake relief, institutions for orphans and the elderly, and memorials for soldiers killed in Afghanistan. Many entrepreneurs have gone beyond charitable contributions to organize local, regional, and national associations. These bodies press their business concerns with government offiicals (including Deputy Prime Minister Leonid Abalkin), organize public rallies to support cooperatives, conduct market research, and take legal action to defend their members. A proposal now circulating among cooperative groups calls for a nationwide political party uniting all citizens engaged in independent work, including private farmers. The contemporary Soviet political climate, in which serious talk of this Free Labor Party is possible, stands in sharp contrast to the political arena of the 1920s.

By no means all voices deplore cooperatives. Some government officials, sounding like earlier champions of NEP, endorse them. The support often stems not so much from zeal for private enterprise as from recognition that cooperatives furnish valuable services beyond the ability of state organizations. The Komi Autonomous Republic went as far as to suspend a harsh tax on cooperatives adopted by its parent Russian Republic. "It is not a demonstration of courage," explained the vice-chairman of the Komi Republic's Council of Ministers. "We did it out of economic interest." Spirited defense of cooperatives also appears frequently in reform-minded journals and newspapers. Here, along with observations that cooperatives help compensate for the state's inability to satisfy society's needs, one finds claims that high prices and shady dealings are the fault of an economy of scarcity and the liabilities placed upon entrepreneurs by bureaucrats. Some articles insist that those who distribute goods produced by others are not parasites but providers of a valuable service. Not only that, advocates maintain, the new businesses have created hundreds of thousands of jobs at a time when the government has finally admitted the existence of unemployment.

Thus, like the Nepmen some seventy years ago, cooperatives face uncertain prospects as the Soviet Union begins a new decade. On the one hand, they are viewed askance by a considerable portion of the population and stifled by officials in many localities. On the other hand, the liquidation of thousands of businesses has been accompanied by determined support for cooperatives from reformers and the opening of an even larger number of new ventures. Even if current trends continue, hardly a safe assumption, their effect on private enterprise is difficult to gauge. Taking the issue of ethnic unrest as an example, several of the republics most determined to break from the Union are regions where public support for cooperatives is greatest. Would their secession leave private entrepreneurs in the remainder of the USSR more vulnerable to official and popular disfavor? Or, if the newly independent states established flourishing market economies, would the Soviet government find this instructive? For that matter, what economic lessons might offiicals draw in Moscow, if market reforms now under way in Poland and other Eastern European countries yield prosperity—or intractable distress?

Domestic *political* reform in the Soviet Union also bears watching. If a multi-party system with genuinely competitive elections becomes a reality, private entrepreneurs may well prove a significant factor—not only through their own parties, but as campaign issues raised by candidates attempting to capitalize on popular resentment of the new rich. This aversion is likely to ferment at least as long as economic hardship prevails. If the present series of crises continues to the point where Gorbachev and his reforms are discredited, the widespread antipathy toward cooperatives that persists in both Party and society suggests that a successor regime's economic policy would not feature private enterprise. Even should Gorbachev fall, however, the course of history since 1917 leads one to suppose that he would not be the final Soviet leader to rename and summon the descendants of Russia's last capitalists.

# Preface

We are now striving to determine the attitude that the ruling
proletariat should adopt toward the last capitalist class—the
fundamental root of capitalism—small private property, the small
producer. This problem now confronts us in a practical way. I think
that we will be able to solve it. In any case the experiment we are
conducting will be useful for future proletarian revolutions, and
they will be better able to make technical preparations for solving
this problem.

—V. I. Lenin

Some four years after what is celebrated as the Great October Socialist
Revolution, the Soviet government felt compelled to retrieve the "bourgeoisie" from the garbage heap of history to help feed and clothe the
Russian people. Far from leaping at once to what the Bolsheviks expected to be the most progressive society the world had yet seen, the
Soviet state—plagued by civil war, foreign intervention, and its own
rashness and inexperience—proved unable to cope with the task of dis-
tributing even essential consumer goods to the population. During the
period from 1918 to 1920, with the economy in ruins and much of Russia's resources outside their control, the Bolsheviks could not offer the
peasantry more than a trickle of desirable products in return for the
grain needed to feed the cities and the army. Still determined, the party
devised a policy of grain requisitioning that saw the Bolsheviks through
the civil war but also spawned peasant revolts in many regions by the
beginning of 1921. In the face of a prostrate economy and a rebellious
peasantry, Lenin jettisoned the hope of an immediate transition to socialism and called for, among other things, the legalization of a considerable amount of private business activity previously banned. Thus was
launched what came to be known as the New Economic Policy, or NEP.

Scholars and others disagree over NEP's chronological limits, as the
policy was neither introduced nor repealed by single decrees. Most
Western historians mark the end of NEP in 1928 or 1929, whereas some
Soviet historians extend its life as far as the second half of the 1930s.

This study will focus primarily on the interval from 1921 to 1929, although some themes will be pursued a few years beyond. The principal subject of this work is the large group of private entrepreneurs, often called Nepmen (the singular *Nepman* being employed in both Russian and English), who played an important role in several lines of business legalized during these years.

One of the first problems encountered in studying the Nepmen is simply deciding what sorts of people and endeavors ought to be considered. A brief perusal of the sources reveals that the meaning of the term *Nepman* varies greatly in the writings of politicians, novelists, and historians. To be sure, any definition of the term *Nepmen* would include at least the large-scale urban traders, manufacturers, financiers, and assorted speculators so labeled in Soviet literature of the 1920s. Nearly as certain to qualify are smaller-scale merchants and artisans whose businesses were their primary occupations. But the consensus breaks down beyond this core of entrepreneurs. Fewer definitions, for example, would encompass the activity of part-time petty vendors and artisans. Fewer still would include peasants, although it might be possible to argue that the peasant who periodically sold produce in the local market should also be considered a Nepman. A variety of private business pursuits will receive attention in the following chapters, but the main focus will be on trade and manufacturing, both large and small scale, conducted by people who were required to register with the state. This requirement for the most part rules out the peasant who brought produce now and then to the market, but includes the other categories of entrepreneurs listed above.

The acceptance, even encouragement, by the state of a private business sector *after* the "socialist" revolution seemed a considerable anomaly to many observers in the 1920s, and the course of Soviet history has done little to change this impression. When contrasted to Soviet economic policies during the years from 1918 to 1920 and the decades following the Stalinist revolution of the 1930s, NEP is often considered merely a brief, albeit fascinating, interlude. Today in the Soviet Union economic measures like those of NEP have not assumed a form more substantial than rumors occasionally associated with speculation over the policies of a new generation of Soviet leaders. But economic programs strikingly similar to NEP (including the legalization of a large private sector) have been implemented in recent years elsewhere in the socialist world—most notably in Yugoslavia, Hungary, and China. Consequently the Nepmen deserve attention both for their importance in the Soviet economy and for the insights their experience can provide into economic reforms adopted more recently by other communist governments.

Western historians, however, have written relatively little about the Nepmen, nothing more than subsections or a few pages here and there in much broader works. Given the nature of these surveys, the discussions of private business are quite brief—and thus hardly more than rudimentary. Further, Western works devote scant attention to the party's position on the Nepmen and the significant changes in the treatment they received during the 1920s. Soviet sources—especially several books and numerous articles published in the 1920s, but also some contemporary publications—are more useful because they contain considerable statistical information from studies of the private sector conducted by government agencies in the 1920s. In addition, recent Soviet works provide a fair amount of information from archives off-limits to Western historians. Unfortunately, the books and articles from the 1920s cover only portions of NEP (generally just the first half or two thirds of the decade, with much less on the period from 1927 to 1930). Again, being mainly statistical (and published in the Soviet Union), they include comparatively little concerning party debates on the private sector or the concomitant shifts in policy toward the Nepmen. Recent Soviet works minimize the fluctuations of official policy through the decade, portraying the party line on the private sector as a consistent development of Lenin's thought leading to the "liquidation of the new bourgeoisie" at the end of the 1920s. This interpretation does not fit the middle years of NEP during the peak of Nikolai Bukharin's influence, when the state treated private entrepreneurs remarkably leniently in comparison with what had come before and what was to follow.

As the research on this project progressed, it quickly became apparent that there are two angles from which to address the topic. On the one hand we must view the issue from the vantage point of the Bolshevik party, to understand the debates and anguish in the party over the question of permitting private enterprise. Also demanding attention here is the fluctuating assortment of policies actually implemented over the years by the state to deal with the private sector. On the other hand we must scrutinize the Nepmen themselves—not only their business activities but also their social origins and reactions to official policies.

This work adopts both approaches. After an introductory chapter on the "War Communism" period from 1918 to 1920, I analyze in chapters 1–3 the succession of policies adopted by the party regarding the private sector in the 1920s. This background is essential to understanding the Nepmen's activity—the heart of this study—explored in the next four chapters. Here the principal topics include the nature and scope of private entrepreneurs' endeavors, the sources of their merchandise and raw materials, and the effects on the private sector of numerous official policy changes. In the concluding chapter I consider the Nepmen's fate and assess their significance in the Soviet economy.

I would like to take this opportunity to express my gratitude for the suggestions and encouragement received from a number of people during the preparation of this work. First and foremost, Samuel H. Baron unfailingly found time to read several drafts promptly and to provide numerous perceptive comments. In addition, the project benefited from criticism and advice offered by the following scholars: E. Willis Brooks, V. P. Dmitrenko, David Griffiths, Gregory Grossman, Gregory Guroff, V. M. Selunskaia, and Vladimir Treml. I must also thank the International Research and Exchanges Board for supporting me during a year of research in Moscow, an experience that immeasurably enriched the present work. I am grateful as well to Colleen Dooling for helping to secure some of the illustrations and to Sheila Levine, Mary Renaud, and Susan Oleksiw of the University of California Press for guiding the manuscript expertly into print. Finally, earlier versions of chapters 1 and 2 appeared as articles in *Slavic Review* (1984, no. 3) and *Soviet Studies* (1985, no. 3), and I thank the editors of these journals for permitting me to use that material here.

# A Note on Conventions

This work employs the Library of Congress system of transliteration, with the following minor modifications: (a) diacritical marks are omitted; (b) certain familiar names (e.g., Trotsky and Zinoviev) are spelled as they customarily appear in English.

Fiscal years (i.e., twelve-month periods beginning on October 1) are designated with a solidus between the years. Thus "1926/27" stands for the period from October 1, 1926, to September 30, 1927. If the reference is to consecutive calendar years, a dash is employed (1926–27).

The translations of quotations from sources with Russian titles are my own unless otherwise noted.

# Terms and Abbreviations

ARA
: American Relief Administration. In the years after World War I, this agency (under the direction of Herbert Hoover) provided relief for famine victims in a number of countries, including Russia at the beginning of NEP.

*Artel'*
: A producers' collective composed of handicraftsmen.

Cheka (Chrezvychainaia Kommissiia)
: The secret police organized by the Bolsheviks after the Revolution. During NEP the Cheka became first the GPU (Gosudarstvennoe Politicheskoe Upravlenie) and then the OGPU (Ob"edinennoe Gosudarstvennoe Politicheskoe Upravlenie).

Gosbank
: The main state bank.

Gostorg
: A state trading agency.

GPU
: *See* Cheka.

*Guberniia*
: A large administrative unit, sometimes translated as "province," now replaced by the *oblast'*.

| | |
|---|---|
| GUM (Gosudarstvennyi Universal'nyi Magazin) | The main state department store in Moscow. |
| Khozraschet | Literally, "economic cost accounting," the accounting basis on which many state enterprises were placed at the beginning of NEP, requiring them to find their own customers and suppliers (state or private) rather than simply rely on the state to provide their raw materials and absorb their output. |
| Kulak | A wealthy peasant (literally, "fist"). The term has a negative connotation suggesting that the kulak exploited other peasants. |
| Kustar' | A handicraftsman. |
| Narkomfin | The People's Commissariat of Finance. |
| Narkomvnutorg | The People's Commissariat of Domestic Trade. |
| OGPU | See Cheka. |
| RKI (Raboche-krest'ianskaia Inspektsiia) | The Workers' and Peasants' Inspectorate. |
| Smychka | Literally, "union." This is the term used by the Bolsheviks for the political and economic alliance they hoped to foster between the proletariat and the peasantry—represented symbolically by the hammer and sickle emblem. |
| Sovnarkhozy | See VSNKh. |
| Sovnarkom | The Council of People's Commissars. |
| STO (Sovet Truda i Oborony) | The Council of Labor and Defense. |
| Sukharevka | The largest outdoor market in Moscow. |
| Tsentrosoiuz | The central agency of the cooperative system. |

| | |
|---|---|
| VSNKh (Vysshii Sovet Narodnogo Khoziaistva) | The Supreme Council of the National Economy. Regional and local economic councils were called *sovnarkhozy*. |
| VTS (Vserossiiskii Tekstil'nyi Sindikat) | The All-Russian Textile Syndicate, a state agency. |
| VTsIK (Vserossiiskii Tsentral'nyi Ispolnitel'nyi Komitet) | The All-Russian Central Executive Committee elected by the All-Russian Congress of Soviets. |
| *Zagotovka* | The purchasing of raw materials, generally from the peasantry; the most important was grain, though the term could indicate the procurement of a wide variety of other products as well. |

# Introduction: The War Communism Prelude

Freedom of trade in grain means enriching oneself with this grain—
and it is a return to the old capitalist way. This we will not allow.
— V. I. Lenin

It would be absurd for the Soviet Power to prohibit petty trade
when it is not itself in a position to replace the functions of this
trade by the activity of its own organs of distribution.
— *The ABC of Communism*

Following the Bolsheviks' seizure of power in November 1917, there
was considerable uncertainty, inside the party and out, as to how and at
what pace the fledgling government would attempt to recast vast, tradi-
tion-bound, underdeveloped Russia in an untried socialist mold. One of
the largest questions concerned the new regime's economic policy, including its plans for the private sector. Would the party proceed at once
to decree complete nationalization of the economy, or would a sizable
number of private entrepreneurs be tolerated well into the future? During the first few months after the Revolution, it appeared that the Bolsheviks would proceed cautiously. In his pamphlet "The Immediate
Tasks of the Soviet Government," written in March–April 1918 and
published in *Pravda* and *Izvestiia*, Lenin spoke of a "new phase" in the
struggle against the bourgeoisie. "In order to continue advancing successfully *in the future*," he contended, "we must 'suspend' our offensive
*now*." Red Guard attacks on capital, appropriate during the revolutionary period, had ceased to serve the interests of the party or the workers.
The task at hand, he stressed, was to digest recent gains: that is, learn
how to administer enterprises and institutions already nationalized before seizing more.[1] To this end, Lenin argued, state factories and agencies had to enlist the services of "bourgeois specialists" (engineers, tech-
nicians, and so forth), even if this required the payment of high salaries,
for these were the people with the expertise to revive the economy.[2] Fail-

1

ure to learn from this segment of the bourgeoisie, he warned, would prevent the Bolsheviks from developing large-scale production, the foundation of socialism.[3]

That Lenin felt compelled to argue repeatedly for utilizing "bourgeois specialists" suggests the suspicion (not to mention outright loath-
ing) with which most Bolsheviks regarded the bourgeoisie—a hostility
that Lenin himself had done much to cultivate in the years before the
Revolution.[4] In the *Communist Manifesto* Marx left no doubt that
bourgeois society was a progressive force while it developed, far superior to the feudal order it supplanted.

> The bourgeoisie, by the rapid improvement of all instruments of production,
> by the immensely facilitated means of communication, draws all, even the
> most barbarian, nations into civilization. . . .
>      It has created enormous cities, has greatly increased the urban population
> as compared with the rural, and has thus rescued a considerable part of the
> population from the idiocy of rural life. . . .
>      What earlier century had even a presentiment that such productive forces
> slumbered in the lap of social labor?[5]

Lenin did not dispute this characterization of the bourgeoisie's role in
general, but early on he reached the conclusion that the *Russian* bourgeoisie was too timid and underdeveloped to carry out properly its historical mission of preparing the social and economic ground for socialism. "In countries like Russia," he wrote during the upheaval of
1905, "the working class suffers not so much from capitalism as from
the inadequate development of capitalism."[6]

According to the conventional wisdom among Russian Marxists at
this time, the Revolution of 1905 could be nothing other than the bourgeois revolution they had long predicted. But Lenin, disgusted at what
he considered the irresolute behavior of various liberal groups, began
to formulate the view that the Russian bourgeoisie could not carry out
a proper revolution and, furthermore, did not even desire one. "We
must," he wrote in *Two Tactics of Social-Democracy in the Democratic
Revolution* (1905),

> be perfectly certain about which are the real social forces opposed to "tsar-
> ism" (which is a perfectly real force understandable to all) and capable of
> gaining a "decisive victory" over it. The big bourgeoisie, the landlords, the
> factory owners, the "society" that follows the [liberal] *Osvobozhdentsy* can-
> not be such a force. We see that they do not even want a decisive victory. . . .
> They are in too great a need of tsarism—with its bureaucratic, police, and
> military forces arrayed against the proletariat and the peasantry—to struggle
> for its destruction.[7]

After widespread rural unrest broke out in 1905, Lenin concluded that the peasantry, not the bourgeoisie, was the class most likely to assist the proletariat in toppling the tsar.

Thus, in Lenin's view, the Russian bourgeoisie not only exhibited vices common to the bourgeoisie everywhere, such as exploitation of the proletariat, but also lacked the virtues of the bougeoisie elsewhere, in particular the revolutionary zeal to carry out the historical tasks described by Marx. Instead, the Russian bourgeoisie preferred to remain beholden to the tsar. Cast in this light of economic greed and political spinelessness (if not outright reaction), the Russian bourgeoisie as depicted by Lenin seemed beneath contempt. Following the fall of Nicholas II in March 1917, Lenin directed his attack on the new "bourgeois" (Provisional) government along these lines. In a pamphlet written the following month he charged: "The bourgeoisie that has found itself in power has formed a bloc (union) with clearly monarchist elements who were extraordinarily ardent supporters of Nicholas the Bloody and Stolypin the Hangman in 1906–1914."[8] Two months later, in a *Pravda* article titled "The Capitalists' Mocking of the People," he claimed that the "government of capitalists" calls itself revolutionary in order to deceive the people while it permits entrepreneurs to amass huge sums through profiteering, with the country on the brink of economic ruin.[9] By September Lenin was contending (in a pamphlet published the following month) that the Russian capitalists were intentionally sabotaging the economy in the hope that the resulting catastrophe would sweep away the Soviets and worker-peasant solidarity in general, thus facilitating the restoration of the monarchy.[10]

The tone of these remarks echoes the attitude of most Bolsheviks toward the Russian bourgeoisie and therefore helps explain the difficulty Lenin had a few months later in convincing party members of the need to utilize "bourgeois specialists." It is important to underscore that when he referred to "bourgeois specialists," Lenin had in mind persons hired to work in state enterprises. He was not yet supporting a revival of independent private trade and manufacturing—a startling policy reversal that would not come until 1921. Meanwhile, even in the period of comparative official restraint that lasted until June 1918, Lenin and the rest of the Bolsheviks were not inclined to pronounce private entrepreneurs capable of essential economic functions in the building of socialism.

Virtually all early socialists were more hostile toward private traders than toward private manufacturers, largely because the former made profits on goods they had not produced.[11] Certainly, Lenin reserved his most passionate attacks on the private sector for traders, or "speculators" as he often called them. Speaking in January 1919 before a joint session of the All-Russian Central Executive Committee, the Moscow Soviet, and the All-Russian Trade Union Congress, Lenin complained that many citizens were still infected with the "capitalist" notion of "every man for himself," which accounted for the wild profiteering evident whenever there was a food shortage.

> That is why all talk on this theme [private trade], all attempts to encourage it are a great danger, a retreat, a step back from that socialist construction that the Commissariat of Food is carrying out amid unbelievable difficulties in a struggle with millions of speculators left to us by capitalism.[12]

Lenin focused his wrath most frequently on the private grain trade, charging that it enriched speculators, impoverished (or starved) the masses,[13] and threatened to drive Russia back to the days of the old regime.[14] Summing up these views in the foreword to a published speech titled "On the Deception of the People with Slogans of Freedom and Equality," he wrote:

> The peasant must choose: free trade in grain—which means speculation in grain, freedom for the rich to get richer and the poor to get poorer and starve, the return of the absolute rule of the landowners and the capitalists, and the severing of the union of the peasants and workers—or delivery of his grain surpluses to the state at fixed prices.[15]

Lenin conceded that for the time being the faltering economy could not produce enough goods to compensate the peasants adequately for their grain. But he urged them to resist the temptation to sell at high prices to private traders—and instead to supply their grain to the state as a "loan" to be repaid once industry revived.[16] If this loan were not extended and free trade flourished, he warned in *Pravda* and *Izvestiia* in August 1919, the consequences would be dire. "With the free sale of grain there are no state grain reserves, the army is powerless, industry dies, and the victory of Kolchak and Denikin [i.e., the "White" or reactionary forces] is inevitable."[17]

During the winter of 1917–18 a number of decrees proclaimed state monopolies on trade in agricultural equipment, some food products, matches, candles, and other goods. Even before the Bolsheviks seized power, the Provisional Government had attempted to ban private grain trading—part of an ultimately futile effort to fend off social and economic collapse while continuing the war with Germany. The Bolsheviks retained this prohibition after the October Revolution and tried to enforce it more rigorously by nationalizing all grain elevators and warehouses. Moreover, they extended this policy to other areas. Private banks were nationalized.[18] In industry, the nationalization campaign during the first half of 1918 targeted individual plants (generally large or abandoned ones) rather than entire branches of production except in the case of the sugar and oil industries. But this relatively gradualist approach, with its grudging and uncertain acceptance of some private trade and industry, was short-lived. In the summer of 1918 the Bolsheviks, whatever their initial plans concerning the economy, opted for a frontal assault on the private sector.

The period from June 1918 through 1920, known as War Communism, was marked by a sweeping nationalization of industry, the banning of private trade, and heavy-handed grain requisitioning. This change (or acceleration) of policy in the second half of 1918 seems largely a consequence of the Bolsheviks' efforts to meet the challenge of civil war and foreign intervention, though there would undoubtedly have been some pressure in the party to "complete the Revolution" in any case. Fighting for its life, the regime strove to extend its control over the economy as far as possible in order to ration supplies and direct production in support of the war effort. At the same time the Bolsheviks (without access to the Ukrainian breadbasket, occupied by the Germans after the Treaty of Brest Litovsk removed Russia from World War I) were faced with the extremely difficult task of collecting enough grain to feed both the towns and the Red Army. Efforts in earlier months to distribute goods to the peasants in return for grain were not successful, because the state had few desirable products to trade and offered them to the peasants at unattractive prices. Now, with the army drawing off a large share of the available resources, the Bolsheviks had even less with which to entice grain from the peasantry. In this position the party saw no other way out than simply to seize the produce it needed. The result was a requisitioning campaign during the next two and a half years that secured enough grain to see the state through the civil war, but so provoked the peasants that Lenin ultimately felt compelled to abandon War Communism.

The tone of War Communism was set at the end of June 1918 by a sweeping decree nationalizing virtually all large-scale factories, mines, mills, and joint-stock companies.[19] Interestingly, the order seems to have been rushed to publication by rumors that the Germans in the Ukraine were planning to transfer ownership of important Russian enterprises to German firms in order to shield the former from nationalization.[20] Though quite broad, this decree was eclipsed by another at the end of the period, in November 1920, that cast the nationalization net over all factories utilizing mechanization and employing over five people (ten people if no mechanization was used). Directors, engineers, and the like were ordered to remain on the job as state employees and keep the enterprises in good working order.[21] Of course, it was one thing to issue decrees and another to actually take over the factories. Lacking the personnel to implement full-scale nationalization, the Supreme Council of the National Economy (VSNKh) was administering only four to five thousand enterprises by November 1920. Even considering that local officials and workers' committees seized some firms on their own initiative, we can safely conclude that a majority of private factories (particularly the smaller ones) eluded state control during War Communism.[22]

At the Fifth All-Russian Congress of Soviets in July 1918, Lenin rejected the appeal of some socialists for free trade and promised that the state would declare a monopoly on the distribution of all products.[23] As we have seen, a number of items had already been placed off-limits to private traders, and during the course of 1918–19 this list of goods expanded. On November 21, 1918, the Council of People's Commissars (Sovnarkom) issued a decree with the express intent of eliminating private trade. Prices of consumer goods were to be fixed, and a network of state and cooperative stores was to be set up, with retail trade placed under the direction of local Soviets.[24] Shortly thereafter a series of decrees from VSNKh banned private sales of virtually all commodities, and private trade was eliminated—at least on paper.[25]

In reality, the state's feeble distribution system and shortage of essential consumer goods meant that the private market, far from vanishing, represented the most important source of supply for the Russian people. Victor Serge offers a vivid description of this part of life during War Communism.

> In spite of my special rations as a Government official, I would have died of hunger without the sordid manipulations of the black market, where we traded the petty possessions we had brought in from France. . . .
> In fact, in order to eat it was necessary to resort, daily and without interruption, to the black market; the Communists did it like everyone else. . . .

> . . . The words of St. Paul that were posted up everywhere, "*He that doth not work, neither shall he eat!*" became ironical, because if you wanted any food you really had to resort to the black market instead of working.[26]

The rough data available for this period fully support Serge's account. In the summer of 1919, for example, the urban population obtained approximately 70 percent of its grain products through private channels, despite Lenin's attacks on the practice. Nor was grain the only product involved. Throughout War Communism private entrepreneurs accounted for the lion's share—between one half and two thirds—of all retail trade.[27] So essential (and difficult to prevent) was this activity that officials in many regions cracked down only intermittently and looked through their fingers the rest of the time. Occasionally, during particularly acute food shortages, the government even felt compelled to legalize some petty private trade.[28]

On the eve of the First World War the bulk of urban trade had been conducted from shops—most small, but nevertheless permanent facilities as opposed to peddlers' carts, temporary stalls in market squares, and so on. This all changed during War Communism as private trade underwent extreme fragmentation. As a general rule, the larger a store, the more tempting a target it represented for nationalization (or at least the requisitioning of its wares) and the more likely its "bourgeois" owner was to flee or be forced out of business. Under these conditions, and because of the difficulty in obtaining merchandise, virtually all private trade during War Communism was conducted by highly mobile, small-scale operators. Many, known as bagmen, journeyed to the countryside in order to trade for a sack or two of food, which they consumed or resold back in the towns. As permanent shops were closed, private trade swelled outdoor bazaars and markets. Here bagmen, peasants (to whom the term *bagmen* was also applied at times), and others offered their wares while the authorities looked the other way or simply dispersed the entrepreneurs, forcing them to seek another location.[29]

Because of the soaring inflation of these years, fewer and fewer sellers were willing to accept cash, and thus the search for goods to exchange for necessities assumed critical importance. As Victor Serge observed:

> In the dead factories, the workers spent their time making penknives out of bits of machinery, or shoe-soles out of the conveyor-belts, to barter them on the underground market. . . . If you wished to procure a little flour, butter, or meat from the peasants who brought these things illicitly into town, you had to have cloth or articles of some kind to exchange. Fortunately the town resi-

dences of the late bourgeoisie contained quite a lot in the way of carpets, tapestries, linen, and plate. From the leather upholstery of sofas one could make passable shoes; from the tapestries, clothing.[30]

The collapse of the currency also prompted many enterprises to pay their workers with a share of the goods they had produced, so that by 1920 over 90 percent of industrial wages were paid in kind. Ilya Ehrenburg recalled that once "all members of TEO [the theatrical section of the Commissariat of Education] were given a tin of shoe polish. We regarded this as a misfortune, particularly as the staff of the Department of Music had been given chickens only the day before." Many workers who received wages in kind joined the ragtag ranks of bagmen and peasants to barter their pay in the markets for other products they needed.[31] As we will see, this sort of primitive, small-scale trade remained important following the introduction of the New Economic Policy (NEP) in 1921. Initially, in fact, before larger-scale operators gained enough confidence in NEP to open permanent shops, private trade differed little from the forms it had assumed during War Communism.

Even though the volume of private trade during War Communism was impressive compared to the trickle of sales in state and cooperative shops, it was merely a fraction of the business conducted in the years before the First World War. This was a consequence of the attempt by the state to abolish private trade and reflected the collapse of the economy in general. During this period the countryside reverted largely to a self-sufficient natural economy, with agricultural production in 1920 roughly three fourths of that of 1912. The situation was nothing short of catastrophic in the industrial sector, where production plunged in 1920 to less than 20 percent of the prewar level. Largely as a result of these developments, the amount of consumer goods supplied to the Russian population in 1920 was less than one fifth of the amount available in 1912.[32]

Startling as these figures are, they do not convey the grimness of the time, the starvation and disease that raged through the land in this period. When Victor Serge arrived in Petrograd in the winter of 1919, he was told: "Typhus has killed so many people that we can't manage to bury them; luckily they are frozen."[33] People abandoned the cities in droves, hoping to find food in the countryside. Weeds normally found in uninhabited marshland were a common sight in Petrograd's main streets. The population of Moscow was estimated to have plunged from about 2,000,000 in February 1917 to about 1,000,000 in August 1920; for Petrograd the drop was from roughly 2,420,000 to 740,000.[34]

Acute shortages of food, fuel, shelter, and warm clothing were commonplace. Livestock died as humans ate the feed normally given to cattle, and many people consumed food considered unfit even for animals in more prosperous times. As the situation grew more desperate, crimes committed to obtain necessities multiplied, and there were even numerous reports of cannibalism in the newspapers. The sociologist Pitirim Sorokin observed that "in Russia at the present time [1918–20] hundreds of bands are stopping trains, robbing everyone they meet, pillaging hamlets, villages, and small towns, etc. The causes of the appearance of such bands are not political—what are politics to the average peasant boy or man? The cause is mostly hunger and the possibility of surviving in a time of famine."[35]

Anatoly Lunacharskii, the commissar of education, complained to Lenin in 1920 that state theaters had not received the food rations promised them: "I myself gave a solemn promise particularly to the starving artists of the orchestra and chorus, stage workers, and so on, that finally their hungry cries would be silenced. But we were quite grievously deceived."[36] On occasion, theater troupes were sent on tours of the countryside, in part to give them an opportunity to forage for food.[37] According to Angelica Balabanoff, some of her most idealistic comrades were transformed by the hardships.

> I saw men and women who had lived all their lives for ideas, who had voluntarily renounced material advantages, liberty, happiness, and family affection for the realization of their ideals—completely absorbed by the problem of hunger and cold. . . . I saw individuals who had devoted their entire lives to the struggle against private property, running home with a parcel of flour or a herring, eager to conceal it beneath their coats from the envious eyes of a hungry comrade.[38]

For many Russians the suffering was ended only by death. There is no way of knowing how many people perished in the three years following the Revolution, though estimates are in the millions. Whatever the actual total, death became so widespread that its shadow appeared in the most unlikely places. There were matter-of-fact reports in the *Protokoly* of the Academy of Sciences, for example, that a scholar's research was passed from one colleague to a second, then to a third, and so on as each died in turn.[39]

By the latter part of 1920 the Bolsheviks had successfully weathered the challenges of the civil war and foreign intervention. But instead of

phasing out the harshest features of War Communism, the party intensified its nationalization and grain-requisitioning drives. Thousands of
peasants, discharged from the Red Army in 1920, found themselves
confronting Soviet requisition detachments back in their home villages.
The results were alarming. In the cities the economy accelerated its skid
into chaos and ruin while peasant uprisings and brigandage spread rapidly through the Ukraine, Crimea, Don, Kuban, Transvolga, and Siberia
now that the justification (the war emergency) for an always-unpopular
policy had vanished. Ilya Ehrenburg recalled these months with a shud-
der: "Gangs of bandits roamed the country. In the villages 'Food Detachments' were shot at. The fields were unsown. The lost children of
the Revolution—*besprizornye*—already loitered near the railway stations. The towns were starving; mortality was rising steeply."[40]

In February 1921 Lenin finally acknowledged the need for a change,
and his view was doubtless reinforced at the end of the month by the
rebellion of sailors at Kronstadt. (Many of the sailors were recent re-
cruits from the countryside, and their demands reflected the peasantry's
discontent.) At the Tenth Party Congress in March, Lenin proposed that
the grain requisitions be replaced by a fixed tax in kind, and shortly
thereafter a series of decrees (for grain and a number of other agricultural products) cast this startling departure into law. The taxes were set
well below the various requisition targets for the previous year, and the
peasants were permitted to market freely any produce they might have
left over after paying the taxes. These measures represented the first
planks of NEP and were joined with further concessions—most notably
the right of the population in general to engage in private trade and
small-scale manufacturing—in the months that followed.

In the aftermath of War Communism there remained the question of
whether it had been simply an emergency policy adopted only until conditions were suitable for something like NEP, or whether it had been a
conscious attempt to enter socialism immediately by liquidating the private sector. Lenin's remarks on this issue were not always consistent. On
a number of occasions he indicated that the party had in fact tried to
hurl Russia directly into socialism-communism but had failed and was
then forced to adopt NEP as a retreat. Speaking to the Second All-
Russian Congress of Political Education Departments in October 1921,
he conceded that "by attempting to go straight to communism, we suffered an economic defeat by the spring of 1921 more serious than any
defeat at the hands of Kolchak, Denikin, and Pilsudski." The implemen-

tation of NEP "cannot be called anything else than a very severe defeat and retreat."[41] In his "Notes of a Publicist" written in February 1922, Lenin compared the adoption of NEP to a mountain climber seeking a long indirect path to the summit after being compelled to abandon an exhilarating route straight up the slope.[42] Such statements suggest that the party had indeed hoped to leap to socialism during the period from 1918 to 1920 and that NEP, far from being the sort of policy the Bolsheviks had planned all along, was necessitated by a disappointing and unanticipated crisis.

Sometimes, though, Lenin's remarks lent support to the opposite position. Attempting to justify NEP to the Seventh Moscow Guberniia Party Conference in October 1921, he argued that in the spring of 1918 the Bolsheviks were contemplating a relatively cautious and gradual transition to socialism (something like NEP) and that only the outbreak of the civil war forced the adoption of more extreme emergency measures. But in the same address he went on to characterize War Communism as more than just a defensive policy. The party had tried "to introduce socialist principles of production and trade through 'direct assault,' that is, in the shortest, fastest, and most direct manner."[43] As to the level of severity with which this approach should now (1921) be criticized, Lenin seemed less than certain. In his speeches to the Tenth Party Congress in March 1921, he appeared to be combining portions of differing interpretations, trying to convince the delegates that War Communism was a necessary emergency measure,[44] though full of ideological excess that NEP would remedy.[45]

Clearly War Communism meant different things to different Bolsheviks. Some, in the 1920s at least, claimed that they considered it all along just a temporary wartime policy,[46] while others viewed NEP as a sellout of the Revolution and mourned War Communism as the true path to socialism. It would probably not be far from the truth to conclude that the harsh measures of War Communism were not contemplated by the party leadership immediately after the Revolution, but began instead as a series of steps taken in response to the war emergency. Undoubtedly, though, many Bolsheviks had no difficulty viewing measures such as the abolition of private trade and industry and the virtual elimination of money (because of inflation) as important steps toward their conception of a communist society. Once set on this course, many (and perhaps most) Bolsheviks were quite willing to follow it, thinking or hoping that it would not only bring them victory in the civil war but also lead them to the social order they desired. This would account for the continuation of War Communism even after the rout of the Bolsheviks' enemies. As time went by and social and economic conditions continued to deteriorate, some in the party, most notably Lenin, began to think a change was needed, while others clung to the spirit of War Communism and were thus cast into despair by the adoption of NEP.

# Part I

## CHAPTER 1

# Building Communism
# with Bourgeois Hands

Small traders were springing up everywhere, crowds swarmed over
the markets, the taverns exhaled their music, barefoot youngsters
ran in the streets at dawn, following the cabs to offer flowers to
lovers.

—Victor Serge

They have coined a new word—*nepman*—and no person who has
not visited Russia can appreciate how mean a word it has become
in that country. *Nepman*—symbol of degradation, object of scorn
and contumely! Pariah, social swine! Villain on the stage, villain in
the motion pictures, villain in everyday life! *Nepman*—label, curse,
anathema!

—Maurice Hindus

To revolutionaries of diverse hues, such as the Menshevik leader F. I.
Dan and Alexander Berkman, an anarchist deported from America to
Russia, the legalization of private trade in 1921 seemed a clear signal
that the Bolsheviks had jettisoned the fundamental ideals of the Revolution. Dan was released from a Bolshevik prison in January 1922 and
wandered the streets of Moscow for a week before being exiled abroad.
He was shocked by the sight of opulent Nepmen strutting around the
capital with impunity.

> This [new private] trade clearly dealt mainly with the luxuries of the "new
> rich," shamelessly standing out against a background of general impoverish-
> ment and appalling hunger, troubling echoes of which reached Moscow in
> the form of reports of widespread death, terrible instances of cannibalism,
> and so on. But all of these reports were received as if they were from another
> planet, and Moscow made merry, treating itself with pastries, fine candies,
> fruits, and delicacies. Theaters and concerts were packed, women were again
> flaunting luxurious apparel, furs, and diamonds. A "speculator" who yester-
> day was threatened with execution, and quietly stayed to the side trying to

avoid notice, today considers himself important and proudly shows off his wealth and luxury. This is evident in every little custom. Again after a number of years one can hear from the mouths of cab drivers, waiters, and porters at stations the servile expression, which had completely disappeared from use—"your honor" [*barin*].[1]

Many Bolsheviks, bewildered by the party's new course, shared Dan's sentiments and bitterly explained the acronym NEP as the New Exploitation of the Proletariat. A bourgeois tide appeared to be sweeping away the cooled lava of revolutionary idealism. Alexandre Barmine, a young Bolshevik in 1921, recalled discussing NEP with some of his comrades:

> We felt as though the Revolution had been betrayed, and it was time to quit the Party. "Capitalism is returning. Money and the old inequality that we fought against are back again." . . .
> If money was reappearing, wouldn't rich people reappear too? Weren't we on the slippery slope that led back to capitalism? We put these questions to ourselves with feelings of anxiety.[2]

These concerns were expressed openly at party congresses and conferences in 1921 and remained common among Bolsheviks throughout the decade. At the end of October 1921, Lenin delivered the closing speech at the Seventh Moscow Guberniia Party Conference and turned his attention to queries passed up on pieces of paper by the delegates: "Questions such as the following are asked: 'Where is the limit to the retreat?' Other notes ask similar questions: 'How far must we retreat?' . . . This question indicates a mood of despondency and dejection that is totally groundless."[3]

To convince such wavering and skeptical party members, Lenin repeatedly outlined the considerations that had compelled the party leadership to legalize private trade. The upsurge of peasant unrest and revolts in 1920 and 1921, spawned in part by War Communism's attack on private trade, was the most immediate threat to the new regime. In a predominantly rural country, Lenin argued, the Bolsheviks could not survive in the face of a hostile peasantry. Or, as Bolsheviks often phrased it, if the *smychka* (the bond of revolutionary solidarity and economic cooperation between the proletariat and peasantry, represented by the hammer and sickle) collapsed, so would the Revolution. Consequently, free trade had to be legalized (along with the replacement of arbitrary grain requisitions by a lower, fixed tax in kind) to help placate the countryside. "We must satisfy the middle peasantry economically by going to free exchange," Lenin told the Tenth Party Congress. "Otherwise it will be impossible—economically impossible—to preserve the power of the proletariat in Russia, given the delay of the international revolution."[4] In less than a decade, Stalin would prove that the party could not only retain power but also industrialize while antagonizing the peasants. But in 1921, as the nascent Soviet state faced revolt in the countryside and economic collapse, Lenin was undoubtedly correct to argue that free trade, by pacifying the peasants and encouraging greater production, would improve the precarious position of the state.

In the spring of 1921 Lenin thought that private trade should and could be restricted to the simple exchange of goods in local markets. The state was to supply the peasants with manufactured goods in return for the latter's surplus food, thus breathing life into the *smychka*.[5] Although this project possessed a certain elegant simplicity, it had no chance of surmounting the obstacles represented by the state's tiny supply of desirable consumer goods and the almost complete absence of a state distribution network in the countryside. Consequently, by the end of NEP's first summer, a wave of private buying and selling had rolled into the void and swept the plan aside.[6] Lenin was quick to acknowledge this setback, conceding, for example, at the Seventh Moscow Guberniia Party Conference in October that "nothing came of commodity exchange [between the state and the peasantry]. The private market proved to be stronger than we, and in place of commodity exchange there arose ordinary buying and selling, trade." In his closing speech to the delegates he added that the party had hoped that "through commodity exchange we could achieve a more direct transition to socialist construction. But now we clearly see that we will have to follow a more roundabout path—through trade."[7] Consequently, by the end of 1921 Lenin was willing to accept not only bartering by peasants but also regular wholesale and retail private trade as the only way to move Russia toward socialism.

According to Marx, capitalists were largely responsible for casting off the commercial restrictions of the Middle Ages, industrializing the West, and thus creating the economic foundation for socialism. Developing this point in his pamphlet *The Tax in Kind* (1921), Lenin argued that capitalism was not an evil in all circumstances. Compared to primitive, small-scale production, it was an improvement, the last leg of the journey to socialism. Consequently, under state supervision and regulation, "capitalism" could be used in the Soviet Union "as the connecting link between small-scale production and socialism, as the means, path, and method of increasing the productive forces." In a speech to the Second All-Russian Congress of Political Education Departments in October 1921, Lenin told the delegates that private manufacturers could help build a Soviet proletariat. This was a crucial task, because an industrial labor force—"which in our country, thanks to the war and extreme devastation, has been made déclassé, that is, knocked from its class niche, and has ceased to exist as a proletariat"—was a *sine qua non* in the Bolsheviks' conception of a socialist society.[8]

Although private manufacturing could help revive the Russian proletariat, Lenin was counting on state industry (labeled the "commanding heights" and including nearly all large factories) to perform the lion's share of this task. But even here, in the development of state industry, Lenin saw an important role for private entrepreneurs. In order to industrialize, the state needed large reserves of grain and other agricultural products both to feed the burgeoning proletariat that would be created by a restoration of industry and to export for Western currency (needed to buy foreign equipment and hire Western specialists). Without such reserves, Lenin warned the Third All-Russian Food Conference in June 1921, "neither the restoration of large-scale industry nor the restoration of currency circulation is possible, and every socialist knows that without the restoration of large-scale industry—the only real base—there can be no talk of socialist construction." Thus private trade was essential, Lenin argued, to encourage the peasants to produce the surplus food needed by the state. Those who increase the exchange of goods between agriculture and industry, even by means of private economic activity, he wrote in May, are doing more for the development of socialism than those who worry about the purity of communism, or those who draft all sorts of rules and regulations without stimulating trade. "It may seem a paradox: private capitalism in the role of socialism's accomplice? It is in no way a paradox, but rather a completely incontestable economic fact."[9]

Actually, as the bewilderment in the party suggested, it was paradoxical in the extreme to use the "new bourgeoisie" in the construction of socialism. Nor was it certain that the Nepmen would scrupulously fill the role of "socialism's accomplice" designed for them by the state. As private traders swept over the land, marketing large quantities of the state's own goods for sizable profits, it was difficult to avoid the conclusion that the Nepmen were fleecing the state at least as much as they were helping to build socialism. To be sure, despite the paradox and uncertainty associated with the legalization of private business activity in 1921, Lenin was almost certainly correct that this was a necessary step for the Bolsheviks. A retreat was essential in order to placate the peasantry, supply the urban population, and revive industry following the Bolsheviks' failure to storm the heights of socialism during War Communism. Clearly some Bolsheviks could accept this with a minimum of trauma. But it is also evident from the foregoing discussion that other party members simply could not bring themselves to regard the Nepmen as "socialism's accomplices."

Faced with this response from many in his own party, Lenin felt compelled to argue his case repeatedly in the last years of his life. "The idea of building communism with communist hands is childish, completely childish," he informed the Eleventh Party Congress in March 1922. "Communists are only a drop in the sea, a drop in the sea of people. . . . We can direct the economy if communists can build it with bourgeois hands while learning from this bourgeoisie and directing it down the road we want it to follow." Such exhortations to learn from the Nepmen, undoubtedly distasteful advice for many party members, were prompted by the reality that most Bolsheviks were unprepared to administer state trading and manufacturing enterprises. As Lenin told the Eleventh Party Congress:

> The point is that the responsible communist—even the best, who is certainly honest and devoted, who in the past endured imprisonment and did not fear death—does not know how to carry on trade, because he is not a businessman. He did not learn to trade, does not want to learn, and does not understand that he must start learning from the beginning.[10]

Just as the Bolsheviks were not afraid to learn from the nonparty military experts during the civil war, Lenin wrote in *The Tax in Kind,* "we must not be afraid to admit that there is still *a great deal that can and must be learned from the capitalist.*"[11]

Since the state in the aftermath of War Communism was unable to produce sufficient amounts of even the most basic consumer goods and distribute them to the population, the party's least objectionable option was to call on the Nepmen. After confronting Bolsheviks and other state employees with such realities, Lenin often left them with instructions similar to those in the following excerpt from a speech given in October 1921:

> Get down to business, all of you. The capitalists will be beside you. . . . They will make a profit from you of several hundred percent. They will profiteer all around you. Let them make a fortune, but learn from them how to run a business. Only then will you be able to build a communist republic.[12]

However sound this advice, Lenin never explained precisely the process by which state officials were to acquire business acumen from private entrepreneurs. Furthermore, even his most general instructions along this line were not readily accepted by many Bolsheviks, most of whom bridled at the prospect of learning anything from a Nepman. It quickly became apparent that some local officials would rather stifle the Nepmen than learn from them, thus hindering the implementation of the New Economic Policy.

Considering Lenin's preeminence in the party and his position as head of the Council of People's Commissars (Sovnarkom), it is not surprising that his views on the legalization of private business activity were rapidly reflected in party resolutions and government decrees. In the early months of NEP Lenin spoke of permitting only local trade by peasants of surplus produce they might have after paying the new tax in kind. This was the conception of the new freedom to trade outlined in a resolution adopted in March 1921 by the Tenth Party Congress. Transforming this declaration into a law, the All-Russian Central Executive Committee (VTsIK) decreed a week later that "exchange [of the peasants' surplus produce] is permitted inside the boundaries of local economic trade [*oborot*] through cooperatives and at markets and bazaars." The state, VTsIK claimed, was assembling a large supply of manufactured goods to exchange for the peasants' surplus grain.[13]

But as Lenin began to realize during the course of 1921, plans to restrict private trade within such narrow limits were rendered nugatory by the swelling army of private middlemen, vendors, and shopkeepers. As the months went by, government acceptance of this new reality gradually became evident in official directives. On May 24 a decree from Sovnarkom permitted not only the free sale of surplus food by peasants but also trade by other citizens of goods produced by small-scale private manufacturers. These sales were not restricted to marketplaces and bazaars but could be conducted from permanent facilities as well as from stalls, booths, and hawkers' trays, for example. Further, state agencies were given permission to market their products through private traders if cooperative outlets were unavailable or not up to the task. Sovnarkom followed this order with another on July 19, declaring that anyone over sixteen could obtain the license that was now required to sell agricultural and manufactured goods from a permanent shop or in a market square. This decree, legalizing an already-existing trade, provided details on obtaining licenses and instructed the local authorities to set trading hours and enforce sanitation and safety regulations.[14]

Even though a good deal of private trade had been conducted in 1921 (and during War Communism) before it was legalized, many other prospective merchants, particularly those thinking of opening permanent shops, were reluctant to begin business in the first months of NEP when its future still seemed uncertain. According to a number of observers, a decree from Sovnarkom on August 9 helped break the ice and call forth a new surge of private trade by the end of the summer. Undoubtedly the portion of the directive most reassuring to Nepmen was Sovnarkom's insistence that state agencies implement more rapidly the decrees issued earlier in the year establishing the foundations of NEP. In case anyone failed to get the message, the text of the decree and a front-page commentary appeared in *Pravda* on consecutive days. "It is necessary," *Pravda* declared, "to realize clearly that under current conditions, the strengthening and development of the revolution are only possible in this way [i.e., through NEP]." The need for extreme state economic centralization had passed with the civil war, and consequently "it has become possible within certain limits to permit free trade and make room for private enterprise." Nationalized firms without great significance to the economy could be returned to cooperatives "and even private individuals."[15]

From August 1921 through 1922 the state churned out several laws that increased the area of legal activity for private traders. Some of the more interesting decrees include one from Sovnarkom on August 8, 1921, that allowed private persons to buy, sell, and own nonmunicipalized buildings, and another on December 12, 1921, that permitted the establishment of private publishing houses.[16] During the course of 1922, private trade in medicines was legalized (though special permission had to be obtained to conduct the trade); private hospitals and clinics were allowed to open; the state monopoly on the sale of agricultural tools and equipment was repealed; the Railroad Charter of the RSFSR (Russian Republic) ended restrictions on freight shipments belonging to Nepmen; horses could once again be bought and sold freely in the RSFSR; and private businessmen received the right to set up credit and savings and loan associations. After April 4, 1922, it was no longer a crime to own foreign currency, precious stones, or gold, silver, and platinum coins and ingots, though Gosbank, the main state bank, retained for a time its exclusive right to buy and sell precious metals and *valiuta* (foreign currencies). Finally, and in contrast to socialist principles, a tax decree of November 11 allowed a person to inherit up to 10,000 gold rubles at a tax rate rising from zero to only 4 percent. With permission from the state, people could pass on larger amounts of wealth to their heirs at a tax rate that increased 4 percent for each additional 10,000 gold rubles and was not to exceed 50 percent.[17] This right to bequeath property freely was an incentive to reinvest profits in a business rather than consume extravagantly to keep them from falling into the state's hands at a person's death.

Just as private traders were being given more legal room in which to operate during the course of 1921, small-scale private manufacturers and artisans were being encouraged by the state. On May 17 Sovnarkom declared that the output of these producers had to be increased, and thus "needless regulation and formalism that hampers the economic initiative of individuals and groups" were to be avoided. These manufacturers had to be allowed to market their products freely unless they had used raw materials supplied by the state under special conditions. In another decree issued the same day, Sovnarkom repealed laws of previous years that had nationalized small-scale factories, though enterprises already put into operation by the state were not to be returned to their former owners. VTsIK and Sovnarkom spelled out the rights of small-scale manufacturers more completely on July 7, announcing that any citizen was free to engage in handicrafts and, if eighteen or older, set up a "small-scale manufacturing enterprise" (*melkoe promyshlennoe predpriiatie*). These producers could legally sell their output on the free market and purchase raw materials and equipment there. According to this decree, a "small-scale manufacturing enterprise" could employ "not more than ten or twenty hired workers," and no one could own more than one firm. This latter stricture, interestingly enough, was omitted from the Civil Code published later in the year. Nepmen (and cooperatives) were also permitted to lease factories from the state, following an order by Sovnarkom on July 5, implementing a resolution to this effect adopted by the Tenth Party Conference in May.[18]

The state not only bestowed its approval on a growing number of private business activities, but by the end of the summer it also began to permit its own enterprises to conduct business with Nepmen. The Eleventh Party Conference declared in December 1921 that state factories had to be allowed to buy and sell on the free market because the state industrial supply and distribution systems were inadequate. This had been obvious for months, and a number of decrees issued in the late summer and fall of 1921 granted state enterprises the right—in fact, forced many of them—to satisfy their needs on the free market. State firms were instructed to take their business first to cooperative buyers or suppliers, and to turn to private businessmen only as a last resort. But the cooperative system was so inefficient and underdeveloped at the beginning of NEP that state enterprises frequently gave business to Nepmen.[19]

The property rights and legalized spheres of business activity that had been granted to Soviet citizens during the first two years of NEP were collected and set down in the Civil Code of the RSFSR, which went into effect on January 1, 1923. Although not a dramatic extension of the rights of private businessmen, the Civil Code, as a compilation of the main points in many of the decrees discussed above, represented a clear reversal of the policies of War Communism. As a result, the code undoubtedly helped convince Nepman and Bolshevik alike that NEP had indeed been adopted, in Lenin's words, "seriously and for a long time." In summary, the key articles of the code concerning the Nepmen allowed private persons to own trading and manufacturing enterprises whose hired workers did not exceed the numbers to be set by special laws. (These numbers were never clearly spelled out for the different branches of manufacturing. A few authors cite twenty as the maximum figure, but some private factories legally employed many more.) Private trade in all items was permitted, except for those officially banned, such as weapons, explosives, aircraft, telegraph and radio-telegraph gear, certain securities, platinum, radium, helium, liquor above the legal strength, and various strong poisons. In a more ominous tone, article 30 warned that all business transactions "harmful to the state" were to be declared null and void, though a reasonably scrupulous entrepreneur had little to fear from this provision in 1922–23.[20]

In any scholarly or political debate in the Soviet Union, those who are able to claim most effectively that their line is consistent with Lenin's thought have a decided edge. Certainly this was clear to both sides in the party debates over the appropriate policy to adopt concerning the Nepmen after Lenin's death in January 1924. During this debate both those who called for continued toleration of the Nepmen and those who desired the "liquidation of the new bourgeoisie" could make a case that they were the true followers of Lenin. The Lenin most prominent in the preceding discussion—the man who argued that private trade and small-scale manufacturing must be allowed in order to satisfy the peasants' needs, gain their support for the Soviet regime, and encourage them to produce the surplus grain needed for industrialization—would tend to support the call for toleration of the Nepmen. On a number of occasions Lenin supplemented his contention that private business activity had to be legalized temporarily with the argument that such a revival of "capitalism" represented no risk or threat to Soviet power.

In April 1921, for example, he told a meeting of party officials from Moscow and the surrounding region:

> Of course free trade means the growth of capitalism; there is no getting around this. . . . Wherever there is small-scale production and free exchange, capitalism will appear. But need we fear this capitalism if we control the factories, transportation systems, and foreign trade? . . . I think it is incontrovertible that we need have no fear of this capitalism.[21]

The following month, in a set of instructions to local government agencies, Lenin wrote that "the workers' state has sufficient means to restrict within proper bounds the development of these relations [free trade], which are useful and necessary for small-scale production."[22] Thus, if we were to go no further, we would have a Lenin who seemed to support posthumously that segment of the party which, in the second half of NEP, maintained that the Nepmen furnished important benefits and posed no fundamental threat to the development of socialism in the USSR.

Nevertheless, Lenin was actually ambiguous on this critical question, at times appearing to consider the Nepmen a serious menace to the new regime. As early as the Tenth Party Congress in March 1921, when he argued for the adoption of NEP, he also felt compelled to warn the delegates that "free trade, even if it is at first not linked to the White Guards as Kronstadt was, nevertheless leads inevitably to White Guardism, to the triumph of capital and its full restoration. We must, I repeat, be clearly aware of this political danger." In the fall of 1921, speaking to the Second All-Russian Congress of Political Education Departments, Lenin asked:

> How can the people recognize that in place of Kolchak, Wrangel, and Denikin we have in our very midst the enemy that has been the undoing of all previous revolutions? If the capitalists triumph there will be a return to the old regime, as all previous revolutions have demonstrated. Our party must make people realize that the enemy among us is anarchic capitalism and commodity exchange. We must clearly understand—and make sure that the masses of workers and peasants clearly understand—that the essence of the struggle is: "Who will win? Who will get the upper hand?"[23]

This struggle was primarily one between the state and the Nepmen to cement a *smychka* with the peasantry. Would the state be able to supply the cooperatives with enough consumer goods to encourage the peasants to join the cooperatives and provide a grain reserve to support the government's industrialization plans? Or would the peasants find it more advantageous to sell their produce to private buyers and patronize private shops? These questions were of extreme importance to Lenin, which is evident in one of his last works, written for the Twelfth Party Congress in January 1923: "In the final analysis the fate of our republic will depend on whether the peasantry sides with the working class, preserving this alliance, or allows the 'Nepmen,' that is, the new bourgeoisie, to separate it from the workers, splitting off from them."[24] Thus here (and on other occasions) Lenin suggested that the Nepmen posed a far more serious danger than was implied in his assurances that the state could control the Nepmen and had nothing to fear from them. At times he even worried aloud that the state had lost its ability to check the swelling torrent of private enterprise loosed by NEP. He confessed late in 1921 to the delegates from the Political Education Departments that the Nepmen, "whom we are letting in the door and even in several doors," were also coming in through "many doors of which we ourselves are not aware, which open in spite of us and against us." By the Eleventh Party Congress in March of the following year, the state seemed even more helpless against the onslaught of private entrepreneurs.

> Here we have lived for a year with the state in our hands, and has it carried out the New Economic Policy the way we wanted? No. We do not like to admit this, but the state has not operated the way we wanted. And how has it operated? The machine has torn itself from the hand that guides it and goes not where it is directed but where some sort of lawless, God-knows-whence-derived speculator or private capitalist directs it. The machine does not go quite the way the driver imagines, and often goes in a completely different way.[25]

This statement must have alarmed the delegates, given the consequences Lenin attached to a victory by the Nepmen. It was also the concern of Lenin recalled a few years later by those in the party who desired a crackdown on the "new bourgeoisie."

All Bolsheviks desired the eventual elimination of the Nepmen, but there was no consensus on when and how this should be accomplished. Part of the problem was that Lenin's ambiguous statements on the duration of NEP left no clear guidelines on how long the Nepmen should be tolerated. During the first months of NEP, Lenin seemed concerned primarily with convincing the party and the public that NEP had been adopted in earnest and was not a momentary zigzag in the state's domestic policy. At the Tenth Party Congress in March, he estimated that the restoration of large-scale industry would take "many years, not less than a decade, and probably more given our economic havoc. Until then we will have to deal for many long years with the small-scale producer, and the slogan of free trade will be inevitable." Two months later, at the Tenth Party Conference, Lenin reiterated more forcefully the need to accept NEP, in an often-repeated phrase, "seriously and for a long time."

> "Seriously and for a long time"—we must definitely get this into our heads and remember it well, because from the habit of gossip rumors are spreading that this is a policy in quotes, in other words, political trickery that is only being carried out for the present day. This is not true.[26]

Although adamant that NEP had been adopted "seriously and for a long time," Lenin was considerably less certain how long a "long time" would be. In March, as we have seen, his estimate was "not less than a decade, and probably more." At the Tenth Party Conference in May, he rejected the guess of another delegate that "seriously and for a long time" meant twenty-five years, but he conceded that he could not predict NEP's duration: "I will not venture an estimate on how long the period should be, but this [twenty-five years], in my opinion, is too pessimistic. We will be lucky to project our policy five to ten years into the future, because usually we cannot even do it for five weeks."[27]

Thus the impression that emerges from Lenin's scattered remarks on NEP's future is one of uncertainty. On balance, his comments tended to support those in the party who felt the Nepmen would be needed for a considerable period of time. But on some occasions he appeared less patient, as in a speech to an All-Russian Congress of Metalworkers in March 1922: "We can now see clearly the situation that has developed in our country and can say with complete firmness that *we can now stop the retreat that we began and are already stopping it. Enough*." Three weeks later he announced to the Eleventh Party Congress that the party was approaching "'the last and decisive battle'" with "Russian capitalism growing out of and supported by the small peasant economy. The battle will be in the near future, though it is impossible to determine the date precisely."[28] Although these statements were not free from ambiguity (for instance, did Lenin understand "'the last and decisive battle'" to mean economic competition or a violent clash?), this did not prevent Bolsheviks who favored a showdown with the Nepmen from contending a few years later that "the near future" had arrived. Stalin, for example, cited remarks such as this—and Lenin's comment at the end of December 1921: "We will carry out this policy [NEP] seriously and for a long time, but, of course, as has already been correctly noted, not forever"[29]—to support his liquidation of the Nepmen at the end of the decade.[30]

Lenin was faced in 1921–22 with the task of designing a policy concerning the Nepmen, who, he had indicated, provided essential skills while threatening simultaneously the very existence of the state. At times Lenin seemed uncertain about how much private enterprise to permit and how to keep it from corrupting the Revolution. In the fall of 1921 he conceded to the Second All-Russian Congress of Political Education Departments that NEP "means the restoration of capitalism to a significant extent—to what extent we do not know." At the Tenth Party Congress he posed a question undoubtedly on the minds of many in attendance: "Can the Communist party really accept and permit freedom of trade? Are there not irreconcilable contradictions here? To this one must reply that, of course, in practice the solution to this problem is extremely difficult to determine."[31] This statement betrays in Lenin more than a hint of the misgivings that were harbored by other Bolsheviks—and that Lenin tried to dispel by claiming that no paradox existed in using Nepmen to build socialism.

Lenin's health deteriorated before he could work out a detailed system of restraints to keep the private sector within limits the party deemed safe. In fact, he had no clear idea even about what these limits might be (and there was certainly no consensus in the party on this score until Stalin imposed it at the end of the decade). On his death in January 1924, Lenin left only his notion of "state capitalism" to guide his successors. "State capitalism," he explained to the Eleventh Party Congress in March 1922,

> is a completely unexpected and unforeseen type of capitalism. After all, nobody could foresee that the proletariat would gain power in one of the most underdeveloped countries, try at first to organize large-scale production and distribution to the peasants, and then, failing in this effort because of the low standard of culture, enlist the services of capitalism.[32]

Specifically, state capitalism as it pertained to the Nepmen was an arrangement whereby the party retained all political power and control of

important economic enterprises but permitted the Nepmen (and a handful of foreign entrepreneurs operating concessions) to conduct business.
The Bolsheviks hoped to restrict this private activity in a number of ways,
as we will see, and guide it into spheres most beneficial to the state.[33]

Some years earlier, in the spring of 1918, Lenin had attached a different meaning to the term *state capitalism*.[34] At this time he argued that
the new Soviet state should engage the services of *large-scale* capitalists—the only people with the expertise to carry out production and
distribution on a national scale. The state, stopping short of nationalizing the enterprises of these businessmen, would limit itself to controlling
or directing them, much the way the government managed the economy
in wartime Germany. This, Lenin maintained, would be a great step forward for Russia—a triumph over the petty bourgeoisie (small-scale
traders, craftsmen, and peasant entrepreneurs) and the last stage in the
transition from capitalism to socialism. By the summer of 1918, however, Lenin abandoned the concept of state capitalism. Few capitalists
were available or interested, and, in any event, as the party entered War
Communism Lenin (and most Bolsheviks) apparently felt that a much
more direct route to socialism was available.

Following the introduction of NEP, Lenin resurrected his pre–War
Communism theory of state capitalism as a means to convince apprehensive Bolsheviks that NEP was not entirely an unanticipated or striking
departure from party doctrine. But once again, few large-scale capitalists (domestic or foreign) stepped forward to work with the Bolsheviks.
Consequently, as the months went by, Lenin began to describe state capitalism as a system of using and controlling *small-scale* entrepreneurs
(the vast majority of Nepmen)—the very people earlier designated as
the principal enemy when Lenin had explained state capitalism in the
spring of 1918.

Toward state capitalism's goal of bridling the Nepmen, Sovnarkom
and VTsIK announced on March 22, 1923 (with a supplementary order
on June 14), that all private businessmen were required to register within
three months with the *guberniia* economic councils (*sovnarkhozy*).
Even Nepmen who had been in business for some time and had already
registered with the state and purchased licenses were required to present
copies of their registration forms to the *guberniia sovnarkhozy*. The
decree instructed *guberniia* officials to scrutinize all registrations by
July 22 and reject those that violated NEP's ground rules. Also that
spring, Sovnarkom and VTsIK reaffirmed the state monopoly of foreign
trade and ordered the People's Commissariats of Justice and Foreign

Trade to crack down on infringements. A number of other decrees and rulings in 1923 addressed narrower lines of activity. For example, private purchases and sales of gold, silver, foreign currencies, and securities were permitted at various state exchanges, but private trade in platinum was forbidden. Further, in August private film production and distribution firms were banned, and a state monopoly proclaimed.[35]

Apart from permitting or forbidding specific economic activities, state capitalism restrained the Nepmen by taxation. The first direct tax on the nonpeasant population after the introduction of NEP was the "business tax" (*promyslovyi nalog*) announced on July 26, 1921, consisting of a license fee and a "leveling fee" (*uravnitel'nyi sbor*). The license fee, which increased with the size of the business, was to be paid every six months, though special three-month and one-month licenses were also available. The leveling fee was a monthly 3 percent tax on production and sales and accounted for a sizable majority of business-tax receipts (about 71 percent in 1922/23 compared to 29 percent for the license fee). In 1921 the bureaucracy was in no condition to assess and collect this tax from all producers and traders, so the tax was implemented gradually, beginning with the fifty-eight largest cities. The following year the tax was extended to the country as a whole, though doubtless many holes remained in the bureaucratic net through which Nepmen could slip.[36]

Individual craftsmen working alone were exempted from the tax, as were peasant handicraftsmen who received help only from family members and also farmed part time. More substantial private manufacturing enterprises were divided into twelve ranks, according to the number of workers employed (from not more than three in rank I to over seventy-five in rank XII), and assessed a license fee that increased with each rank. Private trade was divided into three categories, with the license fee rising from rank to rank. Rank I covered sales by individual hawkers and peddlers from trays, baskets, sacks, and the like in bazaars and market squares. Rank II encompassed sales from tables, stalls, booths, and kiosks, with sales from larger, permanent establishments falling into rank III.[37]

On February 10, 1922, VTsIK and Sovnarkom issued a new business-tax decree, dividing trade into five ranks and introducing a surcharge on the business tax for firms producing or trading "luxury goods." The term *luxury goods* was defined simply by including a long list of individual items such as products made from precious metals and stones, fireworks, photographic equipment, rugs (except those made from hemp or felt), various silk, wool, and linen fabrics, furs, various sorts of footwear, caviar, sturgeon, foreign cheeses, mayonnaise, out-of-season vegetables, cigars, foreign tobacco and cigarettes, art objects, furniture, carriages, cars, "fashionable women's clothes," live flowers, pastries and candies, perfumes, and cosmetics. Producers of "luxury goods" were required to pay half again the normal license fee of businesses their size. Traders of ranks I, II, and III who handled "luxury goods" were ordered to pay an additional license fee equal to 100 percent of the standard fee for rank III. Traders in rank IV were assessed a surcharge amounting to 150 percent of the standard rank III fee, whereas merchants in the fifth rank paid an additional two and one-half times the cost of a standard rank III license. The leveling tax rate on the production and sale of "luxury goods" was raised to 6 or 12 percent, depending on the specific products involved. State and cooperative firms lost their immunity to the business tax in 1922 and were initially taxed at the same rates as private businesses. But in 1923 another business-tax decree raised the Nepmen's rates while the state was busy extending tax advantages to the "socialist" sector.[38]

In November 1922 VTsIK and Sovnarkom introduced an income tax on all individuals living in towns and receiving income from business activity, securities, and other sources. Also taxed were people who lived in the countryside but whose source of income was in a town, and people who lived in towns but received income from the countryside. Most workers' wages were exempt from this tax, and if they had other income, they were taxed at lower rates than Nepmen. The tax was to be levied every six months on a progressive scale that ranged from 0.8 percent to only 14.6 percent, though by 1924 the upper end of the scale had increased to 35 percent.[39]

By the end of 1922, Nepmen were subject to many other taxes and fees besides the business and income taxes. Easily the most substantial of these was the fee for the use of business facilities (rent paid for shops and market stalls, for example), generating twice as much revenue from private traders as the business tax in 1922. The announcement of higher rents in January 1923 accounted, along with the winter weather, for a sharp (40 percent) reduction in the number of private traders in the first quarter of 1923. During this period in Moscow, over one fifth of the applications to rent private trading facilities were withdrawn by the Nepmen themselves. There were also ad hoc taxes, such as the special levy for famine relief funds imposed in January 1923 on producers and traders of "luxury goods." The tax amounted to 50 percent of the license fee and 1 percent of sales or production, and even higher rates were applied to certain enterprises that sold food or drink. In addition, the government drained off some of the Nepmen's profits by requiring them to purchase insurance from the state for their businesses and workers. In 1923, for example, holders of trade and manufacturing licenses and other income tax payers were required to spend on insurance an amount equal to 16 percent of the money they paid in wages. Nepmen were also pressured to buy government bonds, frequently in the tone adopted by G. Ia. Sokol'nikov, commissar of finance, at the Tenth All-Russian Congress of Soviets in December 1922: "If a man is able to support the loan and does not support it, we can and shall interpret this as a refusal to support the Soviet Government in general."[40]

It was one thing to announce these new taxes, but quite another to collect them. Particularly in the early years of NEP, the state's ability to assess and collect taxes and prevent unlicensed trade was extremely limited, both in the provinces and in the large cities. This was the result in large part of the size of the country and all the economic and political disruptions since 1917. But another factor was the disdain of most Bolsheviks for work in a tax bureaucracy. As an official in the People's Commissariat of Finance (Narkomfin) complained on the eve of the Eleventh Party Congress: "Financial and especially tax work is still not at the center of attention of party and Soviet agencies, and thus the old scornful attitude toward financial and particularly tax work is evident."[41] For these reasons, then, a considerable amount of private economic activity undoubtedly eluded taxation.

The state was aware of this problem and took what steps it could to enforce its tax decrees. In May 1922, for example, a Domestic Trade Commission (Komvnutorg) was created and attached to the Council of Labor and Defense (STO). Komvnutorg (which two years later was reorganized and upgraded as the People's Commissariat of Domestic Trade, Narkomvnutorg) was supposed to organize a system to gather data on the Nepmen, study trends in private trade, present drafts of decrees to Sovnarkom and STO encouraging "socialist" trade over private trade, and comment on trade decrees prepared by other agencies. In addition to revamping its own bureaucracy, the state issued a number of orders in 1922/23 requiring trade and manufacturing firms (state, cooperative, and private) to keep business records and make these available to tax agents inspecting the firm. The local police (*militsiia*) were instructed to help register private traders, assist Narkomfin in collecting taxes from Nepmen, and enforce other trade regulations. Unlicensed private businesses and those that did not pay their tax arrears could be closed by the police.[42]

In accordance with his concept of state capitalism, Lenin indicated that the courts would interpret laws the way the Bolsheviks understood them and not in favor of the Nepmen, insisting at the same time that state agencies act within the law and respect the economic rights that were being granted to individuals. "The task before us now," he told the Ninth All-Russian Congress of Soviets in December 1921,

> is to develop trade as demanded by the New Economic Policy, and this requires greater revolutionary legality. . . . The closer we get to firm and lasting power and the further trade develops, the more essential it becomes to adopt firmly the slogan of greater revolutionary legality, and the narrower becomes the realm of activity of the agency [the Cheka] that responds with blows to the blows of conspirators.[43]

A few days later Lenin appealed to the congress for a balanced regulation of private entrepreneurs. The People's Commissariat of Justice, he explained, must "carefully observe the activities of private traders and manufacturers, permitting not the slightest restraint of their activity, but at the same time punishing most severely the slightest attempt to violate the laws of the republic."[44]

This was easier said than done, in part because the restrictions that state capitalism placed on the Nepmen were quite vague. To be sure, certain undertakings such as foreign trade and heavy industry were for all practical purposes closed to the Nepmen, but in domestic trade the legal boundaries were considerably murkier. Initially, as we have seen, the state tried to restrict private trade to the simple exchange of products in local markets, and only grudgingly accepted ordinary private shops and markets when the former scheme was outdistanced by reality. Thus it was next to impossible for even the most alert local official to know which activities were permitted and which not. Provincial officials were not the only ones confused; numerous complaints appeared in leading Soviet economic periodicals in 1922 and 1923 on the lack of a clear and complete body of trade law.[45]

Many Nepmen were also uncertain about the new rules—and not only during the first months of NEP. In May 1923, for example, a correspondent from *Torgovo-promyshlennaia gazeta* (*Trade and Industry Gazette*) talked with a number of private meat vendors in Moscow.

More than anything else they complained that the state had still not worked out a definite set of principles to guide its officials in the supervision of the private sector. As a result, the butchers claimed, they were subjected to widely varying treatment from different state agencies and individual inspectors. Most often this took the form of arbitrary tax assessments, which could fluctuate dramatically even within a single district. Sometimes an individual shop was hit with such heavy tax surcharges that it had to close, while stores nearby remained comparatively unscathed.[46]

Another problem was the concept of "speculation," which the authorities could stretch to ban nearly all private trade, if they chose. Following Lenin's call for a revision of the speculation laws in order to increase state control of the Nepmen, Sovnarkom decreed in July 1921 that anyone who conspired to raise prices or withhold goods from the market was to be imprisoned or have property confiscated, or both.[47] Interpreted strictly, this decree forbade peasants to store their grain until prices improved and made it a crime for a private middleman to offer peasants or any other producers a higher price for their products than that offered by the state. Of course, such open-ended decrees were not enforced with unremitting zeal in the early 1920s. An attempt to do so would have scuttled NEP immediately after its launching. Nevertheless, the police cracked down in one place or another often enough to create considerable confusion about what, precisely, constituted speculation. As Ilya Ehrenburg observed:

> There was a very fine dividing line between permissible profit and illegal speculation. From time to time the GPU arrested a dozen or a hundred enterprising traders; this was called "skimming the NEP." The cook knows when to skim the fish-soup, but I doubt whether all the NEPmen understood which they were: the scum or the fish.[48]

This uncertainty remained, and the state later found it easy to launch offensives against the Nepmen when it wished to, on the basis of existing speculation decrees.

Adding to the legal confusion, the state sometimes resorted to emergency measures in an effort to eliminate manifestations of private trade that the Bolshevik leadership found threatening or unpalatable. In 1921–22, for example, officials were alarmed by the many thousands of bagmen, persons who, generally traveling by train, took a small number of articles to the countryside to barter for food. On May 27, 1921, Lenin sent a telegram to F. E. Dzerzhinskii, head of the Cheka, noting that "all the Ukrainian comrades most urgently insist on intensification of the struggle against bagging in the Ukraine, which threatens to disrupt the purchases of grain for famine-stricken regions of the Republic. . . . I ask you," Lenin continued, "to devote intense attention to this and inform me whether extreme measures are being taken, what these measures are, and their results." Though a number of "administrative measures" were adopted in various localities, such as forbidding bagmen to board trains, confiscating their merchandise, and pressing them into labor gangs, bagging continued to flourish until a more normal food distribution system was established.[49] The state also reserved the right to suspend private trade of particular products, and even shut down local markets completely, in regions where it was having difficulty collecting the tax in kind on these items. By December 1, 1921, private trade of various agricultural products (such as grain, dairy goods, potatoes, wool, and hay) had been banned in five entire *gubernii* and in parts of nineteen others. In some localities all private sales were banned, though it proved impossible, as it did during War Communism, to suppress small-scale private trade completely in these areas.[50]

The ambiguous attitude and policies of Lenin and the central government with regard to the Nepmen were matched by the treatment that private entrepreneurs experienced at the hands of local officials. Part of the problem was simply the result of the mixed signals coming from Moscow. But even when they received clear instructions to tolerate one form or another of private trade, some local officials bridled. Many Bolsheviks had serious misgivings about the legalization of private trade, and those in positions of local authority often showed little inclination "to build communism with bourgeois hands." Thus a number of provincial officials attempted to restrict or suspend private trade on their own authority. In December 1922, for example, local decrees of this sort were issued in Tambov, Simbirsk, Stavropol', Penza, Minsk, Gomel', and other *gubernii*. This activity prompted STO to send out a circular stressing that such decrees violated Soviet law. Local authorities were reminded that they must not take measures that contradicted "the basic principles concerning trade set forth in the decrees and orders of the central government." Besides, STO added, as if for good measure, these attempts to ban private trade simply did not work.[51]

Uneasiness over the Nepmen, however, was too firmly ensconced in the party to be checked by a few circulars. Local officials were particularly concerned about rising prices—which they were inclined to blame on greedy Nepmen—and consequently they sometimes imposed illegal price controls on private trade in their regions. Now and then they went further. In December 1921, *Pravda* reported disapprovingly, an official in Central Asia wrote an article in *Tashkentskie izvestiia* (*Tashkent News*) recommending the use of the Cheka and the "old methods of work" in combating rising prices. Following this advice, the Samarkand Executive Committee, with the help of the local Cheka, arrested many Nepmen and imposed price controls temporarily on all commodities. In *Torgovo-promyshlennaia gazeta,* the author of an article on private trade in the provinces concluded that "the attitude of local authorities toward private trade is not always favorable. . . . Traders live in constant fear of losing their property." This was certainly the case in Voronezh. Following the introduction of NEP, grain and meat appeared again in the market, and prices declined. But the local authorities, hostile to NEP and free trade, confiscated private traders' supplies of these products. As a result, grain and meat vanished almost completely from the market, and the price of what was available skyrocketed.[52]

Early in NEP the press reported that local administrators frequently imposed new taxes on the Nepmen or increased old ones without permission from Moscow. Typical were reports from Saratov, Kolomna, and Bogorodsk (a town near Nizhnii Novgorod), where private traders complained that they were charged too much for, among other things, obtaining trade licenses and renting booths or stands in the market squares. In Nizhnii Novgorod a certain tax was levied on both small-scale and more substantial private traders when, according to the law, only the latter were required to pay it. This helped explain, *Torgovaia gazeta* (*Trade Gazette*) reported, the failure of a considerable number of private traders.[53]

The motive behind these illegal taxes was not always a desire simply to throttle private trade. Such measures could also reflect confusion over the new tax laws or a desperate need to acquire additional operating funds at a time when local officials received little financial assistance from Moscow. In Tambov, for example, the Guberniia Executive Committee levied unauthorized surcharges on, among other things, the normal fines for unlicensed sales, trade licenses, restaurants with billiard tables, and transactions at the local commodity exchange—all in order to raise money to care for victims of the famine that had ravaged the area. In Novocherkassk, among several additional taxes imposed on private traders were two to support a children's home and an old-age home.[54]

This unauthorized taxation of the Nepmen called forth a stream of reprimands and reminders year after year from Moscow to provincial administrators. As late as December 1924, a circular from the Central Executive Committee and Sovnarkom noted that in some localities officials were still requiring private traders to pay various extra fees and "donations." "Such a state of affairs," the circular emphasized, "cannot be tolerated in the future, since it disorganizes the center's tax policy, undermines the trust of the population, and reduces its ability to pay taxes." The effectiveness of all these documents, however, clearly left something to be desired, given the need to reissue them and the continuing reports in the press of local taxation abuses.[55]

According to an article in STO's journal, the treatment of private credit organizations by provincial authorities was better in 1924/25 than it had been in the preceding years. Nevertheless, "in some localities" there were still supporters of a "struggle" with private capital who drove it underground into activities "harmful to the country." Such a "struggle" occurred in December 1925 when authorities "in many provincial towns" misinterpreted a directive from Moscow on combating "speculation" and restricted the operation of private credit institutions with more severity. This restriction, the article complained, produced results opposite those desired by Moscow, for it compelled people to turn to more clandestine and rapacious private usurers.[56]

Thus the treatment of the Nepmen varied wildly from place to place and year to year (even month to month). Given the conflicting, ambiguous statements and measures emanating from Moscow, and the dismay with which many officials regarded NEP, it is hardly surprising that, as a report prepared for STO asserted, the word *chaos* best characterized the implementation of the new trade policy in the provinces. In the spring of 1922, delegates at the Supreme Economic Council's First All-Russian Congress of Trade Officials complained that private entrepreneurs in the provinces were not regulated according to standardized norms. Instead, chairmen of local party committees dealt with private trade as they pleased, encouraging it in some regions and repressing it in others.[57]

Although many Bolsheviks, both in the provinces and the large cities, were wary or resentful of NEP, this was not always the case, as an American Relief Administration official in Iaroslavl' found: "In this community there is less hounding of the 'burgui' [bourgeoisie], less distrust and more cooperation between them and the Communists than in Moscow and Petrograd. To be sure, every now and then the power of the Communists makes itself felt, but on the whole life here is already beginning to flow in the prewar channels."[58]

Similar variations were evident in other localities. In the realm of manufacturing, Sovnarkom had to repeat a number of times its denationalization decrees, since many local officials were hostile (or confused) about the return of factories to private entrepreneurs. Although Nepmen who leased factories from the state were supposed to be allowed to buy raw materials on their own, authorities in various districts feared that such activity would disrupt the state campaigns to obtain the same products and therefore blocked the purchases made by private buyers— even going so far as to arrest them and confiscate their goods. In contrast, other provincial officials, eager to revive the economy in their regions and to unburden themselves of the obligation to administer large numbers of factories and workshops, hurried to return or lease many of them to Nepmen, despite warnings from Moscow to wait for a decree authorizing such procedures.[59]

These wide variations of official behavior at the local level were later matched by sharp fluctuations in the policy of the party leadership— first harsh, then tolerant, and finally merciless—toward private entrepreneurs in the five years between Lenin's death and Stalin's emergence as party leader. Such policy changes underscored the continuing absence of agreement in the party on the questions Lenin confronted repeatedly in the last years of his life: Were the Nepmen more an "accomplice" or a menace to the construction of socialism? What limits should be placed on their activity? How long should they be tolerated? Indeed, should they be tolerated at all? Despite his own uncertainty, Lenin in the first years of NEP could at least mute disputes among Bolshevik leaders on these questions. But his concept of state capitalism was unified only by the general principle of the need to both permit and restrict private economic activity, not by a consistent system of laws reflecting a consensus in the party. In fact, the tenets of state capitalism were sufficiently amorphous to permit the party faction in control at any given time after Lenin's death to alter dramatically the pressure on the Nepmen, while arguing all along that its policies were in harmony with the fundamental principles of NEP spelled out by Lenin in 1921–22.

## CHAPTER 2

# NEP's Second Wind

At the present stage [NEP], the system [does not] involve the actual
prohibition of buying and selling at a profit. The policy is not to
forbid these professions, but to render them precarious and
disgraceful. The private trader is a sort of permitted outlaw, without
privileges or protection, like the Jew in the Middle Ages—an outlet
for those who have overwhelming instincts in this direction, but not
a natural or agreeable job for the normal man.

—John Maynard Keynes

Uncertainty about the morrow gave a special character to the
amusements of the new bourgeoisie. The Moscow that Yesenin
called "Tavern Moscow" lived in a state of morbid tempestuousness;
it was like a mixture of the nineteenth-century gold-fever in
California and an exaggerated Dostoyevskian moral climate.

—Ilya Ehrenburg

Within the limits of "state capitalism," there was ample room to adjust
the pressure on the Nepmen by such methods as enforcing existing speculation decrees with greater or less rigor, and by reducing or increasing
taxes and the flow of goods and credit from the "socialist" to the private
sector. Policy shifts of this sort followed the changes in party leadership
that occurred during NEP, with the result that private entrepreneurs
were subject to widely varying treatment throughout the decade—all
supposedly in the spirit of NEP. These unpredictable policy changes
were a frequent complaint of Nepmen who responded to surveys, spoke
with Soviet reporters, and on rare occasions stated their views directly
in newspaper columns. In 1926, for instance, a spokesman for a private
textile firm wrote in the newspaper of the Commissariat of Domestic
Trade, Torgovye izvestiia (Trade News): "The main factor, from which
private trade and industry suffer a great deal, is that up to now there has
been no regular and consistent policy with regard to private capital. It
would be easier to adapt one's activity to the harshest system than to be
dependent on completely arbitrary and unanticipated developments."[1]
A. I. Sinelobov, a private trader and member of the Moscow Com-

modity Exchange, expressed similar sentiments in *Torgovye izvestiia*. "First of all," he urged, "it is essential that state agencies spell out precisely and definitively their policy concerning private trade." This would enable traders to plan ahead and eliminate the "speculative" leaps of some entrepreneurs from one activity to another.[2] If these views had been restricted to Nepmen, one might be inclined to shrug them off as whining. But this was not the case. The authors of several Soviet studies of the private sector, published in the 1920s, reached the same conclusion. For example, one of the contributors to the Supreme Economic Council's extensive report on the Nepmen concluded that "the main factor negatively affecting the normal development of private trade in the past few years has been the extreme instability and complete uncertainty created in the activity of private capital by the fluctuations of state trade policy."[3]

The problem was not simply the work of arbitrary local officials, uninformed or hostile toward NEP. Several times throughout the decade (first in 1921) party leaders themselves altered markedly their policy toward the private sector. On the national level, the first significant change in the business climate after the introduction of NEP came at the end of 1923 and lasted well into the following year. From the Nepmen's point of view, it was a setback of major proportions. A German correspondent in the Soviet Union throughout NEP described 1924 as "the year of the 'second Revolution.'" He reported, "At that time 300,000 private enterprises were closed in a few months, and a general attack was made on all remnants of bourgeois Russia. Churches were closed. The children of bourgeois parents were driven with merciless fanaticism from schools and universities."[4] William Reswick, a Russian who emigrated to the United States before the Revolution, worked in the Soviet Union in a number of capacities from 1922 to 1934. After a trip to New York in October 1923, he returned to Moscow at the end of December.

> I was struck by the drastic change that had come over the capital in but a few weeks. Again, as in previous winters, the city was immersed in gloom. Stores, shops, and restaurants were bolted and locked. Their ice-crusted windows seemed to stare at me in stern warning of peril. . . .
>
> The Sukharev market . . . was deserted. The feverish activity I had seen there in early autumn seemed to me like a dream. . . .
>
> The obvious signs of fright were the speeding, shrieking Black Marias with their pitiful human cargoes. . . .
>
> The victims of this wave of terror [a Soviet friend explained] are nearly all Nepmen, who had invested their capital in reliance on existing laws and acted in good faith.[5]

Other longtime foreign residents in the Soviet Union were also struck by this sudden change of course, with its wave of arrests and the closing of many private businesses. Nepmen who had made quick fortunes and had gradually lost their fear of an opulent life style suddenly found it risky to flaunt their wealth. Walter Duranty, the *New York Times* correspondent, reported that a lavish New Year's party was held that winter in Moscow's Hermitage restaurant, recently purchased by a group of Nepmen and ornately redecorated. In the midst of the gaiety, which "resembled a New Year's Eve in New York before the Crash," the GPU (secret police) burst in, arrested the host at each table if he was a state or cooperative employee, and announced that a check would be made to determine if all the Nepmen present had been paying their taxes. Shortly thereafter, the restaurant's lease was revoked.[6] The police were not the only ones to implement the harsh new line. State banks, for example, slashed the amount of credit they extended to Nepmen during 1923/24 from 42.4 to 17.8 million rubles.[7]

The reasons for the increased pressure on private entrepreneurs in this period remain shrouded in uncertainty, though undoubtedly several factors played a part. Some party members, as noted previously, were worried by the growth of private trade and feared that the state might soon find itself separated from the peasantry by the Nepmen. In February 1924 I. T. Smilga (a member of the Central Committee) warned a meeting of state economic officials:

> If two years ago private capital made its first timid efforts in the area of trade and petty industry and did not appear a danger to the Soviet state economy, today we can no longer say this. In the person of the private capitalist we have a significant economic force that demands to be considered seriously. In retail trade and especially in trade with the peasants, private capital now occupies the dominant position.

Smilga went on to voice a concern that the "new bourgeoisie" was now positioned between the state and the peasantry, a warning repeated by Stalin a few months later at a course held for local party secretaries: "The merchant and the usurer have wedged themselves between the state on the one hand and the peasantry on the other, thus making it very difficult to set up the *smychka* between socialist industry and the peasant economy."[8] Lenin had based his justification of NEP on the argument that without the support of the peasantry, the state could not hope to industrialize and build socialism. But it clearly seemed to some in the party that NEP, by unleashing private trade in the countryside, was in fact *contributing* to the state's problems there, rather than alleviating them.

Meanwhile, many Bolsheviks were also irritated and alarmed by the revival of lavish "bourgeois" entertainments in the cities. During War Communism, night life of a prerevolutionary sort had vanished nearly completely, but following the introduction of NEP, expensive amusements and public displays of wealth were tolerated. Many observers, Soviet and foreign, dwelled on this facet of NEP—in part because the contrast with War Communism was so stunning and in part because such a life style seemed flagrantly out of place following a "socialist" revolution. NEP's version of the Roaring Twenties went far beyond the reopening of expensive food stores, hotels, and restaurants. Casinos and race tracks also operated legally, the privately owned establishments being required to pay the state a portion of their receipts. Many nightclubs, gambling parlors, and brothels operated semiclandestinely (without licenses or tax payments), and the trade in bootleg liquor flourished. Those in the know had little difficulty acquiring heroin and cocaine.[9] According to Walter Duranty,

> the biggest gambling establishment [in Moscow] was a place called Praga at the corner of the Arbat Square. In the main outer room there were two roulette tables both with zero and double zero, two baccarat tables and a dozen games of *chemin de fer*. Banks at baccarat frequently ran as high as $5,000, a dozen different currencies were used, from bundles of Soviet million notes to hundred-dollar bills, English five- and ten-pound notes, and most surprising of all, no small quantity of gold, Tsarist ten-rouble pieces, English sovereigns, and French twenty-franc coins. As in France, there was an "inner *cercle privé*," where only baccarat was allowed and play was higher, with banks of $25,000 or $30,000.

Among the people at the Praga were prostitutes, "whom N.E.P. had hatched in flocks, noisy and voracious as sparrows. Later in increasing numbers [appeared] the wives and families of N.E.P.-men, the new profiteers, with jewels on their stumpy fingers and old lace and ermine round their thick red necks."[10] In Petrograd, an American famine relief worker attending the opera at the beginning of 1922 found his attention drawn to "a prominent box [in which there] sat a speculator with his richly dressed wife. They placed in front of them a box of delicious sweets, and in the presence of the onlookers peeled an orange (oranges are as rare in Petrograd as in the Arctic), put it on the sweets, and walked out."[11]

It is not difficult to imagine how Bolsheviks (and others as well) could

be appalled at such spectacles and wonder what had happened to the
Revolution. The German ambassador, Count Brockdorff-Rantzau, noted
that the ostentatious revelry of some of the wealthier Nepmen and the
reappearance of casinos and luxury restaurants "have aroused deep resentment among the workers and the rank and file of the Party, who are
asking whether they made the Revolution to enrich a host of private
profiteers." The well-informed Menshevik biweekly, *Sotsialisticheskii
vestnik* (*Socialist Herald*), reported similar discontent among some
workers and party cadre who were demanding "the closing of all 'NEP
restaurants,' the taxation of Nepmen for hundreds of millions, and so
on."[12] This was also the impression left by the anarchist Alexander
Berkman, himself no enthusiast of NEP, describing Moscow in 1921.
"Gay music sounds from the garden nearby. At the little tables white-
aproned waiters serve food and drinks to the guests. Groups gather at
the gate sullenly watching the novel scene. 'Bourzhooi! Damned speculators!' they mutter. The NEP is at work."[13] Perhaps nowhere else than
in the memoirs of Victor Serge is there a better description of both the
amusements of the newly rich and the dismay that this life style provoked among those committed to the Revolution.

> The sordid taint of money is visible on everything again. The grocers have
> sumptuous displays, packed with Crimean fruits and Georgian wines, but a
> postman earns [only] about fifty roubles a month. . . . Hordes of beggars and
> abandoned children; hordes of prostitutes. We have three large gaming-
> houses in town [Leningrad], where baccarat, roulette and chemin-de-fer are
> played, sinister dives with crime always hovering around the corner. The
> hotels laid on for foreigners and Party officials have bars which are complete
> with tables covered in soiled white linen, dusty palm-trees and alert waiters
> who know secrets beyond the Revolution's ken. What would you like—a
> dose of "snow"? At the Europa bar thirty girls show off their paint and cheap
> rings to men in fur-lined coats and caps who are drinking glasses brimming
> with alcohol. . . . You could take the lift to the roof of the Hotel Europa, and
> there find another bar, like any in Paris or Berlin, full of lights, dancing and
> jazz, and even more depressing than the one on the ground floor.[14]

It may also be that as Lenin lay stricken in the winter of 1923–24,
the party leadership (Stalin, Zinoviev, and Kamenev), particularly Stalin, felt compelled by the political uncertainty brought by Lenin's inca-
pacitation and impending death to move against the Nepmen—as an
attempt either to gain additional support in the party or to create an
atmosphere of fear in which political opposition would be more difficult. One of William Reswick's friends, a Soviet journalist with good
Kremlin connections, held the latter view.

Lenin is dying. The end may come tonight, tomorrow, next week, but it cannot be long. The doctors have given up hope. The triumvirate, Stalin, Kamenev, Zinoviev, are in a panic. Hence this new wave of terror. They have practically liquidated the NEP. . . . Stalin's real motive for arresting them [Nepmen] is to create an atmosphere of fright that will tide him over the crisis that must come with Lenin's death.[15]

Not only did a political crisis appear to be in the offing toward the end of 1923, but the country was also beset by the "scissors crisis." The term *price scissors* is a metaphor for a contemporary graph showing that by October 1923 prices of manufactured goods were close to three times higher than those in 1913, whereas agricultural prices were slightly below the 1913 level. This state of affairs provided the peasantry little incentive to produce and market surplus grain, and thus represented a threat to the state's industrialization plans and to the urban population dependent on produce from the countryside. One of the government's responses to the problem of holding down consumer prices was an attempt to eliminate private middlemen-wholesalers by levying higher taxes and sharply reducing the supplies they received from the state.[16] In addition, price controls were set on various common products (though it proved much more difficult to enforce these decrees in private stores than in the "socialist" sector). Thus, even had there been no political motives for shortening the Nepmen's leash, the economic problems of 1923/24 were sufficient to prompt a number of measures detrimental to private entrepreneurs.

As noted above, the drop in state credit available to Nepmen, from 42.4 million rubles to 17.8 million rubles during 1923/24, was particularly dramatic. On May 14, 1924, a special joint session of the Central Control Commission and the Workers' and Peasants' Inspectorate (RKI) ordered state banks to cease "as far as possible" granting credit to private traders. The banks were not slow to comply, and by October 1, 1924, the Nepmen's share of the total credit extended by the country's five main banks had fallen to 2 percent—down from 11.5 percent in October 1923. Following suit, nearly all industrial trusts that continued to sell to Nepmen sharply reduced sales on credit to private customers. To illustrate, of the total sales to Nepmen by cotton textile trusts, the percentage made on credit plunged from 49.3 percent in the first quarter of 1924 to 2.5 percent in May and 0.2 percent in June.[17] In the same spirit, state industry cut back its direct sales to Nepmen during 1924 from 14.7 percent of total sales to 2.1 percent. Some enterprises were ordered to cease all sales to private customers, whereas others were instructed to sell only for cash or in small lots. This was a blow aimed primarily at private wholesalers, who had come to rely on the "socialist" sector for a large portion of their merchandise, but naturally the effect soon rippled down to private retailers as well.[18]

All of these economic and "administrative" measures adopted in 1923/24, along with increased taxes[19] and attempts to control the prices of certain goods in private shops,[20] reduced markedly the number of private traders and the volume of their trade. During 1924 Moscow's newspapers contained numerous reports from around the country with headlines employing the military metaphors so often used in describing the state's relations with the Nepmen, such as "Private capital retreating along the entire front." Looking back on this period from the more hospitable atmosphere of 1925, the Nepman A. I. Sinelobov declared that the campaign to eliminate "speculation" and bring private trade under tighter control had been counterproductive, because the pressure simply forced many traders underground and into more speculative lines of trade. "The more persistently private trade is treated as an evil," he argued, "the more inevitably it becomes an evil," and "in 1924 conditions were created in which normal and loyal private trade became almost impossible."[21] Though Sinelobov's remarks seem partly self-serving, this does not invalidate his assessment of the state policy toward the Nepmen in 1924. In fact, only a year later, articles in a number of Soviet periodicals reached similar conclusions concerning the treatment of private entrepreneurs by the state.

Early in 1924, an article in *Sotsialisticheskii vestnik* predicted that the campaign against private trade would inevitably produce an economic crisis that would prompt the Bolsheviks once again to offer concessions to the Nepmen.[22] The accuracy of this forecast became evident by 1925 when the Nepmen experienced another abrupt change in the business climate, this time a change toward a more hospitable environment. The rationale for this new policy was that in 1924, as during War Communism, the state had bitten off more than it could chew in trying rapidly to replace the private sector. Or, as one observer remarked, it was better for a region to have private traders than no traders.[23]

It cannot be automatically assumed, however, that such considerations would have persuaded the party leadership of 1924 (the triumvirate of Zinoviev, Kamenev, and Stalin) to abandon its policy of pressure

on the Nepmen. The key political development accounting for this economic policy change in 1925 was the party infighting from which N. I.
Bukharin emerged as co-leader with Stalin at the expense of Zinoviev,
Kamenev, and Trotsky (who would later unite to form the so-called Left
Opposition). In late 1924 and early 1925, Zinoviev and Kamenev chal-
lenged Stalin's direction of the party apparatus, prompting Stalin to
join forces with Bukharin (and Bukharin's supporters on the Politburo,
A. I. Rykov and M. M. Tomskii). Stalin's alliance with Bukharin was
primarily one of convenience against a common opponent in the Politburo and should not be interpreted as an indication that Stalin shared
Bukharin's views. But however strained the partnership, Stalin did not
openly challenge Bukharin's line until after the final defeat of the Left
Opposition at the end of 1927.[24] The important point here is that Bukharin was more inclined to tolerate private businessmen than were the
losers in the party power struggle in 1924–25, and consequently the
Nepmen soon felt a relaxation of state pressure.

Like all Bolsheviks, regardless of their positions in the economic debates and political factions of the 1920s, Bukharin regarded industrialization as essential for the construction of socialism in Russia. His
primary differences with the Bolshevik Left were over the means and
tempo of industrialization; he favored a more gradual approach that relied less on "pumping over" resources from the agrarian sector and
more on an expanding consumer market—an approach possible only
with help from private traders. Scholars have repeatedly described and
analyzed the contending positions in the "industrialization debates,"
and there is no need here to trace all of Bukharin's arguments once
again.[25] What were his views on the Nepmen?

Bukharin believed that Russia could industrialize (and thus begin the
construction of a socialist society) only through peaceful "market relations," which meant, among other things, expanding the volume of
domestic trade. Voluntaristic "storming" and "great leaps," though
sometimes appropriate in political revolutions, were useless—indeed
counterproductive, he maintained—as approaches to the economic
tasks facing Russia in the 1920s. During War Communism, Bukharin
wrote in 1925, "we believed it possible to destroy market relations immediately with a single stroke. As it turned out, we will reach socialism
only through market relations." Because the state and cooperative stores
were not sufficiently numerous or efficient to bring about the necessary
revitalization of trade by themselves, private traders had to be tolerated,

even encouraged. They functioned both as additional customers for state industry and as conveyors of goods to people living beyond the less than sweeping reach of the "socialist" distribution network.

> In the towns we are not at all closing the shops of the private trader; we per-mit his "work." As a result we have obtained a greater revitalization of trad-ing in the entire country. This [private] trader is a customer for our state industry and state wholesale trade, while on the other hand he sells our goods—because our own state and cooperative trading network is very weak—in diverse corners of our country. Of course he gains from this and pockets the trading profit or part of the trading profit. But nonetheless, be-cause of the general increase of trade, he facilitates independently of his will the growth of our state trade, the more rapid turnover of capital in the coun-try, including the capital of our state industry and state trade. Thus our pro-duction machinery operates more rapidly, the process of accumulation pro-ceeds more rapidly, and consequently the power of our state industry—this basic foundation of socialist society—increases more rapidly.[26]

Bukharin's contention that the Nepmen played an important role in the restoration of state industry, and hence in the development of socialism in the Soviet Union, resembled Lenin's view after 1921 that communism would have to be built in Russia with noncommunist hands. Pushing this point further, Bukharin noted on a number of occasions that private entrepreneurs were also a source of tax revenue, funds that helped nour-ish the industrial sector. Viewed from this perspective, the Nepmen, in spite of themselves, seemed to occupy a position in the front ranks of the movement to build the world's first socialist state.[27]

In 1925 Bukharin was, in effect, directing his famous "enrich your-self" exhortation at the Nepmen as well as the peasantry, because his analysis had concluded that prosperity in the private sector benefited the state. But the Nepmen could hardly be expected to increase the volume of domestic trade if they were repeatedly harassed by state officials and gouged by rapidly increasing taxes. As Bukharin declared in the spring of 1925, "the development of commodity exchange is possible only with the eradication of the remnants of War Communism in administrative-political work," indicating his disapproval of the state's treatment of pri-vate entrepreneurs in 1924. The time had come for a calmer, less bellig-erent atmosphere, one that Bolsheviks might find less bracing, but at least more conducive to a revival of trade. In *The Path to Socialism and a Worker-Peasant Union* (1925), Bukharin freely acknowledged that the goal of the proletariat and its party in a capitalist society was to inflame class struggle until it reached its most savage form—armed conflict and civil war. But once the proletariat seized power, the nature of the class struggle changed completely, and "the party of the working class in these conditions becomes a party of civil peace."[28]

In the spirit of Lenin's most optimistic statements, Bukharin contended reassuringly in *Path to Socialism* that the Bolsheviks had nothing to fear from the Nepmen, because "the strength and durability of Soviet power is so obvious that the utter hopelessness of any attempt to wage an active and sharp political struggle against the new order is completely clear to the bourgeois elements—the Nepmen—of our society. These elements must willy-nilly reconcile themselves with the existing order of things." But did this mean that class struggle had become inappropriate? Not at all, Bukharin replied. The struggle had simply altered its form and moved to the economic arena. A year earlier, Bukharin had argued before the Communist Academy that the Nepmen should be vanquished, "not by destroying the [private] shops in Moscow and the provinces, but through competition and the growing strength of our state industry and state organizations." It followed from this position— it was the official line by 1925—that the state's principal means of conducting the class struggle were to improve the efficiency of state and cooperative trade and to issue economic decrees placing the "socialist" sector in a privileged position vis-à-vis the Nepmen. Under these conditions, Bukharin maintained repeatedly in 1925, victory in the class struggle would be earned in the marketplace.

> If in the process of competition in the marketplace state industry and trade and the cooperatives gradually drive out the private entrepreneur—this is a victory in the class struggle, not in a mechanical clash of forces, not with the help of armed combat, but a victory in a completely new form that did not exist earlier and was completely unthinkable for the working class and peasantry under the capitalist regime.[29]

Thus class struggle with the Nepmen had become commercial competition, which meant, "not to trample the [private trader] and close his shop, but . . . to produce and to sell cheaper and better . . . than he." The state's success, or lack of it, in this economic arena would be determined by the Russian consumers, because "the consumer shops where the goods are better and cheaper." Consequently, Bukharin declared, the primary task before the Bolsheviks was to demonstrate to the peasants that "the state economy is better able to satisfy the daily demands and needs of the peasantry than is the private capitalist, private trader, private merchant, or private middleman." Although this statement of the challenge before the young Soviet state was far less rousing than the battle cries of the Revolution and civil war, the stakes were every bit as

high. In 1925 Bukharin insisted (as Lenin had at the birth of NEP) that
the crucial question was this: Would the peasantry form a *smychka*
with the state or with the Nepmen?

> The outcome of the class struggle depends on the answer to this question. It
> does not matter at all that this struggle is conducted peacefully, that we are
> carrying on this struggle without the clanging of metal weapons. It neverthe-
> less has truly gigantic significance, for this struggle will decide everything.[30]

Bukharin's call for commercial, rather than violent, competition with
private entrepreneurs is particularly striking in contrast to the development of the Soviet economy in subsequent decades. His reliance on the
consumer as the ultimate judge of acceptable performance is a concept
that Soviet economic reformers have tried to revive without much success in recent decades. At times Bukharin even appeared to regard competition between the "socialist" and private sectors as desirable, a means
of whipping the former into shape. To be sure, he did not expect or want
the Nepmen to remain in the field forever. The advantages of "socialist"
trade—a public service, not an endeavor to extort the highest prices
possible according to the laws of supply and demand—seemed clear
enough to ensure the Nepmen's ultimate defeat. Even though it might
take Bolsheviks a considerable period to learn to trade (as Lenin complained), Bukharin was prepared to wait, rather than expel the Nepmen
from the competition and declare victory. As it turned out, many in the
party were not as patient.

During his period of co-leadership with Bukharin, Stalin made few
public statements concerning the Nepmen. This was in part the result of
what one scholar has recently termed "a rough division of labor between Bukharin and Stalin, between policy formulation and theory on
one side and organizational muscle on the other."[31] In addition, Stalin
could not have been enraptured with Bukharin's views on private entrepreneurs—as his subsequent enthusiastic attacks on the Nepmen suggest—but kept his own counsel for the time being because he needed
Bukharin as an ally against the Left. Indeed, the closest Stalin came to a
fervent defense of NEP's most tolerant principles was in response to attacks from his political rivals on the left. For instance, he delivered the
following reply to a charge from Kamenev that certain party resolutions
of 1925 were concessions to "capitalist elements."

> We introduced freedom of trade, we permitted a revival of capitalism, we in-
> troduced NEP in order to increase the growth of productive forces, increase
> the amount of goods in the country, and strengthen the *smychka* with the
> peasants. . . .

Did Lenin know that speculators, capitalists, and kulaks [comparatively prosperous peasants] would take advantage of NEP and its concessions to the peasantry? Of course he knew. Does this mean that these concessions were actually concessions to the speculator and the kulak? No, it does not. For NEP in general and trade in particular are utilized not only by capitalists and kulaks but also by state and cooperative agencies. . . . [These] state agencies and cooperatives, when they learn how to trade, will prevail (and are already prevailing!) over the private traders, linking our industry with the peasant economy.[32]

Though Stalin said little at this time that could be construed as clear disapproval of Bukharin's program to utilize the Nepmen, his acceptance of Bukharin's views on the private sector must have seemed at most lukewarm to many party members. This attitude was evident at the Fourteenth Party Congress, held in December of 1925. The congress adopted a resolution on the Central Committee's report, which had been given by Stalin, declaring that although industry was growing, so were certain dangers. These included an increase in the amount of private capital, particularly in private trade, and an attempt by the "new bourgeoisie" to establish trade links with the kulaks. But Stalin tempered these warnings by reminding the congress that the Fourteenth Party Conference in April had declared a change [*povorot*] in state policy, entailing among other things more economic freedom to the peasantry and "liquidation of the remnants of War Communism." A little later in his report he identified two possible deviations from the party line: (1) *underestimating* the threat to the state represented by the kulaks and "capitalist elements," and (2) *overestimating* this danger. After arguing that these deviations were equally serious, Stalin added that "in our struggle against these deviations, the party must concentrate on the struggle with the second."[33] This was an opinion Bukharin could share, though he was certainly less inclined than Stalin to warn the party of the danger represented by the first deviation.

Throughout NEP, resolutions of party congresses and other official gatherings contained at least brief, pro forma passages on the harm caused by driving out the Nepmen more rapidly than they could be replaced by state or cooperative operations, even when such dislocations were an obvious result of policies then being pursued (as in 1924 and at the end of NEP). But such warnings punctuated party pronouncements with greater frequency in 1925 than in 1924, suggesting that they were not merely perfunctory nods to one of NEP's tenets, which party leaders would prefer to ignore. The condemnatory references to "administrative measures" and "survivals of War Communism" were both instructions to local officials in contact with the Nepmen and clear criticism of the crackdown on the private sector in the winter of 1923–24.[34] It is also true that some of the pronouncements of official gatherings in 1925 contained passages that reiterated the potential threat to the state (and the *smychka* in particular) posed by an expanding "new bourgeoisie." Apprehensions of this sort appeared now and then in party proclamations throughout NEP. But during 1925–26 these warnings were outweighed by firm condemnations of arbitrary, heavy-handed treatment of the Nepmen.

Although Bukharin's views clearly tinge the resolutions of party congresses, conferences, and other official gatherings in the middle of NEP, these pronouncements understate the magnitude of change in party policy toward the Nepmen in 1925. This is not surprising, given that these sessions generally strove to characterize their proclamations as reaffirmations or logical extensions of positions taken by congresses earlier in NEP, including the Thirteenth Party Congress in 1924. The new atmosphere of 1925 was more clearly reflected in the striking "second-NEP" tone of Soviet newspaper articles on private capital. The new year had hardly begun when the treatment of the Nepmen in the previous year was likened to the policies of War Communism and characterized as mistaken and dangerous. The articles supported a more tolerant, patient handling of private entrepreneurs, resembling the initial dose of NEP in 1921, a resemblance that was underscored when the Soviet press adopted the phrase "new trade practice" (*novaia torgovaia praktika*) to describe the government's more restrained, conciliatory regulation of the Nepmen in 1925.[35]

The justification of the "new trade practice" presented in these articles took the following form. State and cooperative trade agencies had been unable to assume the portion of retail trade relinquished by the Nepmen during the state's onslaught in 1924. The only way the state could conduct a significantly larger volume of trade would be to increase greatly its investment in this area of the economy. But a transfer of funds on this scale could only be accomplished by reducing the rate of industrialization, an unacceptable alternative to Bolsheviks, given the importance they attached to industry. Consequently the Nepmen had to be permitted, even encouraged, to carry on a sizable share of the country's domestic trade so that the state could concentrate its resources in industry.[36]

With the policy of 1924 still fresh in everyone's mind, it would not be easy to reassure the Nepmen and bring about a rapid increase in the number of people engaged in private trade. This realization prompted numerous calls in the newspapers and journals for lower taxes on Nepmen in order to coax entrepreneurs from the sidelines or out of the black market and back into legitimate trade. Some articles even went as far as to characterize state tax officials as either incompetent or crudely hostile to the Nepmen and argued that as long as the state ignored complaints from private traders concerning overtaxation, there was little hope of increasing the volume of private trade. Thus, the argument concluded, the state's task should be to reject "administrative measures," entice the Nepmen back into legal business, and utilize their skills until the day, well down the road, when state and cooperative trade could satisfactorily manage the job alone. As one journalist put it, "It is essential not to destroy private capital, but to accommodate it to the needs of industry. It is a simple matter to spill water, but it does no one any good. To dam it up and force it to flow through our mill will be more difficult, but immeasurably more useful."[37]

Bukharin's relatively tolerant attitude toward the Nepmen also found backing in the Council of People's Commissars (Sovnarkom), the Supreme Council of the National Economy (VSNKh), the Commissariats of Domestic Trade (Narkomvnutorg) and Finance (Narkomfin), and other government agencies. Among the party leaders, Bukharin's most influential supporter was A. I. Rykov, a member of the Politburo and Lenin's successor as chairman of Sovnarkom. Rykov frequently expressed sentiments similar to the following from a speech delivered in April 1925: "It would be exceedingly harmful to prevent the development of private trade by any form of administrative pressure, a thing that has been practiced here and there during the last few years."[38] A. L. Sheinman, commissar of domestic trade, was another prominent spokesman for the new line. Instructing a meeting of state commodity exchange officials, Sheinman made it clear that ideological aversion to the "new bourgeoisie" ran a poor second to economic performance.

> It is naive to speak about liking or disliking private capital. Our policy must be guided by only one consideration—does a particular measure help complete the main task? To the degree that state trade and the cooperatives are still not firmly on their feet and private capital can be economically useful, it [private capital] should be allowed to operate in the market.[39]

In another speech a few months later, he argued that Nepmen should be permitted to handle that portion of retail trade which was beyond the means of state and cooperative stores so that the state could concentrate its investment in industry. Thus, Sheinman declared, the previous year's policy of sharply reducing the flow of goods and credit to private traders would be reversed, and the Nepmen's taxes would be trimmed.[40]

The government also began again to defend Nepmen more vigorously from hostile local officials. In the early spring of 1925, for example, state trade authorities in the Northern Caucasus region instructed officials there to block the development of private wholesale trade (in line with the policy of the previous year). The Commissariat of Domestic Trade's headquarters in Moscow responded with a demand that these instructions be rescinded, adding that such a policy would only be appropriate if state and cooperative wholesalers were able to market enough goods to exhaust the purchasing power of the population. As this was not the case, the dispatch continued, private wholesalers should be allowed to operate, particularly in spheres of trade where the state and cooperatives were weak. It was better to bring Nepmen into the game "than to reduce trade volume artificially because of a fear of the private wholesaler's participation." To cite one more example, a Plenum of the Supreme Court of the Great-Russian Republic (RSFSR) complained in 1925 that some Soviet judges misunderstood the meaning of the "class character" of Soviet courts and convicted Nepmen simply because they were Nepmen:

> The courts must remember that the carrying out of the class attitude concerning the penal policy consists not in convicting the "Nepman" or the "kulak," and not in acquitting the toiler, or the poor or middle-class peasant, but in the clear understanding of the social danger of the act committed by the citizen brought to trial.[41]

Perhaps the most obvious indication of the new mood was a remarkable series of meetings held in state commodity exchanges (*birzhi*) throughout the country during the spring and summer of 1925. The tone of these sessions resembled that of a resolution adopted at a meeting of *birzha* officials in April 1925, which declared that the "new trade practice" was necessary to correct the mistakes "in trade policy of the preceding period [i.e., 1924]," and draw into trade "unutilized, beneficial private capital."[42] This latter goal was generally the main topic of discussion at the individual *birzhi*. What makes the meetings particularly noteworthy is that private traders were invited to exchange views on economic policies with state officials (often from local offices of Narkomvnutorg, Narkomfin, and Gosbank) and representatives from state and cooperative trading enterprises. The fact that these sessions were scheduled amounted to a statement by the government that the party and the Nepmen had certain interests in common—most important, the revival of trade—and that it might pay to listen to the Nepmen's ideas on realizing these aims.

In the discussions, and on other occasions, private traders agreed overwhelmingly that the most necessary reforms were tax relief accompanied by more goods and credit from the state.[43] Early in 1925, a group of private traders from one of Moscow's open-air markets sent a report-cum-petition to an office of local trade officials, asking them to consider the following question: Is private trade necessary and desirable? If the answer was no, the traders continued, then nothing more needed to be done, because private trade would soon be stifled by taxes. But if the answer was yes, substantial tax relief was necessary without delay. The "new trade practice" amounted to an affirmative answer. During the first half of 1925 Narkomvnutorg and Narkomfin prepared tax reduction proposals that were rapidly transformed into decrees. As a result, the Nepmen's overall tax bill crept downward in the months thereafter.[44]

Decrees during 1925 and the first months of 1926 freed small-scale entrepreneurs from certain taxes and softened the impact of these taxes on other Nepmen. Rural artisans, for example, were exempted from the business tax if they employed no hired labor (family members and the first two apprentices did not count as hired labor), while those who employed up to three hired workers were spared the leveling tax. Also, they were no longer subject to a number of local taxes and were permitted to sell their wares without having to buy a trade license. Nearly identical privileges were extended to urban handicraftsmen, and small-scale private traders were taxed at reduced rates. Some levies were abolished altogether, such as mandatory loans to the state and special taxes for local needs and victims of famine. Finally, at the beginning of 1926 the limit on the amount of property one could bequeath to one's heirs was removed, and the red tape on such transactions was reduced. A tax was maintained on these gifts and inheritances, but the state's primary purpose was, as one decree stated, "to make it easier to continue the existence of industrial and trading enterprises after the death of their owners, and also to create more favorable conditions for the circulation of material and financial resources in the country."[45]

The easing of the Nepmen's tax burden is evident in statistics available for this period, which reveal the effects not only of the decrees

noted above but also of the lower assessments made by tax officials—
aligning themselves with the prevailing political current—of individual
Nepmen's income and sales. The percentage of total private sales taken
by the business tax fell from 1.3 percent in April–September 1924 to
1.2 percent in October 1925–March 1926, whereas the figures for cooperatives *rose* from 0.6 percent to 0.8 percent. Data from a special study in
Orlov *guberniia* show that of total business-tax payments (state, cooperative, and private), the Nepmen's share fell from 55.7 percent in
1923/24 to 44.4 percent in 1924/25 and 43.2 percent in 1925/26.[46]

Income-tax data present a similar picture. For example, in 1925/26
income-tax rates for workers increased 28 percent over the previous
year, and rates for government officials rose 45 percent. Among private
traders and manufacturers, however, rates *decreased* 6 percent for small-
scale businesses, 2.5 percent for medium-scale, and 3.8 percent for large-
scale.[47] Perhaps the following statistics are the most revealing. When
combined, the business tax, levy on living space, income tax, mandatory loans to the state, and certain other taxes took in the first half of
1924/25 53 percent of private traders' reported profits and 42 percent of
private manufacturers' reported profits. But by the second half of 1924/
25, these figures had fallen to 36 percent and 35 percent, respectively.[48]

The "new trade practice" was also evident in the increased flow of
goods and credit from the state to the private sector. Reports from
around the country told of expanding sales to Nepmen by state manufacturing concerns, and figures for the nation as a whole show that the
portion of the state's manufactured goods sold directly to private entrepreneurs rose from approximately 2 percent in 1924 to 15 percent in
1925—roughly the Nepmen's share before the crackdown in 1924.[49]
Credit extended to Nepmen by state banks had risen nearly 250 percent
by October 1925 compared to the previous October and remained well
above the 1924 level for the next twelve months. If credit obtained by
private entrepreneurs from state banks via Societies of Mutual Credit is
included in the calculations, the flow of state credit to the private sector
was over 300 percent greater by the end of 1925 than it had been in
October 1924.[50]

As a consequence of the more lenient treatment of the Nepmen under
the "new trade practice," the number of private traders and the value
of their sales steadily increased in 1925.[51] The state now seemed to be
beckoning to private entrepreneurs even more solicitously than in the
first years of NEP. Certainly the series of meetings between state officials
and Nepmen in 1925 suggested less apprehension about working with

the Nepmen than was evident in the party previously. By 1925 the Nepmen had acquired "defenders" at the highest levels of government— Politburo members such as Bukharin and Rykov, who were prepared to accept the private sector for an extended period. But the dismay we have witnessed in the party's ranks over the revival of the "bourgeoisie" did not vanish. Although it is impossible to know with certainty the distribution of views among the party rank and file, it would soon become clear that Bukharin's arguments had not swept the field. In the years to come, as Stalin launched his campaign against Bukharin, Rykov, Tomskii, and their allies, he found ample support of his own in the party for the immediate "liquidation of the new bourgeoisie."

CHAPTER 3

# The Bubble Bursts

We Oppositionists are often asked: What makes you think there is a danger of Thermidor? Our answer is simple and clear. When Bolsheviks are beaten up because they call for turning our fire to the right, against kulak, NEPman, and bureaucrat, then the danger of Thermidor is at hand.

—Leon Trotsky

I'll tell you, citizen, if you don't mind, I'd like to give you a bit of advice, [a shopkeeper informed a professor]. Today a hat is out of style. In fact, it's even unsafe—I mean in the sense of social categories. If you excuse me, who wears a felt hat nowadays? A Nepman! And what's a Nepman, if I may ask? A Nepman is like a splinter of an abolished way of life, something contemptible, not quite a man—an ape, only burdened with obligations. And, let us say, if the finance inspector should visit you, then, having a felt hat, you may altogether undeservedly be clamped into the wrong category.

—Boris Lavrenyov

As the new year dawned following the Fourteenth Party Congress in December 1925, the Nepmen's position had never been more favorable. The party line concerning the private sector clearly followed Bukharin's views rather than the Left Opposition's demands for more aggressive regulation and taxation. Indeed, Kamenev had been heckled repeatedly and even shouted down at the Fourteenth Party Congress when he claimed that the real danger in the party came, not from Zinoviev and himself, but from Bolsheviks who underestimated the threat posed by the growth of "capitalist elements."[1] The state's comparatively lenient policies toward private entrepreneurs were now in place in areas such as taxation, credit, and the supply of goods and underscored the party's repudiation of the harsher approach of 1924. Thus the economic year 1925/26 promised to be the most prosperous the Nepmen had yet enjoyed. It proved also to be the most prosperous year they would *ever* enjoy, for in 1926/27 the party began a transition from Bukharin's com-

56

paratively tolerant position of 1925 to the full-scale assault on the private sector in force by the end of the decade. Just as Bukharin's rise in the party as an ally of Stalin against the Left heralded a moderation of the state's treatment of the Nepmen, so the political decline of Bukharin, from party leader to leader of what Stalin and his supporters branded the "Right Deviation," boded ill for private entrepreneurs.

Few observers in 1926, however, could have anticipated such a dramatic reversal of the Nepmen's fortunes. The Left Opposition certainly did not detect any signs of collapse in the private sector and charged throughout 1926 and 1927 that the "new bourgeoisie" represented an increasingly serious threat. The "Platform of the Opposition" (written in September 1927 and signed by Trotsky, Zinoviev, Kamenev, and many others) warned that the Stalin-Bukharin majority "has been powerless to prevent: (1) an immoderate growth of those forces which desire to turn the development of our country in a capitalist direction; (2) a weakening of the position of the working class and the poorest peasants against the growing strength of the kulak, the NEPman, and the bureaucrat." Worse still, predicted the signatories, policies contemplated by the party majority would result in "a full capitulation on the part of the Soviet power—through a 'political NEP,' a 'neo-NEP,' back to capitalism. . . . The kulaks, the NEPmen, and the bureaucrats, taking cognizance of our concessions, would all the more persistently organize the anti-Soviet forces against our party."[2]

The Left was impatient with party resolutions that continued to emphasize caution in the struggle with the Nepmen. Bukharin and his supporters had not yet been ousted from their party positions, and their views were still prominent in official pronouncements. For instance, a Plenum of the party's Central Committee declared in February 1927 that although "the role of private capital must be systematically reduced . . . it would be an overestimation of our strength and premature if we were now to take up the task of *completely* eliminating private capital from the market and concentrating all trade in the hands of the cooperatives and the state." Similar restraint appeared in a resolution of the Thirteenth All-Russian Congress of Soviets two months later.[3] The congress praised the recent success of state and cooperative trade at the expense of the Nepmen, but added: "Along with this it must be noted [that there have been] a number of excesses in the regulation [of private trade] and incorrect methods of administrative influence on trade that must be resolutely eliminated in the future."[4]

Nevertheless, the tone of official statements on the Nepmen grew less benevolent in 1926/27 compared to the previous year. The change was clearly perceptible and reflected what one scholar has called Bukharin's "reconsideration and significant modification of his policies" in 1926/27.[5] At the core of Bukharin's revised thinking lay the realization that the state could not significantly expand the country's industrial base without, first, a much larger commitment of resources and, second, a greater reliance on planning as opposed to market forces. One of the by-products of his altered views on industrial development was a new attitude toward the Nepmen. Specifically, Bukharin concluded that private entrepreneurs should be taxed more heavily (to secure funds for industrial investment) and regulated more closely (so that their activity would not undermine the state's planning). To be sure, Bukharin continued to accept the basic principles of NEP, including the indefinite existence of a large private sector, but his modified position represented a marked change from his views of 1925.

Not surprisingly, then, party meetings in this period urged state agencies to exert more direct control over activity in the private sector. One way this could be accomplished, a Central Committee Plenum explained in February 1927, was to order state industry to supply only those private traders who agreed not to exceed price ceilings set by the state.[6] Even though such resolutions were not declarations of war on the Nepmen, they were clear indications of the party leadership's concern that private economic activity be more tightly regulated to ensure that it promoted, rather than hindered, "socialist construction."

All of this amounted to a considerable first step in the direction urged by the Left Opposition, though the party leadership was loath to admit it. Indeed, the leaders of the Left Opposition found themselves under increasingly heavy fire as the months went by, making it difficult for them to credit Bukharin's advocacy of a shorter leash for the Nepmen. As Trotsky wrote on November 8, 1927, describing the previous day's celebration of the tenth anniversary of the Bolsheviks' seizure of power:

> In the tenth anniversary manifesto and the speeches of the official orators [supporters of Stalin and Bukharin] there was reference to the need for intensifying the pressure on the kulak and NEPman. Two years ago, according to the Bukharins, the time was not ripe for that. And now, just at the tenth anniversary, it suddenly becomes time. But why is it, in that case, that on November 7, 1927, placards [carried by the Left Opposition in the anniversary parade] demanding that we turn our fire to the right, against kulak, NEPman, and bureaucrat, were torn to pieces? It is enough to contrast these facts to thoroughly expose the policies of the present leadership. Stalin and Bukharin

proclaim intensified pressure on the bourgeois elements in words only. The Opposition wants to apply that pressure in fact. Why, then, do Stalin and Bukharin put the pressure on the Opposition?[7]

Following the final defeat of the Left Opposition a few weeks later, party pronouncements on the private sector embodied even more openly the impatience apparent earlier in the Left's "Platform." In December, for example, a resolution at the Fifteenth Party Congress proclaimed categorically that "a policy of still more decisive economic elimination should and can be applied" to the Nepmen. "The preconditions for a further economic attack on capitalist elements [referring to both the Nepmen and the kulaks] have been created by the previous successes of [state and cooperative] economic development." Party resolutions in the fall of 1927 did still contain occasional reminders that private entrepreneurs should not be driven out of business more rapidly than they could be replaced by "socialist" enterprises. But by now the dominant theme was not the need to patiently tolerate the Nepmen for some time to come, but rather the assertion that the struggle against them could and should be stepped up.[8]

Stalin and his allies supported an intensified struggle with the Nepmen much more wholeheartedly than they did the tolerant statements concerning private entrepreneurs made in party resolutions of 1925–26— suggesting again that the alliance with Bukharin was more a matter of political convenience against the Left than the result of an identity of views. Prior to 1927, Stalin discussed the Nepmen only rarely, but by the end of the year the volume of his comments on the private sector (both the Nepmen and the kulaks) increased dramatically. His concern and point of view were clearly evident during the Fifteenth Party Congress. At one session, instead of concentrating his fire on the now-defeated Left, he took aim in the opposite direction, claiming that some Bolsheviks (not yet naming Bukharin and his top allies) *underestimated* the dangers posed by the private sector, and coupled this charge with a call for a more forceful drive to vanquish the Nepmen.

> The significance of these elements [private traders and manufacturers] is not as slight as it is represented on occasion by some of our comrades. This . . . is a minus in our economy. I recently read comrade Larin's book *Private Capital in the USSR*, which is interesting in every regard. I would recommend that our comrades read this little book. You will notice how cunningly and adeptly the capitalist conceals himself behind the flag of [he lists a variety of cooperative and state trade agencies]. Is everything being done to limit, reduce, and finally eliminate capitalist elements from the economy? I think not.[9]

Such remarks were not completely contrary to Bukharin's position, especially in its revised form of 1926–27, when Bukharin favored increased taxation and regulation of private entrepreneurs. Certainly, Bukharin, Rykov, and Tomskii agreed that the Nepmen would have to be eliminated *eventually* in the campaign to build socialism. But Stalin was clearly more impatient than they were with the prospect of protracted economic competition with the private sector. In focusing on the goal of an offensive against the Nepmen, and virtually ignoring the Right's stress on the dangers of overzealousness, he had begun to formulate a position that he would occupy with increasing visibility and confidence in the years to come.

The year 1928 marked a turning point in the history of the party and NEP.[10] With the final defeat of the Left Opposition in the fall of 1927, Stalin was politically free to oppose Bukharin more vigorously, and the confrontation was not long in materializing. Alarmed by the sharp decline of grain collections in the last months of 1927, the Politburo in January approved the use of "extraordinary" measures that Bukharin and Rykov thought would be limited to a brief campaign against grain "speculators." Stalin chose to supervise personally the grain collection campaign in Siberia and did so with the methods of War Communism, despite the objections of some local officials that this violated the spirit of NEP. Grain was seized from peasants who refused to sell at low state prices, and many local markets were closed—all of which amounted to a repeal of NEP's most fundamental principle, the right of peasants to sell grain freely. The grain collection drives of 1928 were, of course, aimed primarily at the peasants, with private grain traders, millers, bakers, and the like the only Nepmen directly under fire. But as the state adopted harsher measures to wring grain from the peasantry, it also greatly increased the pressure on private entrepreneurs of all sorts. Thus, although the Nepmen's position had already begun to deteriorate in 1927, the new year brought a much higher level of ferocity to the assault on private business.

Indeed, the crushing of the Nepmen in 1928–30 may be viewed as a secondary explosion accompanying the primary upheaval in the villages (first the new grain collections, then collectivization and dekulakization). In other words, the offensive against the Nepmen at the end of the decade represented action on one of several fronts (such as the campaign against "wreckers" in industry, in addition to the turmoil on the "agrarian front") as Stalin and his supporters initiated the "third revolution" to build socialism in Russia at breakneck speed.

Stalin's triumph in the party was not simply a consequence of political muscle or organization. These factors clearly played an important part, but it would be misleading to conclude that Stalin and a handful of allies coerced the party into liquidating the Nepmen. Although Bukharin, Rykov, and Tomskii certainly had supporters in the party, we have seen that many Bolsheviks—not just those in the Left Opposition—were apprehensive about NEP in general and the "new bourgeoisie" in particular. It was difficult for them to wait patiently with Bukharin for the state to eliminate the private sector through peaceful economic competition—all the more because the Nepmen proved to be such tenacious rivals. Thus the prospect of a climactic showdown with the Nepmen struck a responsive chord in many Bolshevik hearts and inclined them to support leaders who argued that the time for an offensive had come.

Similarly, on a more general level, the de facto elimination of the rest of NEP should not be regarded as an overwhelmingly unpopular decision forced on a reluctant party. As Victor Kravchenko, a Bolshevik defector, recalled:

> I was . . . one of the young enthusiasts, thrilled by the lofty ideas and plans of this period. It was a time when my country began to move into a new and in some ways more profound revolution. . . . Stalin and his close associates . . . were intent upon rooting out remnants of capitalist economy and capitalist mentality, in order to lead Russia into industrialization and into collectivization of farming. . . . There was the deep hope in the future of the country, so that it was no accident that I chose precisely this period to join the Party.[11]

Though Kravchenko's enthusiasm for the new course doubtless placed him in a distinct minority of the population (still overwhelmingly peasant), his zeal was far less anomalous inside the party. To be sure, some Bolsheviks would have preferred to continue NEP, and they regarded with dismay the upheavals to come. Such individuals had to be pushed aside or silenced. But by the end of the 1920s, the arguments against NEP had become compelling to many of their fellow party members. In the latter's view, NEP was incapable of sustaining a sufficiently rapid tempo of industrialization, in large measure because of the difficulty of acquiring grain from independent peasants. Furthermore, the existence of a private economic sector seemed at best an obstacle to the attainment of socialism and at worst a corrupter of the Revolution's ideals. Troubled by such concerns, many Bolsheviks embraced Stalin's "solution" of forced collectivization and the replacement of NEP's mixed economy with a centralized, planned economy geared for a massive industrialization drive. The task begun in 1917 was now to be completed.

Following Stalin's Siberian campaign at the beginning of 1928, his statements on the Nepmen (and kulaks) featured a striking new theme. As the Soviet Union approached socialism, he warned, private entrepreneurs' opposition to the state would grow *more* desperate, violent, and widespread, thus necessitating harsher measures by the state to combat this threat. The foundation for this position was evident by December 1927, when Stalin reminded the delegates at the Fifteenth Party Congress that "the characteristic feature of the new bourgeoisie is that, in contrast to the working class and the peasantry, it has no basis to be satisfied with Soviet power." The growth of the socialist sector of the economy hurts the new bourgeoisie, he added, "hence the counter-revolutionary sentiments in this group." In the next few months, Stalin scorned those in the party (not yet by name) who believed that as the "socialist" sector developed, the threat of the Nepmen diminished. In reality, he explained to a Central Committee Plenum in July, the reverse was the case.

> We often say that we are developing socialist forms of economy in the sphere of trade. But what does this mean? It means that we are driving thousands and thousands of small and medium traders out of trade. Is it reasonable to think that these traders who have been driven out of trade will sit quietly and not try to organize opposition? Of course not.

In the next two paragraphs Stalin made the same point with regard to private manufacturers and the kulaks, and then moved to his crucial point.

> It follows from all this that the more we move ahead, the greater will grow the opposition of capitalist elements, the class struggle will intensify, while Soviet power, whose strength will steadily grow, will carry out a policy of isolating these elements, a policy of splintering the enemies of the working class, and finally a policy of crushing the opposition of the exploiters, thus creating a basis for the further progress of the working class and the main mass of the peasantry.[12]

Stalin hammered at this point time and time again in the months that followed. Even as late as 1933 he warned a Joint Plenum of the Central Committee (CC) and the Central Control Commission (CCC) that *former* Nepmen now working in state enterprises had still not embraced the Soviet state and would try to organize sabotage at every opportunity.[13]

The contention that private entrepreneurs would sharpen their resistance to the state as it moved toward socialism may have been inspired in part by the opposition peasants offered to the harsher grain collection campaigns of 1928. As one would expect, heated resistance to grain requisitioning and collectivization was indeed forthcoming in many regions. But there is no evidence that the Nepmen offered widespread, savage opposition to their own elimination. This is in part because the Nepmen were much less numerous than the peasantry and concentrated in urban areas, where they were more easily supervised and controlled. Further, officials could use less violent measures, such as tax increases and reductions in the supply of goods and credit, to drive private entrepreneurs out of business. The state had already begun in this way to reduce the number of private businessmen in 1927, and this generally produced one or more of the following responses: (1) closing the business; (2) concealment or misrepresentation of the business; (3) a shift to small-scale activity less subject to state control, such as street hawking or handicraft work in the countryside; and on at least a few occasions (4) bribery of local tax and regulatory officials. These remained the responses of the vast majority of Nepmen to the heavy-handed "administrative measures" adopted by the state in 1928–29, with most entrepreneurs forced into the first category. Thus the warning that private businessmen, with their backs to the wall, would attempt to "organize opposition" and "intensify the class struggle" proved grossly overdrawn, if not entirely unfounded. But such cries of peril—resembling the warnings about "wreckers" in industry—helped eventually to create an atmosphere in which it was difficult to defend continued toleration of the private sector.

Initially the party did not endorse Stalin's claim that the Nepmen were becoming more hostile as the country moved toward socialism. At the Fifteenth Party Congress (December 1927), where Stalin had begun to formulate this position, a directive on the preparation of the First Five-Year Plan took the opposite view. The resolution maintained that the danger posed by the Nepmen was diminishing because the socialist sector was growing more rapidly than the private sector. But within half a year the party reversed itself, an indication of the spread of Stalin's influence and the decline of Bukharin's. In July 1928, a CC Plenum announced, in words hinting at disagreement in the party, that "the development of a socialist form of economy on the basis of NEP leads not to the weakening but to the intensification of opposition from capitalist elements." By the following April the Sixteenth Party Conference not only came to this conclusion but also added that the Nepmen and kulaks were aided in their struggle by industrial "wreckers," unreliable state officials, and even the international bourgeoisie.

> The kulak and the Nepman will not give up their positions without a fight. . . . [They] are supported by counterrevolutionary wreckers in industry. They are assisted by bureaucrats in our agencies. They are supported in every way and inspired by foreign capitalists. . . .
>
> Only by overcoming wavering and hesitation in our ranks, only by giving a shattering rebuff to the Right deviation, will the party and the proletariat be able to smash the resistance of class enemies and fulfill the five-year plan of the construction of socialism.[14]

Assertions of this kind were obviously incompatible with Bukharin's views, and during the course of 1928 Stalin and his supporters emphasized this fact with increasing boldness. Initially, the targets of their salvos were anonymous; for example, at a July CC Plenum Stalin charged that certain party members harbored "antiproletarian sentiments." These individuals, he claimed, favored the "broadening" of NEP and the "unleashing of capitalist elements," an accusation he would repeat relentlessly in the months ahead. By autumn Stalin frequently tarred his opponents with the labels *Right Deviation* and *Right Opposition,* epithets denoting a failure to appreciate and respond to the dangers posed by the "new bourgeoisie." Such errors, Stalin warned a meeting of Moscow party organizations in October, threatened Russia with nothing less than the restoration of capitalism.

> In what does the danger of the Right, openly opportunist deviation in our party consist? In the fact that it underestimates the strength of our enemies, the strength of capitalism, does not notice the danger of the restoration of capitalism, does not understand the mechanism of class struggle under the dictatorship of the proletariat, and thus freely makes concessions to capitalism, demanding a slowdown of the development of our industry and an easing of conditions for capitalist elements in the towns and countryside. . . .
>
> Without doubt the victory of the Right Deviation in our party would unleash the forces of capitalism, undermine the revolutionary positions of the proletariat, and improve the chances for the restoration of capitalism in our country.[15]

Stalin must have realized that his critique of the Right resembled the charges made against Bukharin and himself in previous years by the Left Opposition. Perhaps this was one reason he also took pains in the speech to describe his differences with the Left (even though it had been shattered the previous year). The fundamental error of the "'Left' or Trotskyite deviation," Stalin charged, was that "it overestimates the strength of our enemies, the strength of capitalism, seeing only the possibility of the restoration of capitalism and not the possibility of the construction of socialism by the forces of our own country."[16] Thus Stalin was claiming that his policies were the only ones that would lead Russia to socialism. On the one hand, he alleged that the Right's blindness to the danger of the "new bourgeoisie" was likely to bring about the restoration of capitalism. On the other, he charged that the Left so exaggerated the strength of the Nepmen and kulaks that it despaired of ever building socialism in Russia without foreign assistance.

In a series of speeches to joint sessions of the party Politburo and the Presidium of the CCC early in 1929, Stalin confronted Bukharin, Rykov, and Tomskii by name. Announcing the discovery of a Bukharinist faction within the party, he charged that the "platform" of this faction advocated "the establishment of complete freedom of private trade and the renunciation by the state of its regulation of trade." This, of course, was a gross distortion of Bukharin's views. No Bolshevik had ever argued that the state should not regulate the Nepmen, but this did not prevent Stalin from flailing Bukharin with the charge, keeping him off balance and on the defensive.[17]

Two months later, for example, Stalin developed his attack with a lengthy speech titled "On the Right Deviation in the Party," delivered to a Joint Plenum of the CC and CCC. He again chastised Bukharin by name and declared that the greatest threat to NEP came not from the Left Deviation but from the Right:

> The danger from the Right, the danger from people who want to abolish the regulatory role of the state in the marketplace, who want to "emancipate" the market and thus inaugurate an era of complete freedom of private trade, is much more real [than the danger from the Left]. . . .
> It should not be forgotten that petty bourgeois elements are working in just this direction—disrupting NEP from the right. It should thus be understood that the cries of the kulaks and prosperous elements, the cries of speculators and profiteers, to which many of our comrades often succumb, bombard NEP from just this direction. That Bukharin does not see this second, very real danger of the disruption of NEP shows without a doubt that he has succumbed to the pressure of petty bourgeois elements.[18]

Although Bukharin's relatively cautious handling of private entrepreneurs was certainly vulnerable to criticism from Bolsheviks eager to eliminate the Nepmen and surge ahead to socialism, it was still brazen of Stalin to accuse Bukharin of contributing to the "disruption" of NEP. At that very moment, Stalin himself was gutting NEP's foundation with his "emergency measures" in the countryside and his crackdown on private trade and manufacturing in the cities. If Bukharin was "guilty" of anything, it was not a desire to scuttle NEP, but rather an attempt to *prolong* it when it could no longer support the pace of industrialization desired by the party.

In the spring of 1929 Stalin added another charge to his indictment of Bukharin's thought on the "new bourgeoisie" by rejecting his contention that Russia could "grow into socialism" during NEP. As early as November 1922 Bukharin had begun to formulate the argument that with the state in the hands of the proletariat, class struggle should be transformed from violent confrontations into economic competition between the socialist and private sectors. On the assumption that eventually the socialist sector would better serve the needs of the population and thus defeat the Nepmen economically, he thought that the Soviet Union could gradually "grow into socialism" without pitched battles and breathtaking leaps. People should be convinced through example, not forced, to join cooperatives, collective farms, and so on. It was an evolutionary approach, then, that Bukharin had in mind when he remarked: "Here there can be no kind of third revolution."[19]

But a "third revolution" was precisely what Stalin had begun in 1929, though he did not bill it as such and claimed to be adhering faithfully to the tenets of NEP. He elected to attack Bukharin's theory of "growing into socialism" from the angle of class struggle, by charging in his report on the Right Deviation that Bukharin meant *Nepmen* could grow into socialists.

> Up to now we Marxist-Leninists thought that an irreconcilable antagonism existed between capitalists in the towns and countryside on the one hand and the working class on the other. Marxist theory of class struggle is based on this. But now, according to Bukharin's theory about the peaceful growth of capitalists into socialism, all this is turned upside down. The irreconcilable antagonism of the class interests of the exploiters and exploited disappears, the exploiters grow into socialism. . . . Have we granted the possibility of the Nepmen growing into socialism? Of course not.[20]

Here again, Stalin was cleverly distorting Bukharin's position by magnifying and focusing on the portion least appealing to other Bolsheviks. Bukharin had meant that the Soviet Union as a whole could make a gradual, peaceful transition to socialism and paid scant attention to the question of whether former Nepmen could become reliable citizens in a socialist state. Only the comparatively benevolent tone of his statements could be construed on occasion as a faint suggestion that some Nepmen might be able to make this transition. But this was opportunity enough for Stalin to press the charge, undoubtedly with telling effort in party circles, that Bukharin favored coddling the "new bourgeoisie."

In addition, Stalin continued to argue that Bukharin's theories had no connection with reality, because Bukharin did not subscribe to the "axiom" that resistance from the private sector would increase as the Soviet Union neared socialism. To charges that his own policies, rather than immutable historical laws, were behind the growing strife in the land, Stalin replied that his accusers had failed to master the dynamics of class struggle set forth by Lenin.

> Bukharin thinks that under the dictatorship of the proletariat class struggle must die out and disappear in order to put an end to classes. Lenin, on the other hand, teaches that classes can be destroyed only through stubborn class struggle, which becomes even more savage under the dictatorship of the proletariat than before it. . . .
> The mistake of Bukharin and his friends is that they do not understand this simple and obvious truth. . . . [They try] to explain the intensification of class struggle with all sorts of fortuitous causes: the "ineptitude" of the Soviet apparatus, the "reckless" policy of local comrades, the "absence" of flexibility, "excesses," and on and on.[21]

Actually, Bukharin claimed not that class struggle would soon cease to exist, but that it should be transformed from violence into economic competition. Competition in the marketplace, however, must have seemed a rather tepid form of class struggle to many Bolsheviks, steeped as they were in the tradition of the Revolution and civil war. Thus it is not difficult to imagine many in the party responding enthusiastically to Stalin's assertions that more vigor was required in the struggle with the "new bourgeoisie." Stalin probably won additional support by representing his notion of class struggle as Lenin's teaching, even though he was on thin ice at this point. As noted above, Lenin's legacy on this score was ambiguous. Certainly, some of his pronouncements appeared to suggest the eventual need for a forceful crackdown on the Nepmen. But Lenin did not argue during NEP that class struggle would intensify as the Soviet Union approached socialism. The dominant themes and tone of his work in the last years of his life were, if anything, closer to Bukharin's position than to Stalin's.

Whatever the validity of Stalin's assertions, the important point here is the appeal of such arguments—repeated endlessly by Stalin's supporters—to many in the party. This appeal, combined with Stalin's organizational leverage, enabled him first to drive Bukharin and his allies rapidly into minority opposition and then to vanquish them. On November 25, 1929, Bukharin, Rykov, and Tomskii signed a confession of their errors (published the next day) that marked the demise of the Right Opposition.[22] The defeat of the Right removed the last major obstacle to the elimination of the "new bourgeoisie." By the end of the decade the state had launched an assault on the Nepmen (not to mention other segments of Soviet society, ranging from peasants to artists) that paralleled Stalin's conflict with the Right—cautious and muted at first, then increasingly open and unrestrained.

As indicated above, Bukharin rethought his position on the private sector in 1926–27 and concluded that the state should regulate the Nepmen's activities more closely. This reappraisal resulted in less favorable treatment for private entrepreneurs, though still within limits that the majority of Nepmen could endure. As in the past, the state relied primarily on its policies of taxation, credit, and supply to restrain the Nepmen and resorted to more forceful, "administrative" measures much less frequently than would be the case in 1928–30.[23] Taxation was the most effective state regulatory device in this period, because many Nepmen did not depend on credit or supplies from the state. Indeed, the Bolsheviks used taxes throughout NEP to restrict accumulation in the private sector, so that even in 1925, a comparatively hospitable year for the Nepmen, the taxes levied on private traders far exceeded the tax burden of prewar traders. The complaints of many Nepmen expressed in petitions, responses to surveys, and even a few newspaper columns in 1925 leave no doubt that taxation was their primary grievance, and it was here that the state applied the most pressure in 1926–27.[24]

During these two years the Nepmen—or "nonlabor elements" as they were sometimes called in tax decrees—felt the bite of the tax man in a number of places. The All-Russian Central Executive Committee (VTsIK) and the Council of People's Commissars (Sovnarkom) issued revised tables for existing taxes, raising the rates for all but the smallest-scale private entrepreneurs, and piled on new levies. Even utility bills and children's education fees, already higher for "nonlabor elements" than "workers and officials," increased in this period for relatively prosperous entrepreneurs.[25] Data gathered by the Commissariat of Finance (Narkomfin) illustrate the growth of the Nepmen's tax burden by 1926/27. Four "personal" taxes (the income tax was by far the most important of these, and they do not include the business tax) rose from 12.9 percent of urban private traders' reported profits in 1925/26 to 18.8 percent in 1926/27, a rate increase of almost 50 percent. A separate study in Orlov *guberniia* found that the portion of private traders' and manufacturers' total volume of business taken by the business tax, income tax, and tax on living space climbed from 4.9 percent in 1925/26 to 8.4 percent in 1926/27. Viewed from another angle, private entrepreneurs in Orlov *guberniia* accounted for 55.6 percent of the total receipts from these three taxes in 1925/26 and 66.7 percent in 1926/27.[26] Thus these studies support two conclusions. The Nepmen's tax burden did increase significantly in 1926/27, but it was not yet unbearable, at least for many entrepreneurs.

Of the new taxes on the Nepmen in this period, the most important was the surcharge on "superprofits," decreed by Sovnarkom and VTsIK in June 1926. Initially, this was billed as a temporary measure directed at large and medium-sized businesses whose profits during the current tax period (six months) exceeded those of the previous period by amounts specified according to the nature of the business. In this form, the law had little effect on all save a handful of merchants and manufacturers. But in May 1927, VTsIK and Sovnarkom issued a new superprofit decree with more teeth. No longer labeled temporary, the new law contained a different definition of superprofits and extended the tax to include somewhat smaller-scale traders. Superprofits were now to be calculated as the difference between a merchant's total income and the "normal income" for a business of that type. This "normal income" was to be specified by regional and local state agencies with guidance from the central office of Narkomfin. As a result, superprofit tax assessments increased significantly, from 0.35 percent of urban private traders' reported income in 1926 to 2.46 percent in 1927.[27] Despite this rise, the superprofit tax was not nearly as heavy on the Nepmen as were a number of other taxes, such as the business and income taxes. But by permitting officials to specify arbitrarily the "normal income" of a business and tax anything more as a superprofit, the tax decree provided an additional means by which to eliminate private entrepreneurs when this became state policy in the following years.

On September 24, 1926, VTsIK and Sovnarkom raised the income tax and the business tax for all but the smallest-scale traders and manufacturers. As before, the business tax consisted of a license fee determined by the size and nature of the enterprise, a "leveling tax" on production and sales, and a surcharge on the production and sale of "luxury goods." The income tax was still assessed according to three separate rate charts—one for workers, officials, and certain professional people; another for small-scale independent craftsmen; and a third for private traders and manufacturers, middlemen, brokers, people living on investments, and so on. The most important changes wrought by the new income-tax decree were two: large numbers of the smallest artisans and vendors were freed entirely from the tax; and the rates in each of the three tax tables were changed, reducing receipts from the first two tables (from 11.9 to 9.2 million rubles, and from 20.6 to 13.6 million rubles, respectively), but increasing the more substantial Nepmen's payments (determined by the third table) from 56.5 to 70.6 million rubles.[28]

The increased concentration of the income-tax burden on Nepmen following the September revision of the law is underscored by data collected from around the country and published by Narkomfin. In 1925/26 the Nepmen represented 15.1 percent of the people subject to the income tax, with 26.8 percent of the taxable income, and accounted for 65.6 percent of total income-tax receipts. The next year, with the new tax tables in effect, these figures increased to 23.1 percent, 37.4 percent, and 79.2 percent, respectively. The impact of this decree on the Nepmen is revealed most clearly by the following figures. From 1925/26 to 1926/27 the percentage of income taken from medium- and large-scale Nepmen by the income tax rose from 10 percent to 15.7 percent—illustrating that this tax, though far from negligible, was not yet a deathblow.[29]

Urban Nepmen also found themselves paying more for their living space in 1926/27, following a rent increase in June 1926. A person's rent was determined by occupation, income, town of residence, and the amount of floor space in the dwelling—with "nonlabor elements" assessed at a much higher rate than the proletariat. A few months later, in October, the housing tax (*kvartirnyi nalog*) was also raised. This tax was directed exclusively at urban residents who paid the income tax according to the third table, which included all but the smallest-scale Nepmen. The assessment was made on the basis of a person's income and floor space, and this was the case as well with a "special housing tax" on Nepmen, proclaimed in March 1927 as a levy to acquire funds for the construction of workers' housing. Lesser taxes on the Nepmen, such as a "contribution" for the armed forces, and the fine for delinquent tax payments also increased in this period.[30] Thus the year 1926 marked a turning point in the taxation of the private sector by the state. By the second half of the year, in accordance with Bukharin's revised thinking on the subject, taxation was clearly being used more aggressively to restrict and regulate the Nepmen's profits and activity while not forcing the majority of entrepreneurs out of business.

As in the past, the state tried to coordinate its tax policy with the volume of goods and credit it supplied to the Nepmen. Consequently, increased taxes in the private sector during 1926/27 were accompanied by a reduced flow of funds and supplies from the state. The Commissariats of Finance and Trade issued numerous directives forbidding state and cooperative enterprises from selling products (often scarce leather and textile goods) to private traders and manufacturers at any price. Though such orders were not always obeyed, they did produce hardship for Nepmen who had come to rely on the state for a substantial portion of their merchandise or raw materials. In part because of the state's revised supply policy (and also from a desire to escape the attention of state tax and regulatory agencies), private entrepreneurs after 1925/26 turned less and less frequently to the state in their search for goods.[31]

Concurrently, the state ordered Gosbank and a number of lesser state banks to curtail their loans to Nepmen. Some banks responded by simply refusing to grant unsecured loans to private customers, and others, such as the Leningrad branch of Gosbank, announced that they would no longer offer any credit to private traders. As a result, the amount of state credit extended to private borrowers fell from 70 million rubles in October 1925 to 51.5 million rubles in October 1926, a drop of over 25 percent. During the following year the plunge was even more precipitous—fully 57 percent—from 51.5 to 22.1 million rubles.[32]

From the beginning of NEP, the Bolsheviks expressed special concern over private grain trading. Few could be content with the thought that Nepmen were bidding against the state for the peasants' surplus production, as this was seen as a threat to both the *smychka* and industrialization. It was axiomatic in the party that Russia could not industrialize and create the foundation for socialism without a sizable grain surplus in the hands of the state (both to feed the proletariat and to export in order to pay for Western technology). Facing this problem in 1921, Lenin had argued that private grain sales had to be permitted to provide the incentive the peasants needed to produce a sufficient grain surplus. But by 1926/27 this argument was losing some of its force in the party as concern mounted over the state's inability to collect what were considered sufficient quantities of grain.

It would be a few years before the state seriously came to grips with this problem, but in the meantime the party hoped to divert a portion of the Nepmen's share of grain purchases (then roughly 20 percent) into the state's hands. This, and a desire to protect the *smychka,* prompted the state in 1926 to tighten the restrictions on private grain trading. With the rout of the Left Opposition in 1926–27, and Bukharin apparently secure as party theoretician, a grain-requisitioning campaign against the peasants seemed unthinkable. Instead, the state tried to make it more difficult for Nepmen to purchase and market grain. During this period state agencies were ordered to cut off credit to private grain dealers; limits were placed on the amount of grain private traders could have milled in state and cooperative facilities; the leases of many large private mills were revoked; cooperatives were forbidden to sell grain to private traders; state and cooperative grain collectors were instructed not to buy grain from private middlemen; and restrictions, including higher freight charges, were placed on private grain shipments by rail.[33]

According to reports from around the country, these measures quickly made themselves felt, particularly on the railways. In the Ukraine, for example, Nepmen shipped 12,736 freight cars of grain during the period July–December 1925, but only 1,572 freight-car loads during the same period a year later. It is unclear, however, to what extent the total volume of private grain trade was reduced in the Ukraine or the rest of the country. Some private cargoes were transported illegally, and the Nepmen also contrived on occasion to circumvent the new restrictions by taking advantage of various legal loopholes (an approach that one Soviet observer labeled *amerikanizm*). As use of the railways became more difficult, many other private middlemen turned to boats and carts to move their grain.[34] Undoubtedly the number of large, long-distance private grain shipments dropped considerably, but the local and regional private grain trade was still far from insignificant.

Thus, the period from roughly the summer of 1926 through 1927 foreshadowed the final assault on the Nepmen. The state policies in this interval, reflecting Bukharin's modified thinking on the private sector, were attempts to regulate and restrict private entrepreneurs more closely, but they did not as yet suggest that the party had elected to liquidate the Nepmen as rapidly as possible. During 1928, however, as Stalin dropped any pretense of agreement with the Right (he ushered in the year with his Siberian grain collection campaign), the atmosphere changed dramatically. Before long, Nepmen found themselves under fire heavier than anything the Left Opposition had proposed. One longtime foreign resident in Moscow reported early in the year:

> We are at present witnessing an anti-NEP wave hardly less violent than that of 1924! . . . The war on trade is being waged more hotly than ever: taxes, refusals of credit by the banks which are all in the hands of the State, prohibitions of goods-deliveries to private individuals, and a thousand irritations

from laws and regulations, to violate any one of which sends the offender off, over the "administrative" route, the route of the G.P.U. to Narim and Solovietski Monastery [i.e., into the forced labor camps]![35]

Naturally, the state did not neglect its "traditional" weapons—taxation and denials of goods and credit—as it stepped up the pressure on the Nepmen after 1927. But with increasing frequency officials resorted to "administrative measures," that is, arbitrarily fining or closing private businesses and sometimes arresting the proprietors. This, for example, is a foreign observer's account of the fate of several private credit organizations: "In Moscow there had been four private banks. One day they were, and the next day they were not. The Government just swooped down and closed them up. Several American friends of mine in Moscow had accounts in these banks, and although they recovered their money, they had considerable difficulty in doing so."[36]

The pretext for such action against a Nepman was often a labor or sanitation code violation that would have been considered minor in 1925. Maurice Hindus witnessed the arbitrary enforcement of such codes while traveling through the countryside. In a village he saw a private trader charged with violating a sanitation law because she had not swept up the sunflower seed shells peasant customers had scattered on the floor of her little shop. That same day he spent some time in the village cooperative with the chairman of the local soviet and a visiting cooperative inspector, neither of whom rebuked the shop's manager or the peasants who were standing around strewing the floor with sunflower seed shells. On occasion, local authorities began trampling the Nepmen so vigorously that they had to be reined in by Moscow. This was the case in a town near Ufa, where in the summer of 1928 officials closed approximately one hundred private leather-working enterprises, allegedly for sanitation violations. Moscow's condemnation of such measures did not prevent them from continuing in many regions, particularly since this criticism from the center amounted to little more than a temporary, insincere concession to the Right from Stalin. As a matter of fact, early in 1929 VTsIK and Sovnarkom granted state labor inspectors even broader powers. A decree of January 2 authorized officials to assess "administrative levies" on employers who, though not violating the labor code, had nevertheless, in the view of the inspector, mistreated their workers.[37]

Local officials (not to mention Stalin during his Siberian campaign) relied increasingly upon "administrative measures" to throttle private grain trade and began to direct their blows not only at the Nepmen and kulaks but also at the majority of the peasants. The markets were closed in numerous localities, and private traders were forbidden to buy grain from the peasants. Where markets remained open, the militia often required peasants to present trading licenses, which only the Nepmen had been required to obtain in the past. The militia and other local officials frequently fixed grain prices and forced the peasants to sell only to the state, sometimes even stopping them on the road and confiscating their grain. In addition, railway freight charges for private cargo were raised again in 1928, and in the following years various state agencies were empowered to forbid private rail shipments of any commodity. In Berlin the editors of *Sotsialisticheskii vestnik* received a report from a small village describing the consequences of the state offensive against private grain trade. "Panic is evident among the local population, caused by the prohibition of buying and selling grain. Repressive measures are being taken against private traders. The renewed arrests, confiscations, and tax increases have almost completely stifled the vitality of the little village of Podoliia." The inhabitants must have detected little difference from the grim days of War Communism.[38]

In a Soviet joke of the period, a Nepman's young daughter answered the door and called to her mother that the tax collector had come. "I'll be right there," replied her mother. "Be a good girl and offer the comrade a chair." "But, Mommy," said the child, "he wants *all* our furniture." This anecdote suggests the growing resemblance of taxation to the more forceful "administrative measures" employed against the Nepmen. Beginning in 1928, tax officials sharply increased the assessments on private entrepreneurs. If a Nepman managed somehow to scrape together enough money to pay the first levy, his taxes were frequently doubled on the inspector's next visit, so that before long he was unable to pay. His property was then confiscated, and he faced possible arrest for tax delinquency. Deputy Commissar of Finance Moshe Frumkin reported to VTsIK in April 1928 that Narkomfin had been directed "to fix the tax so that private mills will close" and added that "in some places we have almost completely abolished private trade by our tax policy." In the following years the state also conducted investigations of its own tax bureaucracy to weed out officials who failed to exhibit sufficient zeal in taxing the Nepmen.[39] It is not difficult to imagine how these purges affected the treatment meted out to Nepmen by those tax inspectors who remained at their jobs.

During the period from 1928 to 1930 the income and business tax rates for private entrepreneurs were raised repeatedly, loopholes were closed, and the period of time over which payments were spread each year was reduced.[40] Income-tax data from the Sokol'nicheskii quarter of Moscow, where many Nepmen lived, reveal the disproportionate burden on those entrepreneurs still in business at the end of the decade. In 1929/30, private traders and manufacturers represented 1.7 percent of the region's income tax payers, with 8.2 percent of the total taxable income, but accounted for 55 percent of the region's income-tax receipts. For small-scale handicraftsmen of the Sokol'nicheskii quarter, the respective figures were 18 percent, 19 percent, and 26 percent.[41]

The Nepmen's taxes increased even more rapidly at the end of the 1920s than did the rates in tax decrees. Financial inspectors often increased arbitrarily their estimates of a private entrepreneur's sales or profits, and at times simply confiscated whatever merchandise or cash happened to be on hand. Toward the end of the decade, for example, an American reporter witnessed a raid on some Nepmen in the apartment building where he lived. A man and his relatives were making stockings without a license and selling them without paying taxes, and another possessed foreign currency worth $20,000. It is not surprising that these people were arrested, but three others, who had retired from business, were told the next day that a new, retroactive tax had been levied on the sales made during their last year in business. The tax happened to coincide exactly with the value of all their possessions. "Within three days they were out in the streets with little more than the clothes they wore and some bedding."[42]

During this period the state also stepped up its pressure on the Nepmen in other ways. The constitution drawn up by the Bolsheviks in 1918, during War Communism, barred certain segments of the population from voting and holding public office. Among these people, who came to be known as *lishentsy* (from *lishat'*, "to deprive") were (1) people using hired labor to make profits; (2) people living on "unearned income," such as interest and income from "enterprises" (*predpriatiia*) and property; and (3) private traders and middlemen.[43] Even though private economic activity was legalized after 1921, the new constitutions issued in the various Soviet republics during the 1920s continued to disfranchise the Nepmen in language identical to that in the constitution of 1918.[44] This must have seemed a perplexing paradox to private entrepreneurs. The Civil Code granted them the right to engage in private business, but the constitution disfranchised them if they exercised this right.

Though it was not proclaimed in Soviet constitutions, *lishentsy* suffered other deprivations as well. They could not have careers in the military or join cooperatives, trade unions, or other semiofficial organizations. Nor could they publish newspapers or arrange gatherings. They paid much higher bills than the rest of the population for utilities, rent, medical care, schooling for their children, and other public services. Nepmen incurred these penalties throughout the decade, even in the comparatively tolerant period from 1925 to 1926. But beginning in 1928, the position of *lishentsy* worsened considerably. As rationing spread across the land, officials wondered aloud why *lishentsy* should be granted food and clothing that were in short supply among workers. "Why must we supply the full 100 percent of the population," A. I. Mikoyan (a candidate member of the Politburo) asked a meeting of cooperative officials in 1928. "Why must we supply Nepmen? The easiest way is to establish a norm, a ration card." Mikoyan meant, of course, that ration cards should be issued to everyone but *lishentsy*, and this is precisely what happened.[45]

In the same spirit, *lishentsy* were expelled from state housing at the end of the decade. Demonstrating their vigilance, many housing committees in apartment buildings searched tirelessly for reasons to disfranchise and expel tenants. The results, as might be expected, were sometimes pathetic. For example, a woman in state housing was disfranchised because her husband, who had been unemployed for over a year, eked out a living by selling cucumbers, bread, and cigarettes at a street crossing. Even former Nepmen, who had since taken up other activities, were vulnerable. Given the acute housing shortage in many cities, it is not difficult to believe reports that the policy of expelling *lishentsy* from state housing was greeted warmly by the urban population. As the Moscow correspondent of the *New York Times* reported at the end of NEP: "In the cities the overcrowding is so great that the news that hundreds or thousands of apartments will be vacated by the expulsion of Nepmen tenants is good news to all." What was to become of people denied work, food rations, and housing seems not to have concerned anyone but the *lishentsy* themselves. Eugene Lyons put this question to

> officials, communist friends, ordinary Russians in the following years, because it was a fascinating mystery. None of them could give me a satisfactory answer, except the amazing tenacity of the human animal in clinging somehow to life.
> Part of the answer of course is that a large proportion of them did not survive. Suicide and death from the diseases of undernourishment decimated their ranks. The rest hung on to existence somehow with bleeding fingers,

doing odd jobs, teaching, begging, "smuggling" themselves into jobs by lying about their status only to be exposed and driven out again before long.[46]

Not only *lishentsy* but their children as well felt the "class principle" of Soviet society more heavily at the end of the 1920s. Throughout the decade, Nepmen were required to pay for their children's primary education at rates several times higher than those applied to the offspring of even the most prosperous workers. Even in the middle of NEP, higher education was out of the question for the children of *lishentsy* unless they could disguise their parentage or pay a large fee. These students had always been vulnerable to expulsion, but at the end of the decade, purges gripped the universities in earnest. Paralleling the eviction of *lishentsy* from state housing, students with "nonlabor" parents were ferreted out of colleges and universities with redoubled vigor. Even other students were enlisted in the hunt. An American student at a Moscow university noticed a banner in the lobby of the main building that bore the words: "Any student who knows why another student should be deprived of his right to vote is obligated to report to the Students' Committee." Some expelled students, overcome by the hopelessness of their position, committed suicide.[47]

Children of *lishentsy* who, despite these obstacles, wished to continue their education often faced the dilemma described in a report from one of *Sotsialisticheskii vestnik*'s sources in the Soviet Union. In a provincial town, two friends of the reporter operated a small cafeteria (without using hired labor). Their daughter finished secondary school and wanted to go on to a university. But with "nonlabor elements" as parents, her way was barred. She then found work in a factory, hoping to gain admission to a university after two years of trade union activity. Soon, however, she learned that factory work would not be enough "to wash away the shame of her bourgeois origins." It was also necessary to make a "complete break" with her parents. Reluctantly, the girl agreed to move out of her family home. But she refused to publicly renounce her parents and cease visiting them, and the trade union would not include her in the group of people it sent on to college. Similarly, Maurice Hindus knew a youth who was denied admission to a university because his father owned a tea house. "He could, of course, disown his father, change his name, declare himself independent, and doors to institutions of learning would open up. Some of his friends had done so. But he could not [that is, did not choose to] follow in their footsteps."[48]

Along with forced collectivization and the elimination of the kulaks, the campaign against the Nepmen reached its peak during the winter of

1929–30. Toward the end of October 1929, representatives from various factories in Moscow met with government officials to organize what were termed "workers' brigades" (or, sometimes, "shock brigades"). These were groups of workers who visited Nepmen delinquent in their tax payments and simply seized whatever property was available to cover the arrears. As one longtime foreign resident of Moscow reported: "The regularly-appointed tax collector, when he calls on private persons, [is] almost always accompanied by a pair of these young stalwarts, who make light of protests and nip resistance in the bud." Given the methods of tax assessment in use, there was no shortage of arrears for these brigades to collect. Following their successful performance against the Nepmen (and kulaks) in the Moscow region, workers' brigades were soon in action throughout the Soviet Union. In many cities and villages, the brigades conducted "trunk weeks," going from house to house in search of anything that could be construed as a supply of goods intended for illicit economic activity. They confiscated items deemed to be hoarded and, if the supply was large enough, had the owner arrested as an illegal trader.[49]

This was also the period of the well-known "gold fever," though, as Solzhenitsyn explains, "the fever gripped not those looking for gold but those from whom it was being shaken loose." As the massive industrialization campaign of the First Five-Year Plan was launched, the state was desperate for gold, which could be used to obtain equipment and specialists from the West. Thus the police arrested anyone they thought *might* be hoarding gold, and many of these victims were, or had been, Nepmen. Private entrepreneurs so detained were generally not charged with a crime and thus rarely journeyed through the penal system to the labor camps. They were simply held in the prisons and tortured until they surrendered their gold. The outlook for those who actually had no gold was bleak.[50]

Toward the end of 1929 nearly all "permanent" private shops were closed. In most regions, the only private traders still tolerated were small-scale, mobile street vendors. As during War Communism, many of these "merchants" were simply peasants bringing food into the cities from the surrounding countryside, now that private middlemen had again been virtually eliminated. During the winter of 1929–30, even these itinerant street traders all but disappeared. This was partly because of the collectivization and dekulakization campaigns (which diminished the volume of surplus produce and the number of peasants free to market it), and partly because of more energetic police measures against such trade. Eugene Lyons described the state's mopping-up activity:

City Soviets would not remain behindhand as against their country col-
leagues and sought to match liquidation of the kulaks with a no less hasty
liquidation of the miserable remnants of private trade. There were days in
which tens of thousands of "speculators" were arrested, imprisoned or driven
from the cities: harried creatures, denied respectable employment by law,
who sold toothpicks, homemade garments, second-hand boots, stale hunks
of bread, matches, a little sunflower seed oil, in the private markets. Further
revisions of living space were ordered in Moscow and elsewhere, so that former Nepmen and other class enemies, whether eight years old or eighty,
might be expelled from their cramped quarters.[51]

Peasants were forbidden to carry sacks of food onto trains and often had
their produce confiscated if they tried to enter cities by other means.
Those who managed to slip through the blockade, along with urban
peddlers, were subject to heavy fines (or worse) if caught.[52]

The aftermath of the state's winter onslaught in the cities was starkly
dramatic. An American mining engineer employed by a Soviet agency,
who had left Moscow for a brief trip to the United States in December
1929, was struck on his return in June by the transformation Moscow
had undergone. "On the streets all the shops seemed to have disappeared. Gone was the open market. Gone were the nepmen. The government stores had showy, empty boxes and other window-dressing. But
the interior was devoid of goods." Another American living in Moscow
observed:

The streets presented a strange appearance to one who had become accus-
tomed to throngs of peasant pedlars. For the first time since the introduction
of the rationing of food the population became almost wholly dependent
upon the supply of food obtainable on their ration cards at the governmental
and cooperative shops. The plight of those people who were deprived of elec-
toral rights, and consequently of the right to have ration cards, was difficult
indeed.[53]

Thus by 1930 the Nepmen's day was over. Private trade was nearly ex-
tinct in all save the remotest regions, and other private ventures such as
medical clinics, dentists' offices, and barber shops were banned at this
time. In addition, Sovnarkom abolished a number of institutions in
which Nepmen had participated, such as credit organizations, commodity exchanges, and fairs (including the famous one at Nizhnii Novgorod). Even defense attorneys, who were state employees, began refusing to accept Nepmen any longer as clients.[54] The campaign against
private entrepreneurs gained such steam in the last years of the decade
that the Nepmen were driven out of business more rapidly than the state

had planned. As late as April 1929, for example, the maximum variant
of the First Five-Year Plan approved by the Sixteenth Party Conference
anticipated that the private share of the country's total trade volume
would not drop below 9 percent by *1932/33.*[55] In reality, the economy
would "achieve" this figure within the year. In many regions, particularly in the countryside, private shops and markets often closed before
they could be replaced by state and cooperative stores, forcing peasants
to travel several kilometers to purchase even essential items.[56]

On March 2, 1930, Stalin signaled unexpectedly (in *Pravda*) that he
was reining in the collectivization campaign then raging through the
countryside. His article, titled "Dizzy from Success," rebuked local officials who had allegedly misunderstood the party line and tried over-
zealously to collectivize their regions. Twelve days later an order from
the CC (to all provincial party committees) condemned "the abolition
of markets and bazaars in a number of places, leading to a reduction in
the supply of [food to] the towns." Party organizations were ordered "to
forbid the closing of markets, to restore bazaars, and not to hinder sales
by peasants, including members of collective farms, of their produce
in the market." As a result of such orders, some peasant vendors reappeared in the streets and market squares. Describing the uncertain
period immediately following the publication of Stalin's article, a foreign
resident of Moscow recalled:

> Everyone wondered, too, whether Nep would be re-established. For some
> time the train of events was confused. The peasant pedlars appeared again
> upon the streets as though by magic. The prices which they charged were,
> however, higher than before their disappearance. On the other hand, the
> shops of the Nepmen were, in most cases, not reopened.[57]

All the while, no decree was drafted to formally abolish NEP, even
though its primary provisions had all been emasculated by the end
of the decade. Instead, Stalin announced that NEP consisted of two
"sides" or "stages" and that the second stage—now at hand—included
a stepped-up offensive against the "new bourgeoisie." Speaking to a
Plenum of the CC and CCC in April 1929, Stalin explained this position
and remarked: "Bukharin's mistake is that he does not see the two-sided
nature of NEP, he sees only the first side." In June of the following year,
while presenting the CC report to the Sixteenth Party Congress, Stalin
scoffed at "the complete absurdity of chatter about NEP being incompatible with an attack [against capitalist elements]."

> Indeed NEP does not only presuppose a retreat and the permission of the
> revival of private trade, the permission of the revival of capitalism with the

state playing a regulatory role—the first stage of NEP. NEP, in fact, also pre-supposes, at a certain stage of development, the attack of socialism against capitalist elements, the shrinking of the field of activity for private trade, the relative and absolute decline of capitalism, the growing preponderance of the socialist sector over the nonsocialist sector, the victory of socialism over capitalism—the present stage of NEP.[58]

With remarks like these, Stalin was again selecting the combative side of Lenin's ambiguous characterization of NEP. Lenin did suggest on a number of occasions that NEP involved first a retreat and then a struggle with the "new bourgeoisie." But was this struggle to assume primarily the form of economic competition, as Bukharin insisted, or did Lenin have in mind the measures adopted by the state in 1928–30? As we have seen, Lenin's works from 1921 to 1923 leave considerable room for doubt that he shared Stalin's conception of NEP on this and other scores. With the defeat of the Right Opposition, however, this became a moot point. As new laws and resolutions abandoned NEP's old principles, police and tax officials had little difficulty gauging the direction and force of the new political winds and adjusted their treatment of private entrepreneurs accordingly.

The renewed toleration of private trade, following Stalin's "Dizzy from Success" article, applied to sales by petty producers, mainly peasants, but not to transactions by middlemen, which had been the heart of the Nepmen's activity. Numerous decrees issued during the 1930s permitted collective farmers and the dwindling number of independent peasants to sell their surplus produce freely in places such as market squares, railroad stations, and boat landings. But as a decree of VTsIK and Sovnarkom added in 1932: "The opening of stores and shops by private traders is not permitted, and middlemen and speculators, trying to profit at the expense of the workers and peasants, must be eliminated everywhere."[59] Private trade, as it had been conducted by most Nepmen, became a crime, punished as "speculation" with a sentence of five to ten years in a labor camp and loss of property.[60]

Meanwhile, Stalin offered an interesting defense of free trade by collective farmers. Speaking to a meeting of party officials in January 1933, he asked the question undoubtedly on the minds of many:

Why did the Council of People's Commissars and the Central Committee introduce [free] collective-farm trade in grain?
     First of all, in order to widen the basis of trade between town and country, and improve the supply of agricultural products to the workers and urban manufactured goods to the peasants. There is no doubt that state and cooperative trade by themselves are not up to this. These channels of trade had to be supplemented with a new channel—collective-farm trade.

Stalin added that these free-market sales would provide additional income for the collective farmers and "give the peasantry a new incentive
to improve the work of the collective farms both in sowing and in harvesting."[61] One wonders if anyone at the meeting perceived the ironic
similarity between Stalin's justification of free collective-farm trade and
Lenin's defense in 1921 of the policies Stalin claimed the Soviet Union
had outgrown.[62]

# Part II

## CHAPTER 4

# "Ordinary Buying and Selling"

The new economic policy turned Moscow into a vast market place.
Trade became the new religion. Shops and stores sprang up
overnight, mysteriously stacked with delicacies Russia had not
seen for years. Large quantities of butter, cheese, and meat were
displayed for sale; pastry, rare fruit, and sweets of every variety were
to be purchased. . . . Men, women, and children with pinched
faces and hungry eyes stood about gazing into the windows and
discussing the great miracle: what was but yesterday considered a
heinous offense was now flaunted before them in an open and legal
manner.

—Emma Goldman

By the end of NEP's first summer, it seemed to many observers that Russia was awash in private trade, especially in comparison to the lean years of War Communism. After moderate growth in the spring and summer of 1921, private trade spread rapidly following a decree from the Council of People's Commissars (Sovnarkom), issued on August 9, that permitted small-scale private manufacturing and the free sale of goods produced by such operations. Two months later, Lenin conceded that the state plan to establish direct commodity exchange with the peasantry had been elbowed aside by "ordinary buying and selling."[1] Armand Hammer, who began his long business relationship with the Soviet Union in 1921, was amazed at the changes that had taken place in Moscow when he returned at the end of August, following a trip to the Urals:

> I had been away little more than a month, but short as the time was, I rubbed my eyes in astonishment. Was this Moscow, the city of squalor and sadness, that I had left? Now the streets that had been so deserted were thronged with people. Everyone seemed in a hurry, full of purpose, with eager faces. Everywhere one saw workmen tearing down the boarding from the fronts of stores, repairing broken windows, painting, plastering. From high-piled wagons goods were being unloaded into the stores. Everywhere one heard

the sound of hammering. My fellow travelers, no less surprised than I, made inquiries. "NEP, NEP," was the answer.[2]

Many other witnesses recorded similar impressions, including the *New York Times* correspondent in Moscow, who wrote in September that the city had recently appeared every bit as barren and dilapidated as many French towns at the end of the First World War. "Now, under the stimulus of the new decrees that are constantly being issued to regulate the changed economic policy, and under the liberty of private trading, shops, restaurants, and even cafés are being opened in all directions."[3] A Canadian living in Moscow during the first years of NEP observed ironically that some foreigners who arrived in the Soviet Union after this revival of trade considered Moscow rather shabby and run-down. But those who had known the city during War Communism, he explained, had a different perspective and were dazzled by the changes NEP produced: "The New Economic Policy had gone further than many dared hope. The Terror had largely vanished. The shops had all reopened, and the streets were now crowded until late at night with people. Even the gaping roadways, always bad in Moscow, were being repaired."[4]

Trade was without question the Nepmen's most important occupation in the newly legalized realm of business, both in terms of rubles and in terms of the number of people involved. Private individuals generally preferred trading to other endeavors such as manufacturing because (1) comparatively little capital was needed to begin trading; (2) the return on investment was generally rapid, an important consideration when long-term business prospects seemed uncertain at best; (3) traders (particularly small-scale vendors) were mobile and better able to avoid taxes, licenses, and other forms of state regulation than were manufacturers; and (4) little business experience was necessary to begin petty trading.[5]

Nearly all private trade was of simple, basic consumer goods. Such merchandise required relatively small amounts of capital to produce and was much in demand, given the widespread shortages of so many necessities. Food—fresh meat, vegetables, dairy products, grains, bread, and processed items—was the commodity most frequently handled by private traders. Particularly in the first months of NEP, the food shortages in most cities and towns ensured that virtually anything edible could be profitably marketed. But even in later years, food represented 40 to 50 percent of the volume of private trade. Most remaining private sales involved textile products and leather goods, such as boots and shoes, and other manufactured (often handicraft) items of use in and around the home.[6]

For licensing and tax purposes, the government divided private traders into ranks according to the nature and size of their business—the higher the rank, the higher the license fee. In the summer of 1921, as we have seen, there were three broad ranks of trade, but as the size and diversity of private enterprises increased, so did the number of categories. Two more were added in 1922, followed by a more detailed definition of the five categories in 1923 and the addition of a sixth in 1926.[7] State agencies used these categories in their statistical surveys of private trade, and consequently much of the available data concerning the Nepmen are expressed in these terms. Therefore, a brief summary of the types of activity included in each trade rank might prove helpful before proceeding with an analysis of the characteristics of private trade.

On the basis of the lengthy definitions in the decree of 1922, the five trade ranks may be described as follows.

Rank I:    Trade (generally in market squares, bazaars, or along streets) by a person selling goods that can be carried by hand, in a sack, in a hawker's tray, and so on.

Rank II:   Trade by a single person, or with help from one family member or hired worker, conducted from temporary facilities (stalls, tables, carts, etc.) at markets and bazaars; or trade by no more than two people from small permanent facilities (such as a kiosk) that the customer does not enter.

Rank III:  Retail trade, by the owner of the business and no more than four hired workers or family members, conducted from a modest permanent shop designed for the customer to enter.

Rank IV:   Partial wholesale trade (*poluoptovaia torgovlia*), i.e., the sale of small lots of goods (worth up to 300 rubles) from enterprises with no more than ten workers.

           Retail trade from permanent stores employing five to twenty workers or family members.

Rank V:    Wholesale trade.

           Partial wholesale trade by businesses with over ten workers.

           Retail trade from large stores with over twenty workers.

The state tried to fill the gaps in its definitions by classifying all firms that did not fit into any category as rank III operations unless their monthly business was less than 300 rubles, in which case they were assigned to rank II. Somewhat more detailed definitions of the trade ranks were included in subsequent decrees, but the main characteristics of each category remained unchanged throughout the rest of NEP.[8]

In the first months of NEP private trade was confined almost exclusively to petty transactions in markets and bazaars, nothing more sophisticated or elaborate than had existed illegally during War Communism.[9] People from many different professions and walks of life—factory workers, intellectuals, demobilized soldiers, prewar merchants, artisans, invalids, peasants, and a large number of housewives—plunged into trade (often the barter of personal possessions) in quest of food, clothing, and fuel. At this time there was no effective network of state inspectors to register and tax private traders, and this was all the encouragement many hungry people needed to try their hand at trade.[10] As a fieldworker for the American Mennonite famine relief organization reported from the Ukraine in November:

> When the people had no more bread their only recourse was to exchange some of their clothing, their furniture or their farming implements for food. Everything imaginable was carried to the "Toltchok" (the "jostling-place" in the village bazaar, where people exchanged or sold personal belongings). The market was soon glutted with such things, so that beds and dressers were selling for ten or fifteen pounds of barley flour, a ten horse-power naptha motor for ten bushels of barley, and other things in proportion.[11]

A traveler in Siberia during the winter of 1921–22 noticed that "many of the homes of Irkutsk were largely empty. The families had sold their furniture bit by bit to the peasants for food."[12]

Private traders often worked only part time or on their days off from other occupations, traveling to rural markets to buy food from the peasants, either for their own families or for resale in the cities. This type of trade, called bagging (*meshochnichestvo*), became an extremely important conduit of food to the residents of cities and towns in 1921 and 1922. Because of bagging's small-scale, itinerant nature and the inability of nascent state agencies to monitor such activity at the beginning of NEP, there are almost no statistics on the volume of such trade or the number of bagmen—one source claims that over 200,000 were riding the rails by the middle of April 1921 in the Ukraine alone. In any case, many people were struck by the crowds of bagmen traveling to and from food-producing regions. The chairman of the Cheliabinsk Guberniia

Party Executive Committee reported in April that "a huge wave of bagmen, impossible to control, has flooded Cheliabinsk *guberniia* and Siberia." Similar telegrams were sent by officials in other cities located in the grain belt.[13]

The railroad was generally the only means of transportation for bagmen, and they often engulfed an entire train like a legion of ants. An *Izvestiia* correspondent wrote in May:

> In the Ukraine bagging has assumed completely inappropriate forms. That which one sees at small stations has blossomed doubly in Kiev itself.
> A sort of gray caterpillar moves along the rails—this is the train, completely covered with a gray mass of bagmen. Under them neither the cars, nor the engine, nor the roofs, nor the footsteps, nor the spaces between the cars are visible. Every space is occupied, filled in. But as the train slows down in its approach to the Kiev station, its gray skin begins to slip off.[14]

The authorities tried to prevent such travel, but without complete success. An American Relief Administration official on a trip from Voronezh to Moscow in March 1922 marveled at the tenacity of the bagmen. No matter how many times the police chased them off the cars, they managed to clamber back on again. As a result, there were more people hanging on outside the cars than there were inside.[15] As the food shortage worsened, desperation drove people of all sorts, from professors to children, into the sea of bagmen.[16] The competition among these traders was understandably fierce, with little to prevent the strong from seizing the provisions of the weak.

Railwaymen were in an ideal position to conduct this sort of trade, since they made daily trips to and from the countryside. It was comparatively simple for them to transport various commodities from the towns to exchange for food with the peasants, and then sell the food for a handsome profit back in the towns.

> This plan [a traveler observed] was general among the railwaymen. One guard on a through express showed me his stock. He took his wife with him, occupying a big compartment, although a number of passengers had been left behind for lack of room. The lavatory attached to the compartment was stocked up. Salt was this guard's medium of exchange. The country people were clamorous for salt. His wife did the bargaining with the peasants, so many pounds of salt for a goose, so many for a suckling pig, and so on.[17]

As in this illustration, nearly all trade between bagmen and peasants assumed the form of barter. The main reason was that most sellers refused to accept currency rendered worthless by the breathtaking inflation that marked NEP's infancy. Such concerns were, of course, not limited to the

bagmen and peasantry. An article in the Commissariat of Finance journal estimated that barter accounted for fully 50 to 70 percent of all trade
in Russia during the first half of 1921/22.[18]

There was virtually no private trade from large, permanent shops at
the beginning of NEP. For one thing, relatively few people possessed the
necessary resources and expertise. But the most important factor was
uncertainty that NEP had actually been adopted "seriously and for a
long time," as Lenin claimed. With the harsh experience of War Communism a recent memory and the Bolsheviks' express desire in the
spring of 1921 to limit private trade to local barter, prospective shopkeepers did not rush to test the waters. An old trader told an acquaintance that he suspected NEP was a ploy on the part of the Cheka (secret
police) to entice merchants to reveal their hidden goods and money. If
they took the bait, he feared, the police would seize their merchandise
and imprison them. In this spirit, individuals capable of conducting
larger-scale trade generally elected to remain on the sidelines until they
were certain of War Communism's demise.[19]

Gradually, though, during the course of 1922, entrepreneurs became
convinced that permanent stores would be tolerated, and the number of
these establishments grew steadily.[20] The lingering uncertainty of some
Nepmen was evident in their tendency to initially give their businesses
official, "Soviet" names such as Snabprodukt (Produce Supply) and organize them, ostensibly, as cooperatives. As time went by, they began to
conduct business more openly under their own names and transformed
the "cooperatives" into private enterprises.[21] Meanwhile, many of the
"amateur" petty street hawkers and bagmen succumbed to the twin
blows of competition from the growing number of permanent shops and
the taxes that the Bolsheviks began to levy on private traders.[22] From the
summer of 1922 to the summer of 1923 the number of licensed private
shops increased 36 percent in rank III, 70 percent in rank IV, and 188
percent in rank V, whereas the number of petty private traders in ranks I
and II *fell* by 23 and 8 percent, respectively.[23] Similar trends are evident
in figures covering a slightly different time period (see table 1). These
developments occurred first in the large cities, with the countryside lag-
ging behind by several months or even a year in areas ravaged by the
famine of 1921–22. During the first third of 1922, for example, the

TABLE I    PRIVATE TRADE LICENSES

|  | July–December 1922 | April–September 1923 |
|---|---|---|
| Rank I | 141,400 | 105,200 |
| Rank II | 288,900 | 222,700 |
| Rank III | 107,000 | 117,600 |
| Rank IV | 9,800 | 12,600 |
| Rank V | 1,700 | 3,000 |

SOURCE:  *Vnutrenniaia torgovlia soiuza SSR za X let* (Moscow, 1928), p. 262.

number of permanent private stores swelled by 83 percent in Moscow, rising from 2,900 to 5,300. At the same time, provincial newspaper correspondents reported from many localities, particularly in the devastated middle Volga region, that large-scale private trade was virtually nonexistent.[24]

The number of Nepmen who had prerevolutionary business experience as merchants or store employees increased after 1921, since these were generally the people opening the larger shops.[25] The dominance of experienced traders in the upper ranks is evident in figures (table 2) collected by the Commissariat of Domestic Trade during an investigation in 1927 of the Nepmen's social origins. As one might expect, the larger a merchant's operation, the more likely he was to have been active previously in trade. Vendors with little or no business experience—most often peasants, workers, and housewives—were concentrated in the first two ranks.

Around the turn of the century the Russian business elite (*krupnaia burzhuaziia* in Soviet studies) numbered approximately 1.5 million merchants, financiers, and industrial magnates.[26] Nearly all these people lost or closed their businesses, emigrated, or perished during the onslaughts of the Revolution and civil war. One exception was Semen Pliatskii, who had been a millionaire metal trader in St. Petersburg. Instead of emigrating after the Revolution, he chose to remain and to work for the state, surviving two arrests by the Cheka during War Communism. Following the introduction of NEP he set out on his own, first as a buyer and seller of scrap metal and later as a supplier of industrial products ranging from office supplies to lead pipe. He had a knack for acquiring even scarce commodities by hook or by crook. Here his many connections

TABLE 2    PREVIOUS PROFESSIONS
OF PRIVATE TRADERS

|                          | Rank I | Rank II | Rank III | Rank IV | Rank V |
|--------------------------|--------|---------|----------|---------|--------|
| Traders, Store employees | 20%    | 38%     | 59%      | 67%     | 78%    |
| Peasants                 | 31     | 27      | 15       | 6       | 4      |
| Workers                  | 10     | 9       | 5        | 3       | 1      |
| Handicraftsmen           | 4      | 5       | 6        | 3       | 2      |
| Office workers           | 5      | 6       | 5        | 6       | 6      |
| Housewives               | 18     | 7       | 2        | 1       | 1      |
| Other                    | 12     | 8       | 8        | 14      | 8      |

SOURCE: *Voprosy torgovli*, 1929, No. 15, p. 65.

with state agencies, often established with bribes, undoubtedly helped. As Victor Serge put it: "This Balzacian man of affairs has floated companies by the dozen, bribed officials in every single department—and he is not shot, because basically he is indispensable: he keeps everything going." It was not unusual for state enterprises to give Pliatskii's orders preferential treatment over those of other state agencies. Before long, he had become a millionaire again.[27] But the ranks of the "new bourgeoisie" contained few prewar merchants of Pliatskii's stature. Nearly all the Nepmen with previous trading experience had been nothing more than small-scale entrepreneurs or shop employees before the Revolution.[28]

After the uncertainty accompanying the introduction of NEP had been dispelled, and trade assumed a comparatively normal form, the distribution of Nepmen in the various trade ranks was roughly as follows through 1926. Half of all licensed private traders belonged to rank II, numbering between 180,000 and 260,000 persons, depending on the year and the season (as a rule, fewer people engaged in trade during the winter). Approximately one quarter (90,000 to 140,000) of all private trade licenses were held by rank III traders, and slightly over one fifth (70,000 to 120,000) belonged to rank I traders. The remaining three or four percent were issued mainly to Nepmen in the fourth rank (8,000 to 18,000), with rank V private traders accounting for less than 1 percent (1,600 to 4,000) of the total.[29] Thus, over 70 percent of all private traders—ranks I and II—did not operate from permanent shops (more specifically, buildings designed for the customer to enter), but traded mainly in the streets, market squares, and bazaars, either from booths or stalls or out in the open. Many small-scale traders avoided registration, and their actual number was thus undoubtedly even greater than the figure presented above.[30]

Private traders in rank III, however, were responsible for a volume of sales roughly twice that of rank II Nepmen, according to data for the period from 1923 to 1926—even though there were twice as many traders in rank II as in rank III. This, of course, is because the permanent shops of rank III were considerably larger operations than the businesses of rank II vendors in the open markets. In fact, the Nepmen of ranks IV and V, who, taken together, numbered no more than 8 percent of the private traders in rank II, accounted for a significantly larger sales volume than did the rank II traders (from 16 to 77 percent larger for the various six-month segments of this period). Data of this sort are not available for rank I Nepmen, though their sales must have been much less than those of private traders in rank II, for the latter were over twice as numerous and ran larger businesses.[31]

As one might conclude from these figures, more private capital was invested in rank III enterprises than in those of any other rank. In fact, data for 1924/25 indicate that the investment in rank III private trade (452.3 million rubles) was nearly as much as the capital invested in the other four ranks combined (454.5 million rubles). Also significant is that large firms in ranks IV and V, which accounted for only 3 or 4 percent of all private trading licenses, together utilized over one third of all private trade capital (138.1 million rubles for rank IV and 194 million rubles for rank V); whereas only 13 percent (114 million rubles) of private trade capital was invested in rank II, and less than 1 percent (8.4 million rubles) in rank I.[32]

This regeneration of larger, permanent private shops was impressive, but even during the peak of the Nepmen's activity in 1925/26, private trade did not regain its prewar level of sophistication. In the years before the First World War, nearly two of every three private trading operations were fixed, permanent shops, whereas in 1925 only about one quarter of all private traders worked in such facilities. The remaining 75 percent, as just mentioned, carried their wares around with them, selling from wagons, booths, tents, trays, and so on, usually in market squares and bazaars. Thus, although there were more urban private traders in the middle of NEP than before the war, their volume of sales was only about 40 percent of prewar urban sales. Rural private traders in 1924/25 numbered only about 20 percent of their prewar counterparts—the figure rose to about 50 percent by 1926/27—and accounted for only about 13 percent of the prewar volume of rural trade.[33]

The predominance of small-scale trade was the result of a number of factors. Even in relatively prosperous times it was impossible for most Nepmen to raise the capital necessary for a large wholesale or retail firm, while modest operations could survive on a small volume of sales and, generally, were less dependent on the state for merchandise. The expenses of such traders were minimal, because they did not have to maintain permanent stores or large numbers of employees, and they were in the lowest tax brackets for private traders. Further, mobile vendors could avoid the attention of state tax officials, the police, and other inspectors more easily than could the proprietors of larger, permanent enterprises. These advantages became virtual necessities for Nepmen during the last years of NEP, when merchandise grew scarcer and the state stepped up its campaign to eliminate private trade.

Throughout NEP, then, the majority of private traders belonged to the first two ranks, whose members were most often found in market squares and along sidewalks. All towns of any consequence had at least one market (*rynok*), and cities such as Moscow, Leningrad, and Kiev contained many.[34] The most famous was the sprawling Sukharevka in Moscow, through which it was not unusual for 50,000 people to pass on a holiday.[35] An émigré's description of the Sukharevka resembles the portraits sketched by other observers.

> Everywhere you look is an agitated, noisy human crowd, buying and selling. The various types of trade are grouped together. Here currencies are bought and sold, there the food products; further along, textiles, tobacco, cafés and restaurants, booksellers, dishes, finished dresses, all sorts of old junk, and so on.
>
> . . . [The merchants cry out to people walking by] "I have pants in your size. Come and take a look!" "Citizen, what are you looking to buy?" "Hats here, the best in the whole Sukharevka!"
>
> Urchins scurry all about with kvass—huge bottles of red, yellow, or green liquid in which float a few slices of lemon. One million rubles a glass [reflecting the severe inflation at the beginning of NEP]. Everyone drinks this poison from the same glass. . . .
>
> . . . In the flea market [*tolkuchka*], where secondhand things are sold, there are no stalls or booths. The trade is just hand to hand. Among these vendors are remnants of the old intelligentsia, selling whatever they have left, from torn galoshes to china, but mainly old clothes.
>
> Solitary policemen stroll through the crowds. It is not clear what order they are to maintain, what laws they are to enforce. The market has its own

customs, its own understanding of honor and honesty. A row of booths sells gramophones and records. As is well known, in the countryside gramophones are valued more highly than pianos, and here in the Sukharevka interest in "musical preserves" is great. Recordings [of famous singers] compete with those of speeches by Lenin and Trotsky.[36]

This scene, including the traditional grouping of traders according to their merchandise, was typical of urban marketplaces during NEP. As one journeyed east, particularly in the direction of the Central Asian republics, markets assumed features of the centuries-old local bazaars. In Astrakhan', a traveler reported:

> We came to a marketplace where the people milled like flies, to the dirty banks of a stagnant canal where the vendors lived in unpainted wooden boats, sleeping over their "live cars" of sudac [pike perch] and swimming sturgeon. There they pulled out flapping fish to sell us. . . . We were offered milk boiled in gourd-shaped earthen urns, hacks of meat from a carcass being skinned, tubs of salted herring, buckets of still-swimming yellow perch, slabs of pink salmon. Chinamen, six feet high, with faces like yellow idols, walked about hung with ladies' garters, second-hand corsets, pencils, knives. . . . A barber shaved men's heads among the tubs of salted fish. . . . [There were also] bales of strange herbs and dyes [and] mounds of many-colored fruits.[37]

Some of the vendors in market squares were not registered in even the lowest ranks of trade. Peasants, for example, generally did not have to buy licenses in order to bring their produce to market in the towns. Nor were most of the smallest-scale traders—people wandering about selling a handful of secondhand wares—required to purchase a license in a trade rank. Doubtless, too, many itinerant traders did not bother to obtain a required license, particularly if they planned to sell their merchandise in a day or two and move on. The majority of the more settled, "professional" private traders in markets operated out of booths, stalls, or tents, which obligated most of them to purchase rank II licenses. The largest markets, such as the Sukharevka and Tsentral'nyi in Moscow and the Galitskii and Petrovskii in Kiev, contained over a thousand merchants plying their trades from "fixed" (*ustoichivyi*) facilities (such as booths). Many other markets in the large cities could boast stalls, covered tables, and the like, numbering in the hundreds.[38]

The number of traders in any given market fluctuated sharply in accordance with the season, the availability of goods, and the level of taxation (particularly the rent charged for a trading spot). In April 1923, for example, the rents and other fees paid by traders in the Sukharevka were raised significantly. As a result, the number of occupied booths plunged from 3,000 to 1,800. In August this financial burden was reduced, and the ranks of traders began to grow once again.[39] Most traders sold food or textiles, and the availability of these products thus had a powerful impact on a market's vitality.[40] The number of produce vendors varied cyclically, peaking each year in the summer and early fall (unless tax and rent increases negated this pattern). Textile traders depended less on nature and more on the state for their merchandise. If the party line of the day or the economic difficulties of the state reduced the flow of goods to the private sector, textile trade suffered greatly. Textile traders in the Sukharevka, for instance, told a Soviet newspaper reporter that they had arranged to receive goods from a state enterprise in return for keeping retail prices under certain ceilings. But, lamented the traders, the enterprise had been able to supply only a minuscule fraction of the textiles they had ordered. Similar complaints resounded in other markets.[41]

The rural equivalent of the urban markets were the village bazaars and local fairs. Nearly every village had a primary market day each week, usually Saturday or Sunday, during which the local population did much of its shopping. These bazaars resembled their urban counterparts, though on a smaller scale. Virtually none of the vendors was a full-time trader in a permanent booth or stall, since the bazaars generally functioned only once (sometimes twice) a week. Instead, nearly all the merchants were peasants, local artisans, and itinerant traders traveling from one bazaar or fair to the next.[42] Most of these people were not required to purchase trade licenses or pay the other parts of the business tax, provisions that the state in any case could not enforce effectively in the seemingly boundless countryside. Though few statistics are available concerning village bazaars, their nature is evident in descriptions left by a number of observers, including a worker in the Quaker famine relief program.

> The roads leading to a good market are always alive with traffic during the night before market day. All manner of livestock, fruits, vegetables, homemade furniture, ox yokes, boots, and so on, to an infinite variety, have been gathered in the square by daylight. All kinds of traders are to be found, from the peasant woman squatting by her bottle of milk or pile of gay carrots, to the swarthy Armenian cloth merchant surrounded by the oriental splendors of fluttering cotton prints that decorate his booth. Among the crowds move scores of itinerant traders with all their wares worn on the sleeve, so to speak. A pair of boots, three or four petticoats, or a half dozen shirts may comprise the entire stock. The vendor of heterogeneous junk, too, is always present with his pile of monstrous rusty locks, an unmated candlestick or so, hinges, door knobs, and a veritable Walt Whitman catalogue of other miscellany.[43]

An American living in the Soviet Union during the last years of NEP recorded the following scenes at a rural bazaar:

> In unending line peasant carts jogged by our window. From the porch of the house we could see three roads, each marked by peasants bound towards the bazaar. . . .
> Following an old custom, the sellers had divided themselves off according to what they were selling. In various corners were calves and colts; wheels, wagon yokes, and harness, all home made; cheese, butter, poultry and freshly slaughtered veal. Peddlers with wood carvings, with bark sandals, roamed about; small boys played games, and idle men crowded the vodka store.[44]

Local fairs took place once or twice a year, generally during holidays, and were usually little more than glorified bazaars with much the same types of trade described above.[45] They had been a common means of trade before the Revolution, especially in the countryside. One study reports 14,432 rural fairs and 2,172 urban fairs in 1894. After nearly vanishing during War Communism, they sprouted up again following the introduction of NEP, particularly in localities where they had existed under the old regime. In Moscow *guberniia* alone, 121 fairs were recorded during 1923, and approximately 440 were reported in the Ural region in 1924. Sometimes, local officials took the lead in organizing these events, but often the fairs reappeared on their own and were registered after the fact. As one Soviet reporter put it, "where they are needed, they appear."[46]

Although rural markets and fairs clearly attracted large numbers of small-scale peddlers and peasant entrepreneurs (a substantial majority of the population still lived in rural areas), approximately 70 percent of all *licensed* private traders did their business in cities and towns during the first four years of NEP. There were much higher concentrations of consumers in urban areas, of course, and the townspeople were more dependent on merchants for the necessities of life (particularly food) than were the peasants. For every inhabitant of a city or town in 1924/25, urban Nepmen made sales totaling 125 rubles, whereas rural Nepmen sold only four and one-half rubles' worth of goods for every person living in the countryside. The sources of these statistics rarely define the term *city* (*gorod*), and there is certainly room for debate over what should be included in this category. Nevertheless, any reasonable definition of the term would not alter the generalization that most *licensed* private traders operated in the towns, with Moscow and Leningrad having much the largest numbers.[47] Furthermore, the larger the shop, that is, the higher its trade rank (see table 3), the more likely it was to be found in an urban area.

TABLE 3    LICENSED RURAL PRIVATE TRADERS AS A
PERCENTAGE OF ALL LICENSED PRIVATE TRADERS

|          | 1923/24 | 1924/25 |
|----------|---------|---------|
| Rank I   | 29%     | 34%     |
| Rank II  | 28      | 35      |
| Rank III | 22      | 27      |
| Rank IV  | 13      | 23      |
| Rank V   | 11      | 16      |

SOURCE: A. M. Ginzburg, ed., *Chastnyi kapital v narodnom khoziaistve SSSR. Materialy kommissii VSNKh SSSR* (Moscow-Leningrad,
1927), pp. 114–115.

In addition, *rural* private firms of rank V had an average of only
14 percent as much capital as the average *urban* private enterprise in
rank V in 1925. The average rural private trader in ranks III and IV had
slightly over half the capital of the average urban firm in each of these
ranks.[48] Consequently, the urban percentage of total *licensed* private
sales volume was very high (roughly 80 to 90 percent),[49] since most
Nepmen, including virtually all the largest private firms, were in cities.[50]

Most of the data on the Nepmen pertains to European Russia as a
whole (roughly the area west of the Urals and north of the Caucasus) or
to individual cities. Some information is available, though, for Transcaucasia, portions of Central Asia, and individual regions of European
Russia that permits a rough comparison of the Nepmen's strength in
each area. In 1926/27, for example, 62.7 percent of all reported private
sales were made in the huge Russian Republic (RSFSR), which was divided into many smaller regions. Of these regions, the most important
were the central-industrial (which included Moscow) with 23 percent of
all reported private sales in the USSR, Leningrad and the surrounding
area with 6.8 percent, the Northern Caucasus with 6.6 percent, the
middle Volga region with 5.2 percent, the central black earth region
with 4.2 percent, the lower Volga region with 3.5 percent, the Ural region with 2.5 percent, and Siberia with 2.1 percent. After the RSFSR,
the Ukrainian Republic accounted for by far the most private trade—
22.3 percent of the country's total—followed by 6.2 percent for Transcaucasia, 5.6 percent for the Uzbek Republic, 2.3 percent for the Belo-

russian Republic, and 0.9 percent for the Turkmen Republic.[51] Nearly half of all private trade, then, took place in the central-industrial region and the Ukraine.

Although comparatively few private traders were located in Transcaucasia and Central Asia, they controlled trade in their regions to a greater extent than did Nepmen in European Russia. These border regions did not come under firm Bolshevik control until the 1920s and, for the government, were difficult locations in which to set up and supply enough state stores and cooperatives to satisfy the needs of the local populations. In the first half of 1925/26, for example, the Nepmen's share of all trading operations was 97 percent in the Uzbek Republic, 97 percent in Transcaucasia, and 93 percent in the Turkmen Republic, but "only" 80 percent in the Belorussian Republic, 81 percent in the Ukraine, 76 percent in the RSFSR, and 79 percent for the Soviet Union as a whole. Data for other years support these figures by revealing that the private share of total retail sales was higher in Transcaucasia and the Central Asian republics than in the republics of European Russia.[52] Just as Georgia is a hotbed of illegal economic activity today, a higher percentage of private trade during NEP may well have escaped the attention of state officials in the distant Transcaucasian and Central Asian border regions than in the heart of the state. If this was the case, the Nepmen in these areas were all the more dominant than were Nepmen in European Russia.

Certain regions, most notably Belorussia and the Ukraine—the old Jewish Pale—were distinguished by a relatively large number of Jewish entrepreneurs. Approximately 60 percent of the Soviet Jewish population lived in the Ukraine and 17 percent in much smaller Belorussia. Thus, even though only 1.8 percent of the Soviet Union's people were Jewish, Jews represented 5.4 and 8.2 percent of the Ukrainian and Belorussian populations, respectively, in 1927.[53] Many of these Jews (and others elsewhere in Russia) had traditionally been traders and artisans. According to the census of 1897, 31 percent of all "economically active" Jews were shopkeepers, hawkers, peddlers, and the like, and 36 percent worked in "industry," mainly handicrafts.[54] A good number of the latter undoubtedly engaged in trade as well. Following the introduction of NEP, many Jews returned to these activities or emerged from the black market to practice them openly. The resumption by many Jews of their former occupations helps account for the fact that in 1927 nearly two thirds of the private traders in Belorussia and over half in the Ukraine had prerevolutionary trading experience, whereas the corresponding figure for the RSFSR (where Jews were not as numerous) was only 38 percent.[55]

If the various peoples of the Ukraine are considered individually, we find that 15 percent of the Jews, 3 percent of the Great Russians, and 1 percent of the Ukrainians were traders in 1926. In the case of "workers" (most of whom, particularly among the Jews, were handicraftsmen and thus frequently traders as well), the figures were 40, 20, and 4 percent, respectively. On the other hand, 91 percent of the Ukrainians, 52 percent of the Great Russians, and only 9 percent of the Jews in the Ukraine were peasants.[56] The concentration of Ukrainian Jews in private business is further evidenced by the fact that Jews accounted for 45 percent of all disfranchised people[57] in the Ukraine while constituting only 5.4 percent of the region's population.[58]

An unfortunate consequence of the comparatively heavy concentration of Jews in private trade was the impulse this imparted to anti-Semitism in the 1920s. A number of observers echoed the words of Maurice Hindus on this score.

> Jews of this group, the successful Jewish Nepmen, have intensified anti-Semitism in Russia. They are conspicuous in all large cities. They are among the most successful of private traders, which does not escape the attention of the Russian proletariat or of the less fortunate Russian nepman. Both point to the Jewish nepman as the real gainer by the Revolution, the man who is turning the nation's agony into personal profit and pleasure.[59]

As historians of more recent decades have indicated, these views did not die along with NEP.

> In many areas a NEP-man had become synonymous with a Jew and he was so treated in some of the belles lettres of the period. When he later [after NEP] served mainly as an employee in a state wholesale establishment or a retail store during the prevailing periods of scarcity, he was accused by the resentful consumers of diverting the scarce merchandise for his own or his friends' benefit.[60]

There was a temporary decline in private trade from the winter of 1923–24 to the spring of 1925. The downturn may even be said to have begun a few months earlier as the "scissors crisis" took its toll on both private and "socialist" trade. At this time, the prices of manufactured goods climbed out of the reach of many consumers, and peasants were discouraged from producing food for the market.[61] But it was not until 1924 that the Nepmen came under the heaviest fire, in the form of tax increases and reductions of supplies and credit from the state.

The effects of these measures were not long in appearing. During this period the number of licensed private traders dropped by approximately 100,000.[62] In Moscow alone, following a sharp tax increase in the spring of 1924, 6,310 of the remaining 16,500 licensed private traders went out of business.[63] This trend is also evident in figures (table 4) available for the Central Market, one of Moscow's largest. As Nepmen were forced out of business during 1924, the volume of private retail sales fell to a level 20 percent below that of 1922/23.[64] Private trade reached its low water mark (that is, until the end of NEP) during the winter of 1924–25. After a drop of over 20 percent in the second half of 1923/24, sales declined an additional 14 percent in the first half of 1924/25.[65] The number of private trade licenses dipped 5 to 6 percent.[66] According to one report, Moscow's host of private merchants shrank fully 39 percent in this period.[67] Since larger enterprises were generally much more vulnerable to the measures adopted by the state than were street hawkers, the sharpest declines (in percentage terms) occurred in the higher trade ranks. In fact, the number of rank I vendors actually increased slightly in the first half of 1924/25.[68]

During 1925, the erosion of private trade was arrested as Bukharin and his allies gained the upper hand in the party. Spurred by the relaxation of state tax, credit, and supply policies (the "new trade practice"), the number of private merchants and their volume of sales rebounded briskly. There were steady increases in the number of private trade licenses from 1924/25 to 1925/26, reversing the earlier decline:[69]

| | |
|---|---|
| 496,454 | second half of 1923/24 |
| 469,692 | first half of 1924/25 |
| 524,400 | second half of 1924/25 |
| 590,203 | first half of 1925/26 |
| 608,280 | second half of 1925/26 |

Moreover, the percentage of all trade licenses (state, cooperative, and private) that were private in the RSFSR rose in every rank from 1924/25 to 1925/26 (see table 5). Private retail trade, after declining from 1,930 million rubles (1913 rubles) in 1922/23 to 1,574 million rubles in 1923/24 to 1,550 million rubles in 1924, rose to 1,825 million rubles in 1925 and then to 2,240 million rubles in 1926.[70]

Impressive as this recovery was, it proved to be fleeting. The private sector environment became less hospitable during 1927 and then turned openly hostile in the years from 1928 to 1930. The results of the measures taken by the state, first to restrict and then to "liquidate" the Nep-

TABLE 4    NUMBER OF BOOTHS IN CENTRAL
MARKET, MOSCOW

|                   | April 1, 1924 | October 1, 1924 |
| ----------------- | ------------- | --------------- |
| Food              | 262           | 133             |
| Textiles          | 277           | 179             |
| Finished dresses  | 15            | 5               |
| Footwear          | 39            | 13              |
| Hardware          | 58            | 29              |

SOURCE: *Torgovye izvestiia*, 1925, No. 28 (June 25), p. 5.

TABLE 5    PRIVATE SHARE OF ALL TRADE LICENSES
IN THE RSFSR

|          | 1924/25 | 1925/26 |
| -------- | ------- | ------- |
| Rank I   | 96.2%   | 99.1%   |
| Rank II  | 93.1    | 94.7    |
| Rank III | 50.0    | 55.9    |
| Rank IV  | 33.1    | 33.4    |
| Rank V   | 18.5    | 24.0    |

SOURCE: *Finansy i narodnoe khoziaistvo*, 1927, No. 33, p. 27.

men, are not difficult to detect. In the following *gubernii*, for example, the number of licensed private traders declined by the indicated percentages in 1926/27 compared to the second half of 1925/26:[71]

| | | | |
| --- | --- | --- | --- |
| Moscow | 42.7% | Vologda | 26% |
| Nizhnii Novgorod | 40.8% | Saratov | 25.3% |
| Voronezh | 37.3% | Kaluga | 24.9% |
| Kostroma | 36.7% | Ivanovo Voznesensk | 23.9% |
| Stalingrad | 31.5% | Tambov | 22.9% |
| Iaroslavl' | 27% | | |

Reported private retail sales fell dramatically after peaking at approximately 5.2 billion rubles in 1926 and dipping slightly to 4.96 billion rubles in 1927. In 1928, sales were off 27 percent, and during the next two years there were consecutive drops of 33 and 54 percent.[72] The

number of licensed private traders (excluding rank I) declined in similar
fashion over the years from 1925 to 1929:[73]

| | |
|---|---|
| 1925/26 | 590,500 |
| 1926/27 | 444,200 |
| 1927/28 | 339,400 |
| 1928/29 | 213,700 |

Reports from various cities underscore these trends. In Kiev, the number of private wholesale and retail firms fell 40 percent during 1927/28,
and sales plunged 47 percent. Of the 3,694 licensed private businesses
in 17 Moscow markets (*rynki*) in October 1927, only 1,571 remained a
year later. Private sales as a whole in the capital plummeted 62 percent
in 1928/29.[74] Such drastic changes were noted by many observers. A
longtime resident of Moscow wrote at this time that private food traders
"have been steadily decreasing both in number and quality and it is very
difficult to find them now, though there are still a few small ones in back
streets and in the very few areas in Moscow that are not well supplied
with shops."[75] According to an American journalist:

> As a matter of common convenience, we met in private cafes and ice-cream
> parlors. We ate in private restaurants, of which there were a dozen along
> Tverskaya [Moscow's main boulevard, later renamed Gorky Street]. We
> shopped in private stores, called in private physicians and used the services of
> private photographers, dentists, and other professional people. Everyone
> else, from commissars down, did likewise. By the end of the year [1928] most
> of this private traffic was ended.[76]

One striking feature of the elimination of private traders was that this
took place more swiftly than the central state planning agency (Gos-
plan) had anticipated and far exceeded the pace at which the "socialist"
(state and cooperative) distribution system was growing.[77] A report prepared for the Commissariat of Trade had noted this problem as early as
1927.[78] The situation only worsened as Stalin and his supporters gained
the upper hand in the party and pressed their attack on the private
sector.

The rapid "liquidation" of the Nepmen, before they could be fully
replaced by state and cooperative stores, had a powerful impact on consumers because the private share of retail trade had been so substantial.
To appreciate the Nepmen's importance, recall that during the first six
years of NEP over 95 percent of all rank I and rank II traders were private, and even a majority of the permanent shops in rank III belonged to
Nepmen. In fact, over 80 percent of rank III enterprises were privately

owned in 1922, and this figure had fallen only to about 60 percent by 1926. Even in ranks IV and V the Nepmen's share of enterprises was far from negligible—70 percent for rank IV and 50 percent for rank V in 1922, down to roughly 30 and 20 percent, respectively, by 1926.[79]

Thus there can be no doubt that during the first years of NEP, the vast majority of consumer goods reached the public through private traders. Few statistics are available for 1921, because state agencies were not yet able to gather such data for the country as a whole. But the Nepmen's percentage of retail trade must have been extremely large, because the "socialist" distribution system was a shambles after the Revolution and civil war. In any event, even as late as 1926, private entrepreneurs accounted for 40 percent of retail trade (more if illegal and unlicensed sales are included), as shown below in the sequence of private shares of retail sales.[80]

| 1922/23 | over 80% | 1926/27 | 37% |
|---------|----------|---------|-----|
| 1923/24 | 58%      | 1927/28 | 25% |
| 1924/25 | 43%      | 1928/29 | 16% |
| 1925/26 | 41%      | 1929/30 | 7%  |

Given this prominence of the private sector in the first two thirds of NEP, the headlong elimination of the Nepmen after 1927 could not help producing fallout across the land. In 1929 Narkomfin's journal declared with considerable understatement (referring to the Ukraine): "There are hardly sufficient grounds to assume that the decline of private retail sales has been covered completely by an increase in sales in the cooperative sector." In 1926/27, the article explained, there were 110 people in Kiev for every retail business, 126 people per business in Khar'kov, 106 in Odessa, and 110 in Dnepropetrovsk. But by 1928/29, the number of people per shop in these cities had risen to "a minimum of 150 to 160."[81] It was not unusual by 1928 to see such newspaper headlines as "Private entrepreneur eliminated but not replaced."[82] *Torgovo-promyshlennaia gazeta*'s correspondents filed reports from around the country on the appearance of "trade deserts" (*torgovye pustyni*), which, as the name suggests, were regions in the countryside where *no* "socialist" shops appeared to fill the void created when the local Nepmen were driven out of business. In such cases, peasants often had to travel several (sometimes even thirty to forty) kilometers to purchase essential products. Even if a village had a cooperative store or two, they were frequently empty of desirable goods. When a shipment of merchandise arrived, the useful items were snatched up in a day or two by customers who had often been standing in line for many hours.[83]

These problems were most acute in the countryside, but the rapid "liquidation" of private traders in Moscow prompted at least one Soviet reporter to apply the expression "trade desert" to the capital itself. A colleague in Smolensk wrote that the elimination of private traders there was proving to be something less than an unmitigated blessing for consumers. "Indeed," he explained, "it is unbelievable, but true, that at present not a single commodity may be purchased in the city without waiting in line. Every day the population wastes many thousands of working hours standing in lines."[84] Such reports would not have provoked an argument from Eugene Lyons, who made the following observation.

> That first winter [early 1928] was an exceptionally bitter one, even by Moscow weather standards. Waiting on queues for bread and other necessities was that much more agonizing. Everywhere these ragged lines, chiefly of women, stretched from shop doors, under clouds of visible breath; patient, bovine, scarcely grumbling. Private trade channels were being rapidly shut off, before the government was able to replace them with official channels.[85]

As pressure mounted on the Nepmen from 1926/27 through the rest of the decade, private trade not only declined but changed in character as well. Virtually all operations able to survive the onslaught of the state were very small scale. The larger enterprises in permanent facilities were most visible, most obviously "capitalist," and thus the first to be eliminated. In 1925/26, for example, 17 percent of all private sales reported to the state were wholesale, whereas four years later virtually all licensed private wholesalers had been driven out of business. This is hardly surprising, for it was next to impossible for large private retail and wholesale operations to escape the attention of state officials, especially wholesale enterprises dependent on the state for much of their merchandise. Taxes and fees levied on large firms were higher than those imposed on petty traders, and Nepmen in the upper ranks could not pick up their businesses and elude a policeman or tax inspector the way rank I and some rank II traders could.[86] An American living in Moscow at the end of the decade wrote that "there are almost no privately owned stores in the city; any who wish to continue the unpopular profession of merchant for their own profit must trade from these rickety stands in the market places or at street corners."[87] The state Central Statistical Bureau reported that by January 1, 1930, nearly two thirds (64 per-

cent) of the 123,000 registered private traders were peddlers and street
hawkers (*raznoschiki*) and that 19 percent operated from tents, booths,
or stalls. Only 17 percent still conducted their business from even the
most modest shops (*lavki*) or stores (*magaziny*).[88]

A demand that far exceeded the supply of most consumer products,
combined with the declining number of private traders, spawned a revival of bagging. The shortages of both food and manufactured items,
labeled the "goods famine" (*tovarnyi golod*) by the press, produced
streams of people traveling in opposite directions—some trekking to the
countryside in search of food and others coming to the towns to trade
for manufactured goods.[89] This type of "amateur" trade continued after
NEP. As famine began to stalk the Ukraine in 1932, for example, a Russian who had emigrated in 1914 and then returned to the Soviet Union
found on a trip to Odessa "that the train guards, conductors, and atten-
dants were all speculators. They were buying food in Moscow, always
better provided for than other cities, and selling it at fantastic prices
down in the stricken southern land."[90] Although bagging seems not to
have been as widespread at the end of NEP as it had been during War
Communism and 1921/22, its resurgence in 1928/29 indicated the in-
adequacy of the "socialist" consumer goods production and distribution system when the Nepmen were driven out of business.

Another consequence of the state crackdown on the Nepmen was
that a greater percentage of private trade was conducted illegally, without licenses. As taxes and harassment from local officials became more
onerous, an important survival skill for many private traders was the
ability to avoid detection. This generally meant operating underground
in the black market or selling goods without a license in the streets and
running whenever the police approached. As one woman was buying
peaches from a private trader in the summer of 1928, "the pedlar and
his enormous tray suddenly disappeared as completely as the vanishing
gentleman of a conjuror's trick. A warning of the approach of a policeman had passed down the line [of hawkers] and the line dissolved. The
vendors are required to have licenses; this one was among the hundreds
who had none." Another foreign resident reported that "the government attempted to restrict this peddling by means of taxation, but the
pedlars always tried to evade these taxes. A frequent sight in Moscow in
1929 was to see a whole mob of petty dealers running before a policeman or two, carrying baskets on their heads or arms, pushing wheelbar-
rows, as they attempted to save themselves from the wrath of the law."[91]
The wife of an American mining consultant in the Soviet Union, noting
that most markets were closed by the state in 1929/30 with the onset of

mass collectivization, indicated that it was still possible to purchase food surreptitiously from resourceful peasants.[92]

Thus private trade came full circle by the end of NEP. As the state stoked up its campaign to "liquidate the Nepmen," adopting "administrative measures" of the sort that had distinguished War Communism, private trade returned increasingly to the forms it had assumed in the years immediately following the Revolution. During War Communism this meant almost exclusively small-scale, unsophisticated, illegal (or barely tolerated) sales and barter, sometimes conducted by bagmen. Little changed immediately after the introduction of NEP except that this activity became less risky and attracted more people. But before long, as we have seen, the number of larger, permanent private shops began to increase (at the expense of many of the marginal petty vendors) and peaked in 1925/26 after suffering a brief downturn in 1924. In 1926, then, the Nepmen were as far from the atmosphere of War Communism as they would get, and thereafter their path turned, slowly at first, back in the direction of an environment bracing for Bolsheviks but bleak for private merchants. The state policies at the end of the decade eliminated virtually all private traders except the very small scale and the surreptitious—the same sort characteristic of the era of War Communism.

Although it is beyond the scope of this work to cover private entrepreneurs in the 1930s, a few words should be added as an epilogue concerning legal private trade immediately after NEP. The state grain-collection and collectivization drives at the end of the 1920s were accompanied by an intense campaign against the Nepmen. But just as the collectivization offensive was halted (temporarily) in the spring of 1930, so too was the effort to eliminate private trade. Though the permanent stores of private traders remained closed, small-scale trade was again permitted in markets and bazaars, primarily because the state was unable to supply adequate amounts of food to the urban population. The bulk of this trade, which continued throughout the decade, was conducted by collective farmers, artisans, and people selling odds and ends, as described by Julian Huxley in the summer of 1931:

> Dingy rows of stalls, with narrow passages between; beyond, men and women squatting in front of the produce they had brought—here eggs, there vegetables, here again potatoes; a few carts belonging to kulaks, laden with vegetables; a row of cobblers; a few sellers of mushrooms and flowers. . . .
> A big-built factory worker was holding out about a pound of raw meat,

half unwrapped from its covering of old newspaper; a neatly-dressed woman, probably a typist in some office, had three eggs, which she proffered in her open hand-bag; an old man was trying to sell two small dried fish; another woman had half a pound of butter. There were city workers who, having bought their supplies at the Cooperatives on their ration cards, were now trying to get money for some luxury by selling them in the open market, where they could get four or five times as much as what they paid for them.[93]

An American engineer, who worked in the city of Groznyi in 1931–32, wrote:

There is still some private trade in Russia, and lately the Government has allowed it to increase. It includes the outdoor markets and some small handicraft shops for shoe repairing, tailoring, blacksmithing, barbering, dressmaking, and the like. . . .

In addition to the small and insignificant booths on the main street belonging to private traders there also existed a huge outdoor market to which the peasants brought their goods for private sale. These markets or bazaars, as the Russians call them, are found in every center and are a necessary source of food supply for the people because the cooperatives cannot yet supply the needs.[94]

Other forms of legal private enterprise led a precarious existence in the cracks of the new planned economy. Private horse-drawn cabs, for example, were tolerated for a time, because not enough cars were produced to fill the need for taxis. At the end of 1935, a new line of trade was approved. In December the party unexpectedly removed the taboo on Christmas trees that had been in force since the end of NEP, announcing that one might celebrate the New Year with a New Year's tree. "The very next morning the markets were full of trees. All night long, axes had been busy in the suburban forests of Moscow and at dawn the roads leading to Moscow saw a procession of peasant carts laden with trees." But ornaments were difficult to find on such short notice after several years without Christmas trees. As a result, old women appeared on street corners selling "old-fashioned Christmas toys, hidden for years, mostly little angels. They did good business."[95]

CHAPTER 5

# Supplying the Nepmen

It is the NEP-man who hurries here and there, and by devices which
are always suspect, obtains exceptionally interesting goods, which
somehow the Cooperatives do not always manage to offer. But why
that is I could not find out.

—Theodore Dreiser

It is difficult to find a more convenient field of operations for all
sorts of pretenders than our expansive country, filled either with
exceedingly suspicious or exceedingly gullible administrators,
managers, and social workers.

—Ilya Ilf and Evgeny Petrov

Throughout NEP the main obstacle facing traders (state, cooperative,
and private) was obtaining goods, not selling them, since demand for
many products far outstripped supply. Soon after launching his first
business ventures in Russia, Armand Hammer discovered that the shortage of most commodities was so great "that any article of general use or
consumption produced inside the country at anything like a reasonable
price is generally sold beforehand." [1] One advantage held by the Nepmen
over the state and cooperative retail network was their ability to acquire
merchandise more efficiently and resourcefully (and sometimes more
deviously). Goods flowed into private traders' hands from a number of
suppliers, whose relative significance varied with the nature of a Nepman's business and with changes in the economic and political climate.

One of the most important sources was the "socialist" sector itself.
During the course of 1921 and 1922 most state factories were ordered
to operate on a cost-accounting (*khozraschet*) basis, meaning that they
could no longer rely on the state to provide them with raw materials,
pay their workers, and absorb their finished products regardless of how
inefficiently they operated. Instead, with the umbilical cord cut, state enterprises found themselves on their own in the marketplace, frequently
in desperate need of funds for raw materials, wages, equipment, and so
on. Many state operations in such straits sold off nonessential goods and
equipment at low prices in order to obtain working capital. This phe-

nomenon was known as *razbazarivanie* (literally, "scattering through the bazaars"), which is usually rendered as "squandering." Very often, the only customers with ready cash were Nepmen. As a Soviet writer remarked in 1924, state firms that "plunged into the anarchy of the market became the source of extremely intensive primary accumulation for the new trading bourgeoisie." [2]

It is, of course, impossible to ascertain the total value of goods involved, but many observers were convinced that a large amount of state property fell into private hands through this process. The state publishing house Krasnaia Zvezda, founded in 1923 to publish military literature, sold cartloads of its paper and expensive stationery to Nepmen at low prices. Somehow, the publishing house also had musical instruments, first-aid kits, and bicycles, which, not surprisingly, it was anxious to sell to anyone available. During the famine in the Volga region at the beginning of NEP, a state livestock breeding agency sold to Nepmen a large portion of its resources (scythes, sugar, salt, oats, and hay). Even some of the agency's purebred stock was sold or rented to private persons for use in horse races. Up to 1927 state enterprises and agencies had sold 1,661 cars and trucks (and 4,000 motorcycles) worth several thousand rubles apiece to private buyers for only 400 to 500 rubles each. [3] As in the case of Krasnaia Zvezda, it was not unusual for a state operation to sell commodities that had nothing to do with its official activity. Agencies as unlikely as Glavchai and Khleboprodukt (which handled tea and grain, respectively) raised cash by unloading large quantities of textiles on the free market in 1921/22. Even Gosbank acquired a variety of goods at the beginning of NEP, some of which it sold to private entrepreneurs. [4]

Not all state sales to Nepmen were haphazard or unsound. Private traders as a rule were more efficient than the state and cooperative retail system, and they could also charge higher prices than their "socialist" competitors (since the latter were supposed to observe price ceilings). Consequently the Nepmen were often able to absorb higher prices and harsher credit terms from state suppliers than could "socialist" enterprises in need of the same goods. As a result, many officials in state factories and trusts, forced to fend for themselves on *khozraschet*, found it possible to overcome any ideological scruples they may have had concerning sales to the "new bourgeoisie." Though this provoked a complaint from Tsentrosoiuz (the central agency of the cooperative system) that "large amounts of goods proceeded from trusts, not to cooperatives, but to the private market [in 1921/22]," such protests were to no

"Nepmen," a watercolor painted in the 1920s by Dmitrii Kardovskii.
(*Serdtsem slushaia revoliutsiiu* . . . [Leningrad, 1980], picture no. 118)

The Sukharevka, Moscow's largest outdoor market. The name of the market was sometimes used as shorthand for private trading in general. (*Illiustrirovannaia Rossiia*, no. 50, 1926, p. 1)

Young street traders in Moscow in 1921. Primitive trade of this sort was most widespread at the beginning and end of NEP. (F. A. Mackenzie, *Russia Before Dawn* [London, 1923], page facing p. 82)

Furniture and other personal possessions for sale in one of Moscow's outdoor markets at the end of NEP. (*Illiustrirovannaia Rossiia*, no. 23, 1930, p. 6)

A group of street traders outside a state shoe store. (*Illiustrirovannaia Rossiia*, no. 10, 1927, p. 1)

A row of clay-pot vendors in a rural market. The dominance of private traders was generally most pronounced in rural localities. (*Illiustrirovannaia Rossiia*, no. 27, 1929, p. 5)

A *baranka* (ring-shaped roll) vendor plying his trade during a village market day. (*Illiustrirovannaia Rossiia*, no. 30, 1926, p. 1)

A state tax inspector and policeman sealing a shop whose proprietor had fallen behind in his tax payments. This scene became a common sight during the last years of the 1920s. (*Illiustrirovannaia Rossiia*, no. 13, 1925, p. 5)

A Soviet poster depicting a Nepman uttering a prayer: "O Lord, help me, a sinner! Help me to cheat and circumvent this [Soviet] power that I hate." (Negley Farson, *Black Bread and Red Coffins* [New York, 1930], page facing p. 208)

A portion of a May Day parade in Leningrad. The sign below the grimacing mask reads: "I buy from a private trader." Below the smiling mask are the words: "I shop in a cooperative." (*Sovetskoe dekorativnoe iskusstvo. Materialy i dokumenty 1917–1932. Agitatsionno-massovoe iskusstvo. Oformlenie prazdnestv. Tablitsy* [Moscow, 1984], picture no. 225)

A clerk in a cooperative store (first frame) admonishes a woman: "Wait a minute, Citizen. Notice that there are many of you, and I am alone. Can't you see that I am busy?" This rudeness sends the woman hurrying (second frame) to a private trader, who greets her much more solicitously. It is interesting to compare the point of this cartoon (published in *Pravda,* January 4, 1928) with the point of the masks in the Leningrad May Day parade (photo on preceding page).

— Подождите, гражданка, будьте сознательной, вас много—я один. Не видите, что я делом занят.

avail. Indeed, a decree of April 10, 1923, permitted state trusts to give their business to Nepmen even when state and cooperative customers were available, as long as the Nepmen offered more favorable terms. Transactions of this sort were particularly common in the first years of NEP, when the state and cooperative retail network was extremely inefficient. But even in 1926, the state salt syndicate announced that it would be desirable to sell to Nepmen 30 percent of the syndicate's output, precisely because private traders could accept less credit and higher prices from the syndicate than could the cooperatives.[5]

That there were comparatively few state and cooperative stores, particularly in the first half of NEP, was another compelling reason for state firms to sell to Nepmen. Otherwise, goods simply would not reach a large portion of the market. For every 10,000 inhabitants of the countryside in 1924/25 there were 6 cooperative shops, 1 state store, and 31 licensed private trading operations. The actual number of private traders was certainly much higher, for it was quite easy to trade on a small scale without a license, particularly in the countryside. As we have seen, private entrepreneurs also dominated trade in the cities during the first years of NEP, handling over 80 percent of urban retail trade in the estimate of the state Central Statistical Bureau. The effectiveness of the private retail network was clear to state officials in the trusts, syndicates, and factories. In the middle of NEP, for example, the state sugar trust maintained that it was essential to market 26 to 28 percent of its products through Nepmen because of the weakness of state and cooperative trade in the countryside. According to the division of the All-Russian Textile Syndicate (VTS) headquartered in Rostov-on-the-Don, private traders were practically the only people available early in NEP through whom textiles could reach consumers. On a related point, an article in one of the Council of Labor and Defense publications noted that during the "scissors crisis" in the fall of 1923, many cooperatives, "artificially supported" by the state, collapsed. Had there been no private traders to market textiles produced by state industry, factories would have been glutted with finished wares, and "it is difficult to imagine the sort of catastrophe for VTS that would have accompanied the autumn crisis."[6] Viewed in this light, sales to Nepmen were in line with Lenin's dictum of "building communism with bourgeois hands."

In 1922 the state system of industrial trusts and syndicates sold roughly 50 percent of its goods directly to private traders. The figure proceeded to fall to 35 percent by 1922/23; 15 percent in 1923/24; 10 percent in 1924/25; and about 8 percent in 1925/26.[7] The declining per-

TABLE 6    DIRECT SALES TO NEPMEN BY STATE TRUSTS
AND SYNDICATES

|          | Millions of Rubles | Millions of 1913 Rubles [a] |
|----------|--------------------|------------------------------|
| 1923/24  | 310                | 157                          |
| 1924/25  | 334                | 160                          |
| 1925/26  | 418                | 189                          |

SOURCE: A. Zalkind, ed., *Chastnaia torgovlia Soiuza SSR* (Moscow, 1927), p. 38; A. M. Ginzburg, ed., *Chastnyi kapital v narodnom khoziaistve SSSR. Materialy kommissii VSNKh SSSR* (Moscow-Leningrad, 1927), p. 130.

[a] The figures in 1913 rubles were calculated according to I. A. Gladkov, ed., *Sovetskoe narodnoe khoziaistvo v 1921–1925 gg.* (Moscow, 1960), p. 456.

centages should not be taken as an indication that the state continually reduced sales to Nepmen during this period. Since the total output of state industry increased markedly in these years, sales to private traders, though falling in percentage terms, did not decline in absolute value after 1923/24 (see table 6). It seems likely that the volume of such sales to Nepmen was off somewhat in 1923/24 compared to 1922/23, as a result of the crackdown on private trade in 1924. But the paucity of comparable data for 1922/23 hinders quantitative comparisons. In any case, volume rebounded in the following years despite the shrinking percentages for those years.

Private merchants were primarily interested in the output of consumer goods branches of state industry, commodities such as food products (tea, coffee, sugar, and salt), textiles, kerosene, tobacco, matches, and leather and rubber items such as footwear. Information is fragmentary for the beginning of NEP, but it is safe to assume that trusts and syndicates in these branches of production generally made between one quarter and one half of their sales to Nepmen.[8] By the middle of the decade, record keeping had improved sufficiently to permit more detailed estimates (see table 7). Approximately 80 percent of direct private purchases from trusts and syndicates were concentrated in just a half dozen or so branches of production. In 1924, textiles alone (primarily cotton cloth) accounted for over half such sales to private entrepreneurs. But the demand for textiles far exceeded the state supply, and as the number of state and cooperative stores increased, textile trusts and syndicates were instructed to sell more of their goods to "socialist" enterprises.[9] The results were apparent as early as 1925 and were striking by 1926 (see table 8).

TABLE 7    PERCENTAGE OF TRUSTS' AND
SYNDICATES' SALES MADE TO NEPMEN

|  | 1923/24 | 1924/25 | 1925/26 |
|---|---|---|---|
| Tea and coffee | no data | 37% | 36% |
| Kerosene | no data | 27 | 33 |
| Alcoholic beverages | no data | 11 | 16 |
| Rubber goods | 33% | 14 | 9 |
| Glass and porcelain | 19 | 12 | 11 |
| Tobacco | 34 | 18 | 21 |
| Salt | 23 | 12 | 16 |
| Sugar | 12 | 8 | 14 |
| Leather goods | 26 | 20 | 10 |
| Textiles | 22 | 12 | 6 |
| Wood products | 6 | 9 | 7 |
| Metal products | 4 | 3 | 2 |
| Makhorka (coarse tobacco) | 18 | 4 | 5 |

SOURCES: A. Zalkind, ed., *Chastnaia torgovlia Soiuza SSR* (Moscow, 1927), p. 39; A. M. Ginzburg, ed., *Chastnyi kapital v narodnom khoziaistve SSSR. Materialy kommissii VSNKh SSSR* (Moscow-Leningrad, 1927), p. 130; and Ts. M. Kron, *Chastnaia torgovlia v SSSR* (Moscow, 1926), p. 31.

NOTE: In some cases the figures are estimates made by averaging the percentages available for the first and second halves of the year.

TABLE 8    DISTRIBUTION OF PRIVATE PURCHASES
FROM TRUSTS AND SYNDICATES

|  | 1923/24 | Second Half of 1924/25 | Second Half of 1925/26 |
|---|---|---|---|
| Textiles | 52% | 42% | 23% |
| Leather goods | 7 | 11 | 7 |
| Sugar | 6 | 9 | 22 |
| Tobacco | 6 | 7 | 9 |
| Tea and coffee | no data | 5 | 7 |
| Alcoholic beverages | no data | 5 | 11 |
| Other products | 29 | 21 | 21 |
| Total | 100% | 100% | 100% |

SOURCES: A. Zalkind, ed., *Chastnaia torgovlia Soiuza SSR* (Moscow, 1927), p. 41; A. M. Ginzburg, ed., *Chastnyi kapital v narodnom khoziaistve SSSR. Materialy kommissii VSNKh SSSR* (Moscow-Leningrad, 1927), p. 130.

In addition to legal, direct purchases from state agencies, private traders could obtain goods from the "socialist" sector by various illegal, semilegal, and indirect means, much the same way large quantities of state property reach private hands today in the Soviet Union. Although little quantitative information on this activity is available, it is clear that a considerable volume of commodities reached private traders through "informal" channels. Few Bolsheviks knew how to trade during the early years of NEP, as Lenin lamented repeatedly, and state enterprises often had to hire people with experience in private trade to help market goods or obtain raw materials. These people were then in a position to divert state supplies into the private sector, because they were often more aware of what materials were on hand than were the nominal managers.[10] It was not unheard of at the beginning of NEP for a private trader to have a second "full-time" job in a state enterprise. In 1922, for instance, the state trading agency Gostorg had a number of employees who simultaneously operated private businesses that were well stocked with Gostorg's wares. Occasionally a private contractor or supplier for a state agency who was also an official in that agency could buy and sell goods to and from himself—on rather unattractive terms for the state, one might suspect. One Nepman even wrote letters proposing transactions to himself in his other capacity as an official in a state firm.[11]

Some of the first private stores opened in 1921 were owned by former state employees who had used their official positions to acquire the goods they then sold on their own. Other people remained in state service, registering their shops under someone else's name (often a close relative), and then supplied the stores with products they controlled as state officials. The search for goods was also joined by relatives scattered about in the "socialist" sector (*nevesta v treste, kum v GUM, brat v narkomat;* "a fiancée in a trust, a godparent in GUM [Moscow's leading department store], and a brother in a People's Commissariat," as Mayakovskii once quipped). In 1922, for example, an agent of Gostorg at the Nizhnii Novgorod fair delivered supplies at low prices to the private firm Transtorg, whose director happened to be his brother. Nor did the ties between the two enterprises end here. A member of the board of directors of Transtorg was also head of a division of Gostorg, and the founder of Transtorg was at the same time an agent for Gostorg—all quite legally.[12]

In December 1922, on the heels of similar directives and draft decrees prepared by several state agencies, the Council of People's Commissars (Sovnarkom) adopted a law making it illegal to engage in private business activity while employed by the state.[13] If Sovnarkom's intent was to dam the "unofficial" flow of state resources into the private sector, the decree was futile for a number of reasons. First of all, the accounting practices in many state enterprises, especially at the beginning of NEP, were sloppy or nonexistent, and it was relatively easy to steal goods from an agency that did not even realize it possessed them. The disappearance of supplies from state and cooperative operations as a result of poor record keeping and other sloppy practices was dubbed the "four u's"—*utruska, usushka, utechka,* and *ugar* (roughly, "spillage," "shrinkage," "leakage," and "waste"). Eight years after the Revolution, for example, officials at the Leningrad naval yard had still not made an inventory of the vast amount of goods lying around the facility. Entire warehouses, listed as empty in the naval yard's books, were actually full of valuable commodities at the mercy of thieves and the elements. Millions of rubles' worth of state goods were stolen across the land, and much of this loot found its way into the hands of private traders. To illustrate, a Nepman named Brounshtein, representing a private firm with virtually no capital, contracted to supply a state factory with nine hundred tons of oil in return for some steel pipe. After promising the steel pipe to another enterprise in exchange for some roofing iron, Brounshtein stole the oil he needed from the Leningrad naval yard. He then carried out all of the transactions described above, leaving himself with a supply of roofing iron, which he sold. Part of the proceeds went to certain naval yard employees who had helped him steal the oil. In 1922, American Relief Administration officials in Rostov-on-the-Don learned that bands of thieves were stealing state supplies from railroad freight yards and selling them to private wholesalers. These Nepmen sometimes bribed the station agents to ship their newly acquired goods to various markets by rail. At times the thieves could be brazen. Employees in the state factory Treugol'nik stole cable from the factory and then sold it back to the factory through a private firm, Kontora Martinova, they had set up.[14]

Even Walter Duranty, Moscow correspondent of the *New York Times,* and Herbert Pulitzer, son of Joseph Pulitzer, were peripherally involved in the theft and resale of state property at the beginning of NEP. As Duranty tells it:

> Among our flock of American wage-slaves there was one white crow in the person of Herbert Pulitzer, the principal owner of *The New York World,* in whose vineyard he then chose to labor as a mere reporter. The knowledge of his wealth must have reached Moscow, for one day a Russian came to his

room at the Savoy, where I was sitting, and circumlocutively invited him to
buy a carload of sugar. I think the price was $1,200, and the Russian, who
had a note of recommendation from the restaurant in the Arbat where we
always took our meals, declared that it could be sold immediately for $5,000.
There would be some small commissions, he smiled knowingly, but we could
count on a clear profit of at least 200 per cent. I was interested, but the rich
Pulitzer asked crudely, "Who owns the sugar now, and where is it?" "Oh,"
said the Russian airily, "it is Government property stored in freight cars at
one of the Moscow depots. But they've forgotten all about it, and of course
some of it would go to sweeten the only official who knows anything. I assure
you there is not the slightest risk."

During another meeting over a good deal of French champagne, the
Nepman coaxed $500 from Pulitzer and $100 from Duranty and raised
the rest elsewhere. After completing the transaction, he spent half of his
thousand-dollar profit on a lavish banquet (to which Pulitzer and Duranty were invited) and gambled the rest away the same evening. Duranty learned later that in the following months he had made approximately $50,000 in similar business operations and then slipped out of
the country to Paris.[15]

Despite warnings and decrees from the state, some Nepmen maintained cozy relationships with state officials (frequently with bribes) in
order to obtain merchandise or special services. This system, called by
some wags *krugovaia poruka* (an old Russian term meaning mutual responsibility), was the next best arrangement to being both a Nepman
and a state employee oneself.[16] The businessman I. D. Morozov, for instance, had had many connections in the West before the Revolution,
and after opening a store in Moscow during NEP, he decided to try to
renew some of these old ties in order to obtain Western goods. To this
end he enlisted the aid of the chairman of a Soviet trust who was about
to go abroad on a business trip—and who had been the director of one
of Morozov's factories before the Revolution. The director of the Northern Section of the Association of State Workers Artels (ORA) illegally
rented the services of one workers' *artel'* of five hundred men to a private contractor of ORA, named Kornilov, for four months at the rate of
one ruble per head. Kornilov employed these workers in his own business ventures, which had nothing to do with ORA (such as cutting,
loading, and unloading firewood).[17]

To be sure, few Nepmen contemplated international maneuvers or
rented brigades of state workers. Most of the collusion between state
officials and private entrepreneurs bore a greater resemblance to the fol-

lowing cases. In 1921 a man named Alkhazov was arrested for cocaine trafficking and sentenced to a year in prison. Following this setback he managed to install himself as an official in a state trading agency (Dagtorg) and soon began to conduct shady transactions. In Moscow he met an old acquaintance, now a director of a private firm, and they contrived to be of use to each other. On one occasion Alkhazov went to the Nizhnii Novgorod fair and purchased (from another state agency) a large quantity of textiles in Dagtorg's name, even though Dagtorg had instructed its representatives not to buy textiles. According to the sales agreement, the goods were to be sold to the people of Dagestan (in the eastern portion of the Caucasus), but Alkhazov hurried back to Moscow and sold half the textiles to his friend. The rest reached private traders through other channels. To cite another example, in 1922 the OGPU charged the director of a state tobacco-processing factory and two former private wholesalers with creating a "black trust" that sold 90 percent of the factory's output to Nepmen.[18] In some instances, state agencies that officially had nothing to do with the trade of various products obtained them anyway from trusts and syndicates for resale to private wholesalers.[19]

Nevertheless, most private traders were small-scale vendors in markets and bazaars and thus in no position to strike special deals with influential state officials. If such junior Nepmen (and many larger-scale merchants as well) wished to obtain goods directly from the "socialist" sector, they had to tap the state distribution system farther down the line. This would often entail bribing a clerk in a state or cooperative store to withhold goods and sell them to the private trader. On other occasions "socialist" clerks, store managers, and others took the lead in these transactions, knowing that they could sell merchandise to private traders at prices well above the official ceilings. This activity was widespread, prompting the Supreme Council of the National Economy (VSNKh) in July 1924 to send out a directive to the enterprises under it forbidding the practice. But this and numerous other official complaints proved futile, and the sale of goods to Nepmen from state and cooperative wholesale distribution agencies and retail stores continued to flourish.[20]

If bribes seemed too risky, a private trader could simply purchase merchandise from state or cooperative stores as a normal customer and then resell the items. It was not difficult to find people willing to pay more for the products than the prices charged by the state, particularly in the provinces, where shortages were acute.[21] A report of the All-Russian Textile Syndicate issued in the fall of 1925 describes this phenomenon.

> Squeezed in the grip of a goods shortage in the provincial market, private trading capital has moved to Moscow, and here, in the streets of Moscow, conducts the sort of transactions for cotton cloth that Moscow has not seen before. Crowds of unemployed people and invalids stand in lines for textiles outside retail stores of trusts and syndicates. Those who obtain goods sell them to bagmen who pay twenty to thirty kopecks per meter. The bagman brings the goods to the market where they are bought by a provincial retailer, who in turn sells them in the countryside, marked up 100 to 150 percent.[22]

It was not uncommon for a larger-scale private trader to mobilize relatives and friends or hire people (often invalids and the unemployed, as stated above) to stand in lines at state and cooperative stores to buy goods for resale elsewhere. Nepmen used these hired buyers throughout the decade, though the latter became particularly numerous in the final years of NEP as the state began shutting off the direct flow of its goods to private traders.[23]

Soviet correspondents and store employees estimated that as many as three fourths of the people standing in lines outside state and cooperative shops intended to resell the merchandise they purchased. Whatever the actual figure, there was no doubt that small armies of hired buyers were involved. More than a few Nepmen had good contacts in the "socialist" distribution system and seemed to be more aware, one correspondent observed, of which scarce commodities were in various state and cooperative stores than were some of the state's own marketing officials. When word leaked out that a desirable product was about to go on sale in a particular store, a line of surrogate buyers generally formed well before the doors opened.[24] Toward the end of the decade, as rationing was introduced, surviving Nepmen turned more frequently to trade unionists, people in members-only cooperatives, and others with access to newly restricted merchandise. Some of these people were induced either to buy goods for the private traders or to "rent" their documents to the latter, who then made the purchases themselves. Other Nepmen eliminated the "middleman" by obtaining multiple copies of cooperative membership books and ration cards.[25]

As we have seen, both Lenin and Bukharin believed that the cooperatives had to win the economic struggle with the Nepmen if socialism were to triumph in the Soviet Union. In order to tip the scales in favor of the cooperatives, the state granted various supply, credit, and tax privi-

leges to them. These measures, while improving the cooperatives' position, also encouraged some private businessmen to disguise their operations as cooperatives (or other favored organizations) in order to share
the benefits of cooperatives and escape their own heavier obligations.
More specifically, one advantage of the ruse was easier access to state
goods (as depicted by Ilf and Petrov in *The Little Golden Calf*), since
supply agencies were often instructed to show special favor to the cooperatives.[26] Toward the beginning of NEP, for example, a man named
Vitkun arrived in Moscow from Siberia with only a hundred rubles in
his pocket. Along with his wife and some friends, he announced the formation of a joint-stock gold mining company. Shortly thereafter, one of
the "partners" was dispatched to the Urals, whence he sent back telegrams describing the work in the fictitious gold fields in glowing terms.
Armed with these cables and exploiting the desire of the state to increase the output of gold, Vitkun obtained provisions on credit from
various state agencies, allegedly to supply workers in the gold fields.
In reality, the goods were resold. The ploy even worked for a fourteen-
year-old boy in Leningrad, who proclaimed the organization of a producers' cooperative, the Detskaia artel' imeni t. Lenina. The Commissariat of Finance gave him eight thousand rubles to get started; the
Commissariat of Communications provided free travel tickets for the
use of the cooperative; and the Leningrad Soviet donated seventy-two
hundred pounds of clothing. Actually, the cooperative was just a front,
and the youth (who may have been a front himself) used the money and
various resources he had been given to open a movie theater.[27]

It is impossible to determine precisely the amount of goods that belonged at one time to the "socialist" sector but were marketed ultimately by private traders. The shadier the transaction between a state
enterprise and a Nepman, the less likely it was recorded accurately or at
all. This, along with the chaotic or nonexistent bookkeeping of many
state operations, particularly in the early years of NEP, renders statistics
on this score rough estimates at best. An extensive study of private capital in the USSR, prepared for VSNKh in 1927, estimated that close to
half the output of state industry in the middle of NEP reached consumers through private traders.[28] Whatever the actual percentage, there is
no doubt that the "socialist" sector represented an important source of
goods for Nepmen until the closing years of the decade, when the state
tried to turn off the flow. In 1925/26, urban private traders received approximately 40 percent of their merchandise from state and cooperative
enterprises, agencies, and stores—an estimate that fell to 33 percent in

1926/27, 25 percent in 1927/28, and 17 percent in 1928/29.[29] As it became more difficult to pry manufactured products from the state, some Nepmen were forced out of business. But the more nimble and resourceful among them turned to other sources of supply.

Over half the Nepmen's wares originated in the private sector. A significant portion was produced by the peasantry, since food products were the items most frequently sold by private entrepreneurs. The number of peasants in collective farms and producers' cooperatives was negligible during NEP, which meant that virtually all the fresh, unprocessed food (vegetables, meat, eggs, dairy products) in private shops and markets was produced on individual peasant farms. Lenin had hoped that the peasants would shun the Nepmen and sell their goods to the state via cooperatives. In return the peasants were supposed to be supplied with manufactured goods at reasonable prices in the cooperative stores. This arrangement was intended to strengthen the *smychka* between the workers and peasants and draw the latter voluntarily into the cooperatives, thus preparing the foundation for socialism in the countryside. Throughout NEP, however, private middlemen competed successfully with state agencies for that portion of the peasantry's products which the peasants did not consume, save, or market themselves.

One reason for the Nepmen's success was that the state and cooperative *zagotovka* agencies (whose task was to buy grain and other products from the peasantry) had relatively few officials out in the countryside and inadequate supplies of cash and commodities to offer the peasants. In fact, the official *zagotovka* network was so underdeveloped that many state agencies were forced to buy from private *zagotovka* enterprises.[30] Probably the Nepmen's main advantage was their freedom to offer the peasants higher prices than could state *zagotovka* agents (who were supposed to operate under price ceilings). In the cities and towns the demand for farm products generally exceeded the supply, enabling private middlemen to outbid the state buyers and still resell the products for a profit.[31] Private buyers also profited frequently from closer relations with the peasantry than those maintained by state *zagotovka* personnel. The success of a private mill operator named Klassen was based on such factors: (1) Klassen accepted all the crops that the peasants brought him rather than just some, which was the practice at state and cooperative agencies; (2) he did not pass on local fees to the peasants, which state and cooperative agencies did; (3) he knew the peasants personally and paid the transportation costs of those who, he knew, had to have their grain brought across the river (unlike the state and cooperative mills); and (4) he provided free sacks. As a result of these measures, in 1924 he collected 2,160 tons of grain, which he shipped all over the country.[32] Undoubtedly, Klassen was able to provide all these services for the peasants because he knew he could command a high price for his flour.

The peasantry was an important source of goods for private traders throughout NEP, but particularly at the beginning of the period (before consumer goods industries had recovered from War Communism) and at the end (when the state tried to cut off the flow of manufactured goods from the "socialist" sector to the Nepmen). The *smychka*, which seemed so crucial to Lenin and Bukharin, had little chance of becoming a reality during NEP, because the state refused to offer the peasants free-market prices for their crops and a significantly larger supply of manufactured consumer goods. These and similar policies were not forthcoming from a government committed to channeling its modest resources into industrialization. Consequently, the peasantry seemed as inclined to form a bond with private traders as with the state, a development that caused considerable concern in the party. One wonders how or whether Lenin, who in his last years repeatedly warned against alienating the peasants and driving them into the arms of the Nepmen, would have tried to preserve and strengthen the *smychka* in the second half of the decade while pursuing at the same time a policy of industrial growth.

Most of the private traders' merchandise not produced by the "socialist" sector or the peasantry came from private manufacturing enterprises inside the Soviet Union, that is, from other Nepmen. We will consider these undertakings in the following chapter, and for the present need only note that nearly all the private "industrial" output came from small artisan shops. The craftsmen in these facilities generally produced clothing, footwear, food products (mainly bread), or various common household utensils, that is, items in demand by consumers and hence by private traders. Not surprisingly, most (approximately 80 to 90 percent) of the output from private manufacturers found its way to consumers through Nepmen.[33]

By the second half of the decade, private traders began to obtain increasing percentages of their wares from artisans (see table 9), largely as a response to the growing difficulty of tapping state industry.[34] A study

TABLE 9    PERCENTAGE OF URBAN PRIVATE RETAILERS'
GOODS PURCHASED FROM ARTISANS

|                                       | 1926/27 | 1927/28 | 1928/29 |
|---------------------------------------|---------|---------|---------|
| Footwear and other leather goods      | 54%     | 65%     | 73%     |
| Dishes, pots, pans, etc.              | 31      | 33      | 34      |
| Clothing, textiles, haberdashery      | 18      | 28      | 45      |
| Metal products                        | 11      | 26      | 34      |
| Bread and confectionery               | no data | 46      | 71      |

SOURCE: N. Riauzov, *Vytesnenie chastnogo posrednika iz tovarooborota* (Moscow, 1930), p. 37.

in Irkutsk revealed that although the total volume of private trade there declined in 1926/27, sales in some branches of trade were up. Nearly all of the increased business involved merchandise (leather goods, dresses, hats, pottery) produced by artisans. The authors concluded that as a general rule, most of the private traders still active in Irkutsk obtained their wares from small-scale producers. Some Nepmen went as far as to close their shops, purchase goods from artisans, and resell these items as if they themselves were the producers. In this way they disguised their position as middlemen or "nonlabor elements" and so avoided the license fee and heavy taxes levied on private traders.[35]

Thus the peasantry and small-scale manufacturers, always important suppliers to the Nepmen, emerged as their most dependable sources of merchandise at the end of the 1920s. Of course the "socialist" sector continued to provide goods to private traders, both knowingly and otherwise. But the increasing unreliability of this connection forced most surviving Nepmen to search for merchandise among rural private producers—peasant farmers and artisans—in the waning years of NEP. This trend was reported from many regions, including Kiev, where a Soviet journalist wrote at the end of 1928 that those private traders still in business were supplied almost entirely by peasants and handicraftsmen.[36] The other side of the coin was the shrinking portion of goods received by Nepmen from the state (see table 10).

Smugglers provided a smaller but by no means negligible quantity of goods to private traders, particularly in the early years of NEP when

TABLE IO    PERCENTAGE OF URBAN NEPMEN'S
MERCHANDISE OBTAINED FROM SOCIALIST SECTOR

|  | 1926/27 | 1927/28 | 1928/29 |
|---|---|---|---|
| Metal products | 51% | 41% | 27% |
| Candles, soap, and other household chemicals | 51 | 50 | 40 |
| Paper products and toys | 46 | 48 | 40 |
| Processed food products | 41 | 36 | 24 |
| Wood products | 40 | 28 | 28 |
| Textiles, clothing, and haberdashery | 36 | 29 | 19 |
| Dishes and other household utensils | 35 | 35 | 31 |

SOURCE: N. Riauzov, *Vytesnenie chastnogo posrednika iz tovarooborota* (Moscow, 1930), p. 36.

domestic manufactured products were scarcest. Probably the largest volume of illicit imports came in across Russia's western border with Estonia, Latvia, and Poland, though a considerable quantity also flowed across the vast Central and East Asian frontiers.[37] Although few statistics are available for such surreptitious activity,[38] markets in many towns (especially those near the border) were reportedly well stocked with contraband.[39] According to customs estimates for October–December 1923, illegal imports equaled slightly over one third the value of legal imports.[40] During the two previous years the figure was undoubtedly even higher. A report at the end of 1922 by the Central Commission in the Struggle Against Contraband, noting that "our most important markets, not only in border . . . regions but also in the largest urban centers, are flooded with contraband," concluded that the influx of smuggled goods "far exceeded" legal imports.[41]

The bulk of this trade involved textiles, yarn, haberdashery (*galantereia*), and footwear, with sugar, tea, cocoa, medicines, narcotics, liquor, perfume, and technical equipment accounting for most of the rest.[42] Prices for these commodities were considerably higher in Russia than in neighboring countries, and thus many people were willing to accept the risks associated with smuggling. Staging areas, transit camps, and inns sprang up all along the western side of Russia's European border where deals were struck, money changed, and loads of merchandise assembled for the trip east. Authorities in Poland, Estonia, and Latvia winked at this activity, and consequently smugglers had only to employ their ruses against Soviet border officials.[43] The state estimated that only about one tenth of the contraband entering the country was intercepted, and, ironically, even this one tenth found its way to private traders more often than not. Most of the illegally imported items seized by the state were sold at auction. The ubiquitous Nepmen attended these auctions, purchased the goods, and then resold them—all within the law. Frequently the auction prices were lower than the cost of a special import license and customs duties.[44]

Private traders also received foreign products through the mail from relatives or partners living abroad. These goods were known as "semi-legal contraband" because it was illegal to resell them but not to receive them. To avoid attention some Nepmen had packages sent to friends and relatives, and a few large-scale operators had receiving networks of up to one hundred people scattered through several cities.[45] On occasion, private entrepreneurs acquired merchandise in packages from the American Relief Administration (ARA) during its campaign against the famine in the first years of NEP. Upon receipt of ten dollars for food or twenty dollars for clothing, the ARA put together a parcel to be delivered to the person designated by the American making the payment. Many Jews in particular had emigrated to the New World in the preceding decades, and through this service were able to send packages to friends and relatives who had remained behind. The process was often initiated in Russia, where ARA officials distributed cards printed in English and Russian requesting such aid. People filled in the name and address (sometimes no more than the name of a state or the word *America*) of a prospective benefactor in the United States and mailed the cards.[46] The contents of these parcels were very much in demand and thus were sometimes resold.[47] They became in effect, as one observer put it, "the foundation of many small businesses."[48] There were even employees at Gosbank who obtained goods through the mail and posted advertisements for their wares around the premises. Daily announcements such as the following appeared in the women's restrooms at Gosbank: "Foreign shoes for sale, inquire at the debits section." On March 15, 1926, higher postage rates and a five-kilogram limit were applied to packages mailed from abroad, apparently in an effort to bring this trade under control. Whatever the intent of the measure, it did sharply reduce the number of packages in the mail.[49]

The last resort for private traders with no access to any of the sources of goods mentioned above was to sell their personal property. This trade was generally conducted in market squares and along sidewalks by people desperate for funds to purchase food, fuel, and shelter. In Moscow, much of this activity took place in the large, open-air Smolensk market, where on Sundays people without trading licenses could sell their wares. A foreigner in Russia toward the end of 1928 described the scene:

> Imagine a bitterly cold day with the thermometer registering twenty to thirty degrees of frost, and the ground covered with snow. The trams pass through the centre of the street, and with tingling bells drive great lanes through this immense crowd. Furniture and household goods stretching for miles are piled up on both sides of the road, leaving the pavements clear for prospective purchasers. Outside this mass of junk stand men, women and young girls of all ages, mostly belonging to the [prerevolutionary] upper and middle classes to judge by their looks and general demeanour. Here they stand or squat shivering in the snow for hour after hour in the hope of selling the few remaining articles left in their homes in order to raise a few roubles for the purchase of food. Many are blue in the face, paralyzed with hunger and cold, and all have a dumb, expressionless, resigned look, as if all hope had long since departed from their souls.
> . . . You could furnish your home with second-hand articles by just moving along this line of frozen survivors of the old brigade. Double beds, single beds, pianos, wardrobes, wash-hand-stands, pots without handles lie in the snow side by side with hundreds of sacred Ikons, and piles of old blankets and worn-out sheets. Old tin tubs, knives, forks, plates, glasses, and dishes lie jumbled together. There are old clothes of all shapes and sizes, pokers and shovels, musical instruments, family portraits, paintings, photographs, odd toilet requisites, looking-glasses, electric fittings, boxes of nails, worn-out shaving brushes, second-hand tooth-brushes, toothless combs, and half-used cakes of soap. There are a number of odd boots and shoes, because many Russians only have one, and are looking for another to match it.[50]

Many of the people selling their possessions were members of the nobility or other wealthy and privileged segments of society before the Revolution. Now the tables had been turned, and they were called "former people" (*byvshie liudi*). Most were denied work in state agencies, state-subsidized housing, and food ration cards when these were introduced at the end of NEP. Consequently, as many observers noted, these people were forced into petty trade, generally of their personal possessions, in a struggle for life's necessities.[51] Sometimes the goods for sale were so worn or useless that the spectacle of these "former people" was pathetic.

And here, standing in the mud, is a [formerly well-to-do] woman, about fifty years old, in a dilapidated velvet coat and broken shoes. Her face is grey and motionless, her eyes dead. Straight before her she holds the single article which she has to sell: a plush-mounted stereopticon, one of those instruments in vogue a quarter of a century ago into which one stuck photographs and colored cards, to see them magnified.

No one in the market seemed at all interested in it.[52]

The three main sources of goods for private trade, therefore, were the state, the peasantry, and private industry (mainly small-scale artisans), with a considerably smaller amount of merchandise coming from smuggling operations and personal belongings. As a general rule, to which there were many exceptions, large private retail and wholesale operations depended on state enterprises for a higher percentage of their goods than did less sophisticated forms of private trade. It was often the easiest and sometimes the only way for large businesses to obtain sizable quantities of manufactured products. This comparatively heavy reliance on the "socialist" sector was one of the reasons large private firms were particularly vulnerable when the state cracked down on the Nepmen in the last years of the decade. Those private entrepreneurs, mostly smaller-scale businessmen, who did not succumb at once to the pressure found themselves more dependent than ever on peasants and artisans for merchandise. A growing number of traders in the second half of NEP tried to eliminate *all* contact with the state by supplying artisans with raw materials purchased from the peasantry and then selling the artisans' products to consumers. These arrangements, known as "closed circles," are treated in the following chapter, where we will see that the evolution of private manufacturing in the 1920s had much in common with the development of private trade.

CHAPTER 6

# At the Foot of the
# Commanding Heights

New millionaires are enslaving the *kustar'* workers
[handicraftsmen] and all small producers in general. Is everything
being done to restrict and eliminate by economic means these
exploiting elements who link the *kustar'* workers with cooperatives
or state agencies? There is no room for doubt that far from
everything is being done in this area. In the meantime this is a
serious problem for us.

—I. V. Stalin

Both state trade and industry prefer to place their orders [for small-
scale metal goods] with private manufacturers, independent *arteli*
[groups of craftsmen working together], and the like, assuming that
since this is a private entrepreneur, he will do the job better and
on time.

—*Torgovo-promyshlennaia gazeta*

A survey of party pronouncements concerning the Nepmen leaves no
doubt that the Bolsheviks were more worried about private trade than
private industry. This was undoubtedly in part because of the conspicu-
ous swarms of private traders stirred up by NEP in the cities and towns.
Many in the party, not to mention some ordinary citizens,[1] viewed most
private traders as crafty, parasitic speculators, taking advantage of shortages to net huge profits by selling goods they themselves had not produced. The term *Nepman*, especially when employed with a sharply
negative connotation, almost always suggested a person engaged in ava-
ricious trade (generally labeled "speculation"), not industry. Lenin, for
example, remarked that "this word [Nepman] first appeared in jour-
nalese as a joking name for the small trader or person using free trade
for all sorts of abuses."[2] Even worse, given the importance the Bolsheviks attached to the *smychka*, private traders appeared to be menacing
the very foundation of the young Soviet state as they carved out a large

127

share of rural trade and competed effectively with the state for the peasants' surplus produce.

The existence of private manufacturing seemed less alarming to the Bolsheviks. As larger factories—the so-called commanding heights of industry dominated by the state—were brought back into production, the Bolsheviks found their position considerably more hegemonic in industry than in trade. To be sure, there was the specter of workers being exploited once again in private factories. But the vast majority of private "industrialists" during NEP were small-scale handicraftsmen, not titanic robber barons. Though many private manufacturers also engaged in trade (usually to market their finished products), the party generally viewed them more favorably than it did private middlemen, who profited from goods produced by others.[3] Comparatively speaking, then, Bolsheviks felt less anguish convincing themselves that private "industry" (as opposed to private trade) was necessary as a temporary supplement to the "socialist" sector.[4] The need for such a supplement was certainly clear to Soviet consumers, who relied heavily on private manufacturers for many essential goods throughout NEP.

One of the early indications that NEP was more than a set of concessions to the peasantry appeared on May 17, 1921, when the Council of People's Commissars (Sovnarkom) issued two decrees legalizing private manufacturing. One law stressed the need to increase "small-scale and handicraft" industrial production, particularly by producers' cooperatives but also by independent manufacturers. It was imperative, Sovnarkom declared, to "avoid needless regulation and formalism that hampers the economic initiative of individuals and groups of the population." Thus small-scale producers were allowed to dispose of the fruits of their labor on the free market, unless they used raw material supplied by the state under special conditions.[5] This decree was followed on July 7 by an announcement that any citizen was permitted to engage in handicraft (*kustarnyi*) work, and, if he was at least eighteen years old, operate a "small-scale manufacturing enterprise" employing up to "ten or twenty" hired workers. These producers, too, were allowed to sell their output to anyone.[6]

Sovnarkom's second decree of May 17 abolished a law issued by the Supreme Council of the National Economy (VSNKh) on November 29, 1920, that had nationalized all factories with over five workers (ten workers if the factory had no mechanization). Those enterprises that had not yet been actually taken over by the state, Sovnarkom announced, were to be returned to their owners as private property.[7] Many local officials were confused by, if not hostile to, this policy change, and VSNKh felt compelled three months later to reiterate the main points of Sovnarkom's decree, adding that private factories could no longer be nationalized except in unusual cases and only with special permission from the highest state agencies. On December 10, 1921, Sovnarkom and the All-Russian Central Executive Committee (VTsIK) reaffirmed the decree of May 17 and also ordered that smaller-scale workshops not in fact nationalized by April 26, 1919, could again become the property of their former owners upon the latter's request.[8]

Information concerning the number of denationalized factories, and the people who gained ownership of them, is fragmentary. To further cloud the picture, rumors anticipating the denationalization decrees prompted some former owners to sell "their" businesses to people willing to gamble that the enterprises in question would be denationalized. During War Communism approximately 37,000 "factories" were nationalized (at least on paper), most of them quite small. Only one third employed at least sixteen workers per plant, and roughly 5,000 had only one or two workers each. Following the decree of May 17, which elicited a considerable number of petitions from expropriated owners, VSNKh itself returned 150 factories by the end of 1921/22 and 76 in 1922/23. Local officials doubtless returned many more, as a report from Smolensk *guberniia* indicates. There, by the beginning of 1922, former owners regained 60 "enterprises" and 1,300 grain mills.[9]

The state returned numerous factories to the private sector on lease, that is, temporarily and under specific conditions. Some provincial authorities, not wanting the responsibility of administering thousands of workshops, began leasing them to nearly anyone available in the spring of 1921, despite warnings from VSNKh to wait for a decree permitting such activity. The decree to which VSNKh referred was issued by Sovnarkom on July 5 and spelled out the procedure by which private persons and cooperatives could lease industrial enterprises from the state. In the following years this decree was joined by several supplementary provisions, including the stipulation that the lease had to run for at least one year. This, it was felt, would discourage rapacious exploitation of the plant and encourage the leaseholder to make repairs and improvements. In no case, however, was the lease to exceed twelve years.[10]

Over half the leases granted to state, cooperative, and private manufacturers were approved during the last quarter of 1921. Thereafter the total number of leases increased gradually for two years before peaking in 1923/24 at close to 6,500 factories. To this sum should be added approximately 7,000 grain mills, a sizable majority of which were leased to private operators.[11] Data available for the years 1921 and 1922 indicate that 28 percent of the leased enterprises (excluding grain mills) manufactured food products and 21 percent tanned hides. Of the remaining operations, the most numerous were devoted to metalworking (11 percent), chemicals (10 percent), and woodworking (10 percent). Textile mills represented only 6 percent of these undertakings but accounted for many of the largest enterprises and thus an impressive 23 percent of all workers in leased industry. Taken together, the various branches of leased factories were responsible for 13 percent of the output of all nationalized industry in 1922.[12] Were grain mills included in the data, the figure would be still higher.

Even after allowing for a number of cooperatives and producers' collectives (*arteli*) that were organized by private entrepreneurs as fronts through which to lease factories, most estimates place the private share of leases at approximately two thirds. The rest were taken by cooperatives, state agencies, and genuine *arteli*.[13] Numerous reports from around the country illustrate the Nepmen's importance as leaseholders. Of the 731 enterprises (including 380 bakeries) leased in Moscow by October 1924, 72 percent (including 76 percent of the bakeries) were operated by private entrepreneurs. In the Ukraine, where 1,709 factories had been leased by October 1923, Nepmen accounted for 80 percent. In the region including Rostov-on-the-Don, the private share was 71 percent in 1921/22 and 65 percent in 1922/23. Finally, from Siberia came a report that by the end of 1922, half of all leased enterprises in the Novonikolaevsk region were in private hands.[14] As one would expect, a significant portion of private leaseholders—roughly 50 percent—were former owners of the factories they operated.[15]

Generally, factories leased to state and cooperative organizations were considerably larger than those leased to Nepmen. In Moscow *guberniia*, for example, the average number of workers per private operation was 33, less than half the average in enterprises leased to the "socialist" sector. For the country as a whole in 1923/24, 16 to 18 people worked in the average factory leased to a private entrepreneur. As we will see, this was a large operation compared to most ordinary (nonleased) private workshops, though tiny in relation to the average state plant, which employed 230 workers in 1924/25.[16]

The overwhelming majority of these small, privately leased enterprises, many of them simply glorified handicraft shops, turned out the same types of items that dominated private trade—simple, essential consumer products. Given the shortages that prevailed, especially in the countryside, it was not difficult to market such wares. Again, the uncertainty of the Nepmen's future prodded private manufacturers into the production of basic consumer goods, since these items could be turned out rapidly, with a minimum investment, and often with raw materials purchased from the local peasantry. Figures for the end of 1922 (which do not include grain mills) indicate that one quarter of all factories leased to Nepmen produced food, most cases being bakeries or breweries. Enterprises that turned out leather and fur products were nearly as numerous, accounting for 21 percent of all privately leased operations. The shares of other important branches of production were distributed as follows: textiles, 14 percent; metalworking (frequently smithies), 11 percent; brick making, 9 percent; chemical production (including household products such as soap and candles), 8 percent; and woodworking, 7 percent. In these areas of production Nepmen generally received at least 50 percent of the leases granted by the state, whereas in the case of food (including flour), textiles, and leather products, the share of leases held by the private sector was closer to 80 percent.[17]

Leases usually involved an agreement on the Nepmen's part to some combination of the following obligations: (1) repairing the factory; (2) getting production up to specific levels by specific dates; (3) paying the state either a percentage of production or a certain amount in cash or kind; and (4) giving state agencies preferential treatment over other customers—lower prices and priority handling of orders, for example.[18] Of all the lease payments due the state in 1921–22 (from both the "socialist" and private sectors), roughly 90 percent were to be made in kind. Though this was understandable, given the instability of the currency at the time, the apparatus for collecting and storing these products was woefully inadequate. Largely as a result of this, only 31 percent of the fees in kind due the state by October 1922 were actually received, as opposed to 85 percent of cash payments. Not surprisingly, then, the state converted most lease payments to cash in 1923 when inflation succumbed to monetary reform.[19]

These rents, in kind or cash, varied sharply in different regions. The fees were so low in some areas that they did not even cover depreciation of the equipment, whereas elsewhere they were sometimes prohibitive. Figures for the period ending on October 1, 1922, indicate that approximately 10 percent of all leases were annulled, often because the leaseholder could not carry out the terms of the lease or pay the taxes. Nepmen, interestingly, were apparently better risks in this regard than were "socialist" agencies. State investigators, assessing the results of leasing enterprises in the period from 1921 to 1923, concluded that private leaseholders, and especially former owners, were the most conscientious in fulfilling the obligations they had assumed with the leases.[20]

Most leases to Nepmen, as well as to state and cooperative organizations, were for relatively short durations. In fact, a majority were scheduled to last for periods of no more than three years, and virtually none exceeded six years. Nor did the state renew most leases as they expired, because by the middle of the decade it was better able to operate these facilities itself.[21] This was the reason that, as previously noted, the number of private leaseholders began to decline after 1924, well before the state launched its final crackdown on the Nepmen.

Private producers were organized in ranks for licensing and tax purposes by a string of business-tax decrees in the period from 1921 to 1923. Under these laws, private manufacturers paid the same levies as private traders, namely, the license fee, leveling tax, and surcharge on the production of luxury goods. Private "factories" were divided initially into twelve ranks, determined by the number of workers (including family members) involved in the operation. According to a decree of July 26, 1921, rank I workshops had 1 to 3 workers, rank II firms had 4 to 6, rank III enterprises 7 to 10, and so on up to rank XII, which was reserved for factories with over 75 workers. As in private trade, the higher the rank of a business, the higher its license fee. Very small scale operations could often qualify for exemption from the business tax. These included peasant farmers who engaged in handicrafts as a subsidiary occupation and employed no "special equipment" or extra labor beyond family members. Also exempt were certain craftsmen who used no additional labor, even from family members.[22] A series of subsequent decrees made some changes in the number of workers that delimited each "industrial" rank and later added three ranks to the original twelve. But the basic features of the system were not altered.[23]

Those private manufacturers who were required to purchase a license in one of the twelve (later fifteen) ranks of the business-tax table are often divided by Soviet statistics into two categories, called census and noncensus industry. Census firms were large-scale operations, at least by the standards of the private sector, and may be defined broadly as all mechanized enterprises with at least fifteen workers and all nonmechanized factories with at least thirty workers.[24] Nepmen preferred to lease census factories from the state rather than risk the sizable, long-term investment (of which few private entrepreneurs were capable, in any case) needed to build large new facilities. In 1923/24 and 1924/25 nearly 70 percent of all private census plants were leased rather than privately owned, and these leased enterprises accounted for over three fourths of all private census production. Even in 1926/27, when the number of private leaseholders had been declining for two years, slightly over 70 percent of private census output still came from leased factories.[25]

Nearly all private census operations were much smaller than state plants. Even though they represented close to 20 percent of all census factories during 1923/24 and 1924/25, private enterprises employed less than 3 percent of all the workers in census industry.[26] Viewed from another angle, the average number of workers per private census factory ranged from a low of 21 in 1923/24 to 34 in the first half of 1925/26, whereas the average state plant employed approximately ten times as many workers.[27] These figures, in addition to casting light on the nature of private census enterprises, indicate that many of these operations violated the twenty-worker limit announced, rather vaguely as we have seen, at the beginning of NEP. The uncertainty surrounding this matter was never dispelled, and over one hundred private factories operated freely with labor forces exceeding three hundred workers.[28] Nevertheless, the important point for our purposes is that although a number of private census firms exceeded the twenty-worker "restriction," few exceeded it by much.

There are numerous gaps in the statistics concerning the development of private census industry during the course of NEP, particularly early in the decade, when there was administrative chaos in many regions. Nevertheless, the information available is more than sufficient to indicate a number of important general trends. For example, the number of private census factories (leased and privately owned enterprises taken together) increased from under 1,000 in mid-1922 to a peak of somewhat under 2,000 operations in 1923/24. This total fell to slightly under 1,800 in 1924/25 and remained at this level in 1925/26. The decline after 1923/24 was primarily the result of the government decision in the middle of the decade not to renew most leases, since the state was now more capable of operating these facilities itself.[29] The harsh measures taken against private capital in 1924 (such as reductions of supplies and credit) may also have played a part, though this crackdown seems to have mainly affected private traders.

Although there was virtually no increase in the number of private census enterprises after 1924—in contrast to developments in private trade—the output of these factories continued to grow as it had since at least 1923/24 (and probably since 1921). More specifically, private census factories decreased in number by about 8 percent from 1923/24 to 1924/25, but at the same time boosted their production by 30 percent. During the following year production rose by almost 50 percent, but the number of enterprises increased only marginally.[30] These results indicate that many private census firms were growing larger in this period. The total number of workers engaged in private census production swelled from 41,000 in 1923/24 to 61,000 in 1925/26, so that, as noted above, the average number of workers per factory climbed 65 percent, from 21 to 34.[31] Thus, according to the data, for large-scale private industry as well as for private trade, 1925/26 was the most prosperous year. In fact, the private percentage of total (state, cooperative, and private) census production reversed its decline and increased a few tenths of a point (to about 4 percent) in this period, despite the continued growth of industry in the "socialist" sector.[32] But as we will see, this prosperity began to wither by 1927 and thereafter vanished as quickly as it had come.

Just as most private trade was conducted by small-scale entrepreneurs, so nearly all private "factories" hired only a handful of workers. In each case the reasons were much the same, since both lines of activity were conducted in the same uncertain business climate. Given the shaky political prospects for the private sector and the economic collapse accompanying the civil war, small handicraft shops had a number of advantages over larger operations: (1) small shops needed comparatively little capital for equipment and raw materials; (2) small enterprises were less visible and could often elude the attention of state officials, particularly in the countryside; (3) in any case, endeavors without hired labor were generally less subject to inspections of various kinds; and (4) taxes on artisans were much lower than those on entrepreneurs in census industry. Thus, through 1924/25 approximately 80 percent of the manufacturing licenses issued to Nepmen for the twelve ranks of the business-tax table were for rank I, that is, operations with no more than three workers.[33] Even in the following years, when most small-scale producers were freed from the business tax, a majority of the private manufacturers still paying the tax were in rank I.[34]

In contrast to private traders, who were concentrated in cities and towns, roughly two thirds of private producers with business-tax licenses worked in the countryside, according to data for 1923 and 1924/25.

This was primarily because many small-scale artisans were or had been peasants. In addition, such craftsmen obtained most of their raw materials from peasants and sold the bulk of their output in the countryside. Not surprisingly, private census factories were more likely to be located in cities—Moscow and Leningrad in particular—than were petty handicraftsmen. This point is underscored by a government report revealing that in 1923 Moscow and Petrograd contained a merely respectable 14 percent of the licensed private "industrial" enterprises, but fully 35 percent of the hired workers in these operations.[35]

The private sector's share of all business-tax manufacturing licenses was impressive, though somewhat deceptive. Because of the numerous small-scale private operations, approximately 90 percent of "industrial" licenses went to private entrepreneurs until 1925. Nearly all the enterprises in ranks I and II (from 1 to 3 and from 4 to 6 workers, respectively) were privately owned in these years, and over half the businesses in the next two ranks belonged to Nepmen. Even as late as 1927, in rank V (from 21 to 30 workers in a factory without mechanization or 13 to 20 workers plus mechanization) one quarter of all firms were in private hands. At this time in the capital itself, on the eve of the final campaign against the "new bourgeoisie," private entrepreneurs ran over 90 percent of the sum of all enterprises in ranks I through V.[36] But it must be borne in mind that the state enjoyed a similar hegemony in the top half of the fifteen (by 1926) industrial ranks, thus rendering the Nepmen's share of total industrial production considerably smaller than their share of licensed "factories."

Private manufacturing was slower to develop than private trade and did not hit full stride until the end of 1922/23. As late as the end of 1922, only about 60,000 private "industrial" licenses had been issued, but during the next nine months, the total swelled to about 250,000. After modest gains early in 1923/24, the number of licenses dropped slightly (not as precipitously as in private trade), reflecting the tougher line of the state against private entrepreneurs. This decline was short-lived, however, and during the first half of 1924/25, the number of private manufacturers with business-tax licenses peaked at over 300,000. Then the figure suddenly plunged toward the end of 1925 to approximately 80,000, where it remained during 1926. At first glance this drop might seem puzzling, coming as it did during the most lenient treatment of the Nepmen by the state. Actually, the decline was a direct result of several decrees that exempted most small-scale producers, including some with hired labor, from the business tax. Such artisans were now only required to obtain an inexpensive "license for personal productive activity" (*patent na lichnoe promyslovoe zaniatie*), and a wave of roughly 350,000 individuals did so by the second half of 1925/26.[37]

Up to now we have only considered private producers who belonged to the twelve (later fifteen) ranks of "industry" defined by the business tax. The tax reforms of 1925, which drained approximately 200,000 people from rank I alone, direct our attention to the largest group of private manufacturers.[38] These made up the vast sea of handicraftsmen, often called *kustari,* who operated either with *lichnye promyslovye* licenses or with no licenses at all.[39] Less information is available concerning these people, because they do not appear in business-tax statistics and were heavily concentrated in the countryside. The scope and nature of their activity resembled that of producers in the lowest "industrial" ranks, which is indicated by the large number of the latter who obtained *lichnye promyslovye* licenses in 1925. At times it will be convenient to refer to both *kustari* and private manufacturers with low (noncensus) business-tax licenses as a single group under the label petty private industry. *Kustari* made up over 90 percent of this category, which meant that most petty producers were simply handicraftsmen working at home or in a nearby shop, either alone or with help from family members, apprentices, and occasionally a hired hand.[40]

The number of people engaged in petty industry grew from approximately two million in 1922/23, to three million by 1925/26, and reached nearly four and a half million by the end of the decade. An overwhelming 75 to 80 percent of these artisans worked in the countryside, which one would expect on the basis of the foregoing discussion of small-scale manufacturers. In particular, a large percentage of *kustari* were peasants who engaged in handicrafts during the agricultural off-season. According to figures for 1924/25, peasants with small plots (up to 5.4 acres) obtained over half their income from such activity.[41]

At the beginning of 1922, the Central Committee sent a directive to *guberniia* party committees complaining that party work among *kustari* was still "extremely weak" and urging local officials to organize *kustari* into producers' cooperatives. This was easier said than done, however, in the far-flung countryside, and nothing significant came of such demands from Moscow until the end of NEP. In the early years of the decade, the private sector reigned virtually unchallenged in petty industry, accounting in 1923/24 for over 90 percent of the workers and just under 90 percent of the total output in this category of manufacturing. By

1926/27 these figures were still in the neighborhood of 80 percent, and as late as 1929/30, only 45 percent of the *kustari* were to be found in the state system of producers' cooperatives.[42]

Thus private "industry" during NEP was overwhelmingly small-scale. One might think that private census factories, often mechanized and considerably larger than peasant handicraft operations, would have accounted for an impressive percentage of total private industrial production. But even in the middle of the decade, when private census industry was at its peak, the millions of petty enterprises accounted for over 80 percent of the total private industrial output.[43]

Taken as a whole, the private sector made a particularly large contribution to the Soviet Union's industrial production in the first years of NEP, when the "socialist" sector was a shambles. Unfortunately, little statistical information could be collected on this (and most other) topics given the disruptions and chaos that had to be overcome. Furthermore, one suspects that the data published for 1921/22 and 1922/23 (and, to a lesser degree, throughout NEP) understate the Nepmen's role in industry, for many private entrepreneurs, particularly in the countryside, undoubtedly managed to escape the scrutiny of the nascent state bureaucracy. Even so, figures for 1922/23, which include only the twelve business-tax ranks (i.e., not *kustari*), place the Nepmen's share of industrial production between 40 and 50 percent. Thus, if information on the value of goods manufactured by *kustari* were also included in the calculations, the portion of total industrial production attributable to the private sector at this time would be more accurately measured at well over 50 percent.[44]

As the state gradually brought large factories back to life, it assumed the leading role in the industrial activity of the country. Even though private production continued to increase in absolute terms, the portion of total industrial output that it represented dropped to about one quarter in 1923/24 and to one fifth in 1924/25 and 1925/26.[45] Though comparable statistics are surprisingly scarce for the last years of NEP, there is no doubt that private manufacturing dropped off sharply in this period. It is somewhat misleading, however, to speak simply in terms of the Nepmen's share of total industrial production. Private manufacturers had virtually no desire or capability to produce heavy capital equipment and were nearly all engaged in turning out consumer goods.[46]

Thus, an understanding of the Nepmen's significance in industry requires a more specific assessment of their activity in several branches of light industry.

The entire group of private producers concentrated in the same lines of activity as private leaseholders, and for the same reasons. Five categories (see table 11) dominated private manufacturing completely, in terms of both the number of people involved and the ruble value of output. In each division, certain products and occupations were more important than others: (1) textiles: finished articles of clothing, felt boots, wool, linen, and cotton fabrics; (2) food: bread baking, milling of flour, groats, and vegetable oil; (3) processed animal products (not including wool): footwear, other leather products such as harnesses, furs, sheepskin coats, and processing of hides to produce leather; (4) wood products: furniture, barrels, carts, sleighs, spinning wheels, charcoal, and pitch; (5) metalworking (mostly by blacksmiths): common household and agricultural tools and utensils.

Information from numerous localities supports the contention that private manufacturers were concentrated in the five branches of production listed above. The main differences from region to region were in the distribution of people and resources within these five branches, which was dictated by the characteristics of each area. For example, in the Ukraine and other regions where agriculture was important, a large number of private grain mills magnified the already impressive position that food production occupied in private industry. Journeying from the Ukrainian countryside to a city, one would find that food production (most often in bakeries), though still significant, had to share more of the spotlight with private entrepreneurs turning out clothing, footwear, and metal products. Sometimes the location of a city or region encouraged specific industries such as fishing in Rostov-on-the-Don and Astrakhan', flax and linen production in Belorussia, and gold mining in Siberia. But everywhere, regardless of these local variations, the five categories of production listed above reigned supreme in the private sector.[47]

Although it is easily established that private manufacturers were concentrated in certain lines of activity, the question remains: What portion of the Soviet Union's total output in these areas did they contribute? An author in Sverdlovsk, addressing a similar question in an article on the Ural region, instructed his readers simply to take a walk in the countryside. There, he declared, they could not fail to notice that nearly all the peasants' agricultural equipment, household utensils, furniture, and clothing were produced by *kustari*.[48] Indeed, the entire population, not

TABLE II    BACKBONE OF PRIVATE
MANUFACTURING, 1923/24

| | Percentage of All Workers in Private Industry | Percentage of All Private Industrial Production (in terms of ruble value) |
|---|---|---|
| Textiles | 27.5% | 9.7% |
| Food | 20.9 | 66.6 |
| Processed animal products | 19.2 | 14.7 |
| Wood products | 15.4 | 2.9 |
| Metalworking | 11.5 | 4.8 |

SOURCE: Calculated from data in A. M. Ginzburg, ed., *Chastnyi kapital v narodnom khoziaistve SSSR. Materialy kommissii VSNKh SSSR* (Moscow-Leningrad, 1927), p. 87.
NOTE: These figures do not include private census industry. Were census factories included in the table, there would be no significant changes. Petty manufacturing completely dominated census industry in the private sector, and private census industry was, in any case, concentrated in the same branches of production.

just the peasants, relied on private producers for a number of essential goods. As late as 1926, nearly half of all processed food products were turned out by private manufacturers, and earlier in the decade the private sector's share of production must have been even greater.[49] Private bakeries, for example, accounted for close to 90 percent of the nation's bread in 1923—an impressive figure, given the importance of bread in the population's diet.[50]

Nor were private producers important only in the realm of grain products, for in 1926 roughly 80 percent of the Soviet Union's footwear and 60 percent of its fur products (as well as related items such as sheepskin coats) were manufactured in the private sector.[51] Private individuals, working mainly in modest tailoring enterprises, were also responsible for approximately 70 percent of the clothing (*shveinaia*) industry's output in the middle of NEP. At this time private entrepreneurs turned out between one quarter and one third of common wood and metal consumer goods, hauled in 75 percent of the fish catch, and mined most of the country's gold. In addition, private manufacturers were quite strong in the *makhorka* (coarse tobacco) and vegetable oil industries, accounting for 30 to 40 percent and 50 to 60 percent, respectively, of total production in 1923.[52] Finally, Nepmen were able to maintain considerably more than a toehold in grain milling, despite the state's concern that private entrepreneurs in this activity constituted a particularly grave threat to the *smychka*. As late as 1925/26, the private share of flour production was 20 percent, and it had been close to 40 percent in 1923/24.[53] Given the weakness of the "socialist" sector of the economy at the beginning of NEP, private millers must have ground well over half the country's flour in 1921/22. In light of such figures there is no room to doubt that private "industry" was close to indispensable for Soviet consumers in the 1920s—a view supported by estimates that place the private share of total consumer goods production at 44 percent in 1923 and 32 percent in 1925/26.[54]

We have seen that the Nepmen's position began to deteriorate gradually by 1926/27 when their taxes increased, and supplies and credit became more difficult to obtain from the state. These developments, combined with the decrees of 1925 that exempted many small-scale producers from the business tax, brought about striking changes in private manufacturing during the last years of the decade. One of the Nepmen's responses to higher taxes and more aggressive regulation was to shift their activities to the countryside, where state officials were far less numerous. This also had the advantage of bringing private producers closer to their only reliable source of raw materials, the peasantry. Even at the beginning of NEP such considerations helped account, as we have seen, for a majority of private craftsmen working in rural areas. But once the state stepped up the pressure on the Nepmen in 1926/27, so-called closed circles (*zamknutye krugi*) multiplied rapidly throughout the countryside. These were networks of private manufacturers and traders that shunned any contact with state agencies or officials. More specifically, private craftsmen obtained raw materials from peasants, either directly or via private middlemen. They sold their finished products to private traders, who then retailed them to private customers. The "system," then, was a response to both increased taxes and regulation on the one hand and the state reduction of supplies to the private sector on the other. Consequently, the arrangement was far more prevalent after 1926 than in the first half of NEP.[55]

Another way for private producers to avoid large tax bills was to atomize their businesses. After most artisans were freed from the business tax in 1925, many owners dissolved their workshops and transferred

their operations to a "putting-out" or "domestic" system. By this arrangement an entrepreneur provided raw materials and some form of
payment to ostensibly independent craftsmen (who often worked in
their homes) and then marketed the finished products.[56] The advantages
were that no factory existed on which the business tax could be levied,
and the scope of the organizer's activity was camouflaged. For these reasons some Nepmen had used the domestic system since the beginning of
the decade.[57] It became more widespread, however, in the second half of
NEP, after most small-scale artisans were exempted from the business
tax, and as taxes on private factories steadily mounted. In a sense, this
trend was a reversal of the traditional pattern of industrial development,
a reversion to a more "primitive" (pre–Industrial Revolution) mode of
production. Such arrangements were popular with Nepmen for much
the same reason that *zamknutye krugi* were, and it is hardly surprising
that the latter frequently took the form of domestic systems. By 1927,
estimates place approximately one quarter of all *kustari* in domestic systems, some of which involved several hundred and even a thousand
handicraftsmen.[58]

Other Nepmen chose not to abandon their factories but to disguise
them as *arteli* (producers' cooperatives). These false *arteli*, as they were
called, assumed a number of forms. Sometimes an owner would "give"
his factory to an *artel'* and appear to join the *artel'* himself while actually continuing to function as the director of the enterprise. More often,
the owner simply had his workers registered as an *artel'* while he himself remained inconspicuous. He would supply raw materials, sometimes "lease" the facility to the workers, and market the finished product. Thus it was frequently difficult to be certain whether an *artel'* was
genuine or merely a front.[59]

Private manufacturers formed false *arteli* for several reasons. First of
all, by the beginning of 1925, most *arteli* had been freed from a number
of taxes (including the business tax), which made them, like *kustari*, attractive to private businessmen.[60] Another advantage of the *arteli*, one
not shared by independent *kustari*, was that the former were considered
part of the "socialist" sector. Consequently, they had greater access to
raw materials, credit, and other products from the state than did the
Nepmen. It was not unusual for false cooperatives and *arteli* to be
formed primarily to exploit this opportunity. In Moscow, for example,
there appeared a cooperative called Moskredkoop (Moscow Credit Cooperative), organized ostensibly to supply its member *kustari* with raw

materials and other goods from various state agencies. As it turned out, several members were Nepmen who saw to it that Moskredkoop resold most of its goods to private entrepreneurs.[61]

The activity of the sewing *artel'* Proletarii (Proletarian) was more brazen, matching the prior antics of its founder. Previously he had been a circus performer, billing himself as "Mister Sem, possessor of the Tibetan secret of divining the present, past, and future." One of his first exploits after organizing Proletarii was to have it classified as an *artel'* of invalids, a move that initially paid handsome dividends. As a representative of such an organization, he was successful in securing official documents requesting that other state enterprises give him privileged treatment. In the end, the *artel'* was caught selling textiles and other goods obtained illegally from an army warehouse.[62]

Though false *arteli* sprouted throughout NEP, they appear to have multiplied most rapidly in the second half of the decade. This was probably because of both the tax benefits (not to mention other privileges) that most *arteli* had received by 1925 and the worsening position of legitimate private manufacturers after 1926. In other words, as NEP waned, the advantages of false *arteli* must have seemed increasingly attractive to private producers struggling to stay afloat.[63] In any case, the Commissariat of Finance estimated in 1927 that two thirds of all producers' cooperatives were false; VSNKh set the figure at 80 percent. If one remains skeptical of these estimates, there is nevertheless no room to doubt the sardonic assessment made in 1927 by a Soviet observer: "It must be said that if our country feels a shortage of something, it is not of illustrations of the fact that producers' cooperatives very often turn out to be false cooperatives."[64]

Predictably, private manufacturers suffered heavy losses during the assault on the Nepmen launched by the state in 1928. In addition to using stiff tax increases and "administrative" pressure, which could be directed at any private entrepreneur, the state aimed a number of measures specifically at private industry. One of these was simply to nationalize private, especially census, factories. After a campaign to do so in 1928/29, only 177 private census enterprises remained in the Soviet Union. In fact, many of these were too small to be considered census operations within the traditional definition, for they employed altogether a total of only seventeen hundred workers.[65] As early as 1926/27 the state began annulling many leases on factories operated by Nepmen, particularly in branches of production such as grain milling and leather working, where the private sector was firmly ensconced. During 1928/29, nearly all remaining "private" leases were revoked, so that in Leningrad, for example, only eight such factories (with a total of sixty-six workers) remained by May 1929. For the country as a whole, the value of production in privately leased census enterprises plunged from 149 million rubles in 1926/27 to 25 million in 1928/29. Total private census production (i.e., from leased and privately owned factories) fell to less than 1 percent of the country's census industrial output.[66]

Private census operations, like private traders in "permanent" facilities, were eliminated more completely at the end of the decade than were small-scale entrepreneurs. One reason, of course, was that large factories were more visible and immobile. From the point of view of the Bolsheviks, large factories were more irritating ideological eyesores than were the independent artisans, because the former, with their comparatively large complements of hired labor, were more clearly "capitalist" enterprises. In the realm of small-scale private production, the primary goal of the state campaign was to break up domestic systems and false *arteli*. Local officials were ordered to scrutinize the cooperatives in their regions and not only drive out but also prosecute any "capitalists" they uncovered. *Arteli* were instructed not to sell to private middlemen products made with goods supplied by the state. Little information is available concerning the results of these decrees, though it is known that out of 3,716 *arteli* investigated in the Russian Republic (RSFSR) during 1928/29, 630 were liquidated.[67]

Even more difficult to measure, though undeniably important, were the problems created for artisans by the concomitant campaigns of the state against private traders and the peasantry. The collectivization drive, for instance, affected craftsmen in a number of ways. It disrupted the activity of many peasants who worked part time as *kustari* and made it more difficult for other producers to obtain raw materials (since these had generally been supplied by the peasantry). The crackdown on private trade created other difficulties. Those producers who marketed their own wares, including peasants who continued to sell their surplus grain, were by 1928 more vulnerable to the charge of "speculation," which some local officials extended to cover virtually all private trade. Further, as private middlemen were forced to abandon the field, many artisans found it difficult to get their goods to market. For instance, *Torgovo-promyshlennaia gazeta* reported that a large number of private metalworkers had to close up shop after the traders who purchased their goods were driven out of business. The "socialist" distribution system was still too underdeveloped to replace the private middlemen and market the artisans' output.[68]

The state coupled its offensive against false *arteli* and domestic systems with an attempt to draw *kustari* into the network of producers' cooperatives. The party, however, clearly considered this task less urgent than the industrialization and collectivization efforts of the day, and by 1930 the cooperative system had absorbed less than half the total number of *kustari*.[69] Much as it permitted free collective-farm trade to supplement "socialist" trade after NEP, in the 1930s the state tolerated (and even extended tax incentives to) independent artisans who used no hired labor.[70] These craftsmen continued to turn out the same basic consumer goods they had produced in the 1920s, which were still in short supply. As late as 1939, approximately 1.3 million *kustari* had not yet, in the words of a Soviet historian, "linked their fate with the socialist sector of the economy."[71] They, along with collective-farm traders, were the primary legal remnants of the private economic activity that had flourished during NEP.

In conclusion, private manufacturing, like private trade, consisted of a comparatively modest number of large enterprises and a swarm of petty entrepreneurs. However diminutive these handicraft operations were individually, they still accounted collectively for one third of the Soviet Union's total consumer goods production as late as the middle of NEP. But it was not only consumers who benefited from private manufacturing. As a number of articles in Soviet periodicals explained in the 1920s, private producers, by helping to fill vacuums in light industry and turn out goods essential for day-to-day living, supplemented rather than harmed state industry.[72] In other words, far from menacing the commanding heights, these Nepmen freed the state to invest more resources in heavy capital-goods production. Of course, as the "socialist" sector expanded, competition was bound to develop with private manufacturers for both customers and raw materials. But when this occurred, one article explained, the state would represent a threat to the private sector, not vice versa. Certainly, something of the sort happened. By the end of the decade the state had pushed private producers far back from the positions they had held in 1925/26. This, however, could be attributed not only to a burgeoning complex of large-scale state factories but also to "administrative" pressure of the sort described in previous chapters. Just as Nepmen were driven out of trade before the state and cooperatives were capable of replacing them, so the state was unable at the end of NEP to satisfy the population's demand for manufactured goods. Had the competition with the "socialist" sector been solely a test of economic competence, private producers would not have succumbed as rapidly as they did.

## CHAPTER 7

# Secondary Endeavors

Cooperatives not only do not dominate the market; they even utilize
the services of private individuals as contractors. . . . The trusts
have ceased being masters of their own affairs and have found
themselves in the hands of [private] middlemen. They appear to be
state institutions in name only, in reality depending on private
people and serving their interests.

—Report presented at a meeting of the
Petrograd Party Central Committee

Private capital has seized the initiative and almost completely
dominates the *zagotovka* market.

—*Torgovo-promyshlennaia gazeta*

In addition to conventional trade and manufacturing, smaller numbers
of private entrepreneurs engaged in a wide variety of other activities.
These businesses included cafés, restaurants, boardinghouses, inns, bath-
houses, and shipping operations (using cars, trucks, horse carts, and
boats on inland waterways). There was even a private airline (expropriated in 1929) based in the Ukraine and serving Khar'kov, Rostov-on-
the-Don, Odessa, Kiev, and Moscow. One could also obtain a license to
operate facilities such as private theaters, billiard halls, ice-skating rinks,
gymnasiums, tennis courts, and the like.[1] In addition, a government survey in 1923 (excluding Moscow and Petrograd) indicated that 9 percent
of the "legitimate theaters," 29 percent of the cinemas, and virtually all
variety theaters were privately owned.[2] This list of activities might also
be stretched to cover the "free professions" (doctors, dentists, archi-
tects), even though these individuals were not included in the same harsh
tax category as most other private entrepreneurs.[3] Although there is comparatively little information on private ventures outside trade and manufacturing, there is sufficient material to sketch at least the outlines of
selected realms of endeavor—book publishing, middleman transactions,
*zagotovka* work, joint-stock companies, and credit organizations—distinct in one way or another from the activities covered in previous
chapters.

Book publishing was one of the few lines of private business not out-lawed during War Communism. In 1918 there were 111 private pub-lishers registered with the state, and during the next three years at least some of these operations issued books, both on their own initiative and to fulfill orders from the state publishing agency (Gosizdat). Neverthe-less, the state effort to eliminate private trade during War Communism applied also to the *sale* of books, and this greatly hampered the activity of private publishers.[4] The initial decrees heralding the transition to NEP said nothing of the book trade, and it was not until late in the sum-mer of 1921 that the Moscow Soviet permitted the free sale of books by independent publishing houses.[5] Only in December did the Council of People's Commissars (Sovnarkom) officially extend NEP to the publish-ing business and announce a new set of rules for this activity. As spelled out in Sovnarkom's decree, licensed private publishers were allowed to own printing equipment, sell their output at free-market prices, and im-port books (after obtaining special permission). All manuscripts had to be approved by the state, and Gosizdat reserved the right to buy at whole-sale prices all or any number of the copies of a book being printed.[6]

Following Sovnarkom's decree, the number of private publishing houses swelled rapidly, so that by the end of May 1922, there were 319 registered in Moscow and Petrograd (though only a handful in the rest of the country). But many of these were ephemeral operations or fronts for other business schemes and published few if any works. In Moscow, for example, of the 220 private publishers registered by May 26, 1922, fully 133 did not submit a single manuscript to Gosizdat for approval in the period after mid-November 1921. Another 60 firms requested clear-ance for one to five books each, and only 10 sought permission to pub-lish at least eleven titles per enterprise. The situation was similar in Petrograd, where, during the period from January 31, 1922, to May 29, 1922, 44 of the 99 registered private publishers did not approach Gosiz-dat with a manuscript, and only one operation submitted as many as eleven.[7] Either Gosizdat's censors were not particularly strict or most publishers limited themselves to safe works (including books issued under contract for Gosizdat), because only 41 of the 1,003 manuscripts presented for approval were rejected.[8]

As a general rule, private publishing was most heavily concentrated in the humanities, accounting by the beginning of 1923 for a third of all titles on philosophy and psychology, for over 40 percent in the area of poetry, belles-lettres, and literary criticism, and for half the books on painting, theater, and sports.[9] The private share of all books published

TABLE 12    PRIVATE PUBLISHERS' SHARE
            OF THE MARKET

|      | Share of All Titles Published Privately | Share of Total Pages Published Privately |
|------|------------------------------------------|------------------------------------------|
| 1922 | 20.0%[a]                                 | 18.0%[a]                                 |
| 1923 | 25.0[a]                                  | 22.0[a]                                  |
| 1924 | 11.5                                     | no data                                  |
| 1927 | 7.1                                      | 6.4                                      |
| 1931 | 0.1                                      | 0.1                                      |

SOURCE: A. I. Nazarov, *Oktiabr' i kniga* (Moscow, 1968), p. 254; E. I. Shamurin, *Sovetskaia kniga za 15 let v tsifrakh* (Moscow, 1933), pp. 25–26.
[a] Private and cooperative publishers together.

was under 20 percent in 1922 and under 25 percent a year later (see table 12).

In absolute terms private publishing declined dramatically at the end of the decade, paralleling the fate of the Nepmen in general. If their output in 1927 is labeled 100, then private publishers issued 61.9 titles in 1928, 49.6 in 1929, 14 in 1930, and 2.4 in 1931.[10] All of these figures may prompt one to conclude that private publishing was insignificant. Certainly it cannot be considered one of the Nepmen's major areas of activity, with regard to either the number of people involved or their impact on the state and population. Nevertheless, by virtue of their concentration in the fine arts and the willingness of some to issue works from a variety of literary circles, private publishers contributed to the cultural richness and diversity that help distinguish NEP in Soviet history.[11]

Whereas the endeavors of private publishers were less than critical to the nation's economy, another group of entrepreneurs—private middlemen—played a significant economic role in the "socialist" sector itself. We have already noted the Nepmen's importance in marketing goods produced by the state and will focus here on their activity as supply agents for state and cooperative organizations.

Raw materials and other supplies were frequently as scarce as finished consumer goods, and many inexperienced "socialist" enterprises, thrust out on their own in the marketplace, were forced to engage the services of private middlemen even to obtain products from other state agencies. Soviet scholars such as I. Ia. Trifonov concur on this point: "Lacking experience and skill in trade-money operations, state enterprises [at the beginning of NEP] appeared helpless, carrying on isolated and unorganized trade. Even business between state enterprises could not be conducted without private middlemen."[12] Some Nepmen sold products to state agencies as just a part of their operations, continuing to deliver goods to private customers as well. But often a middleman was more closely linked to a state firm, making purchases and sales in the latter's name and agreeing (not always sincerely) to conduct no additional business on the side. Under this arrangement, a Nepman could garner a handsome commission (generally at least 10 to 15 percent of the transaction) without investing any capital of his own.[13] These private middlemen, acting as plenipotentiaries for "socialist" enterprises and traveling with official documents and passes, were a common sight on trains in the first years of NEP.[14]

Data available for October 1922 indicate that fully 32 percent of state industry purchases were made from Nepmen (dropping to 11 percent in September of the following year). Even in Moscow, where official supply agencies were concentrated, some state stores in 1922 relied heavily on private middlemen for manufactured consumer goods such as textiles.[15] The situation was similar with the cooperatives. As a general rule, the farther one looked into the countryside, the weaker the state distribution system became, and the more cooperatives depended on Nepmen for supplies. On the periphery of Moscow *guberniia,* for example, cooperatives obtained roughly 45 percent of their merchandise through private middlemen in 1922. Taken as a whole, the cooperative system bought between 30 and 40 percent of its wares from Nepmen at this time. According to a report from the Petrograd Guberniia Party Committee, some cooperatives even received loans from the private sector.[16]

In the case of nonagricultural products, a private middleman delivering goods to a state enterprise generally acquired them from a second state agency. At an official congress on trade and industry in Rostov-on-the-Don, delegates from around the region told of the poor or nonexistent relations between "socialist" operations in 1922, which resulted in the "'organic' functioning of private middlemen in transactions between various state trade agencies." Similar reports elsewhere emphasized that this state of affairs was common throughout the land.[17] At times, the helplessness of state enterprises was breathtaking. "It would seem apparent," complained an official in the Workers' and Peasants'

Inspectorate (RKI), "that oil and coal could be bought from state fuel agencies, electric lamps from the Electric Trust, but even here [state firms] often run for help to middlemen." To cite but one example: In 1922 a Nepman contracted to supply GUM (the main state department store) with two million *pudy* (36,000 tons) of coal at sixty-five kopecks per *pud*. He simply took the advance payment from GUM over to Torgugol' (a state agency whose name indicates that it sold coal), where he was able to buy coal at thirty-eight kopecks per *pud* and thus have a considerable quantity of coal left over after delivering GUM its share.[18]

In such conditions it is not surprising that Nepmen often made large profits, either from hefty commission fees and gross overpayments by incompetent state agencies or in more underhanded ways such as using bribes to obtain scarce commodities or simply disappearing with the advance payment. Semen Pliatskii, whom we encountered in a previous chapter, sold a Petrograd trust 30,000 *pudy* of metal that happened already to be in the trust's own warehouses.[19] These and other abuses and the profits streaming into private pockets sparked numerous outcries and reform proposals in the press.[20] At the same time a number of government bodies were discussing ways to control the activity of private middlemen. RKI, for instance, proposed among other things that large sales be registered with the state commodity exchange and that commissions be limited to 1 percent of the value of the transaction.[21] By an order issued on December 4, 1922, the Moscow division of the Supreme Council of the National Economy forbade state agencies in Moscow from using private middlemen in dealings with other state enterprises. State organizations could still employ Nepmen in transactions with the private sector, but could not pay commissions at a rate exceeding 3 percent.[22] Finally, on January 2, 1923, Sovnarkom issued a decree for the country as a whole that banned private entrepreneurs from conducting business between two state agencies. Instead, state enterprises were permitted to retain their own in-house middlemen to facilitate sales and purchases.[23]

These measures, along with increased business expertise in many state and cooperative undertakings, reduced considerably the number of private middlemen by the second half of NEP. In December 1927, a resolution of the Fifteenth Party Congress spoke confidently of the "socialist" sector's dominant position in the economy and recalled the prevalence of private middlemen at the beginning of NEP as simply an indication of how much progress had been made since.[24] But despite the state's undeniable economic gains, investigations and reports throughout NEP indicated that many "socialist" enterprises continued to rely on Nepmen (not necessarily illegally) for the supply of raw materials and other services.[25] This is hardly surprising, since shortages and resource distribution problems refused to succumb completely to state policies. Even today, in a planned economy, these difficulties continue to plague both manufacturing and distribution operations. As a perusal of the satirical journal *Krokodil* confirms, some state enterprises still hire people to scour the country for scarce supplies.[26]

Thus, just as Soviet consumers were partially dependent on private retailers, many state enterprises relied at least to some extent (especially at the beginning of NEP) on private middlemen. But even though most Bolsheviks were willing to tolerate Nepmen in the market squares for a number of years, they were considerably less patient at the spectacle of private entrepreneurs servicing the "socialist" sector. At the First All-Russian Congress of Commodity Exchange Officials early in NEP, Rykov asserted: "In the area of trade, private capital is trying to fill the cracks between our state production organizations and devoting too much of its attention and capital to middleman activity." Although there was certainly room for private capital to play a "large and useful role" in the development of trade, Rykov added, private involvement in transactions between state agencies was inappropriate.[27] In a similar vein, the aforementioned congress (on trade and industry) in Rostov-on-the-Don declared that private retail trade was "desirable"; private wholesale trade "only tolerable"; and private middleman activity between "socialist" enterprises "completely impermissible."[28]

In other words, even though there was widespread agreement that many nascent state undertakings had little alternative to dealing with private entrepreneurs,[29] the official "solution" seems to have been almost exclusively a determination to eliminate private middlemen and improve at once the efficiency of the "socialist" sector. This in contrast to retail trade, where the state was more willing to accept the presence of Nepmen for a time. To the Bolsheviks, the Nepmen's transactions with state and cooperative agencies seemed a much graver threat to the development of socialism in Russia than did private sales to individual consumers.

Another important occupation of the Nepmen was the purchase of food and various raw materials in the countryside. This *zagotovka* work, mentioned briefly in a previous chapter as a source of merchandise for private traders, merits additional attention here for both eco-

nomic and political reasons. Private buyers roaming the countryside
sought a wide variety of goods, ranging from grain, meat, vegetables,
and eggs to hides, wool, and flax. These products, the vast majority of
which were purchased from the peasantry, were then resold to private
manufacturers and traders, "socialist" agencies, or directly to consumers. The grain *zagotovka* clearly assumed paramount urgency for the
party, both because bread was the staple of the people's diet, and because the Bolsheviks desired to amass a grain surplus to support industrialization. Here, as in the case of private middlemen, the party found
itself in the position of needing the Nepmen, but fearing their presence
would undermine state control of a vital sector of the economy. Before
pursuing this point, we need to examine the extent of private participation in the *zagotovka* of grain and other products.

There is little statistical information on the size of private grain purchases in the first years of NEP, because this activity was largely beyond
the monitoring ability of the fledgling state bureaucracy. Certainly,
though, the Nepmen's share was substantial, given the chaos plaguing
state *zagotovka* efforts and the peasants' suspicion of (not to mention
hostility to) state grain collection campaigns in the wake of War Communism. During 1922/23 in Tambov *guberniia,* for example, private
buyers obtained over four times as much grain as state and cooperative
*zagotovka* agencies.[30] By the middle of NEP the private percentage
of the grain *zagotovka* had fallen but was still far from negligible—
roughly 30 percent in 1924/25, 20 percent in 1925/26, and 15 percent
in 1926/27.[31] In the Ukraine, private middlemen bought approximately
40 percent of the grain marketed by peasants in 1924/25 and accounted
for over half the procurement in many regions of the country.[32]

The Nepmen's share of the *zagotovka* of all agricultural products
taken together has been estimated at 40 to 50 percent in 1924/25, 30 to
40 percent in 1925/26, and in the neighborhood of 30 percent the next
two years.[33] In the case of a number of products, including meat, butter,
eggs, furs, and hides, the private sector's role was even more impressive
(see table 13).

A significant portion—47 percent in 1926/27 according to one estimate—of the Nepmen's purchases in the countryside was resold to state
and cooperative enterprises.[34] It is difficult to determine the share of the
state's total *zagotovka* that came through the hands of private middlemen, because "socialist" *zagotovka* agents sometimes bought goods illegally—grain, for example—through the private *zagotovka* network.[35]
Figures available for 1925/26 indicate that Nepmen supplied roughly 40

TABLE 13     PERCENTAGE OF *ZAGOTOVKA*
ACCOUNTED FOR BY NEPMEN

|                   | 1924/25 | 1925/26 |
|-------------------|---------|---------|
| Makhorka          | 30%     | 20–40%  |
| Hemp              | 45      | 30–50   |
| Seeds (for oil)   | 20      | 40–60   |
| Wool              | no data | 50      |
| Hides             | no data | 50      |
| Furs              | 60      | 60      |
| Meat              | no data | 67      |
| Flax              | 9       | 3       |
| Cotton            | 4       | 3       |
| Tobacco           | 21      | 24      |
| Butter            | 64      | 63      |
| Eggs              | 54      | 61      |

SOURCES: *Sovetskaia torgovlia*, 1927, No. 7, pp. 7–8; *Torgovye izvestiia*, 1926, No. 99 (September 11), p. 2; *TPG*, 1928, No. 283 (December 6), p. 4; A. Zalkind, ed., *Chastnaia torgovlia Soiuza SSR* (Moscow, 1927), pp. 49, 62, 65; and I. Mingulin, *Puti razvitiia chastnogo kapitala* (Moscow-Leningrad, 1927), pp. 75–76.

percent of the state's *zagotovka* of hides and furs,[36] and undoubtedly considerable quantities of other products followed similar paths to the "socialist" sector.

Though conceding that private *zagotovka* activity was necessary to help acquire raw materials and food, Bolsheviks also harbored serious misgivings about Nepmen in this sphere of the economy. The party's concern went well beyond the risk of some "socialist" enterprises becoming dependent on private suppliers. The private *zagotovka* network was extensive and could offer the peasants free-market prices, in contrast to "socialist" *zagotovka* agents, who were supposed to observe price ceilings.[37] As a result, the Nepmen proved to be effective contenders for the peasants' produce, and thus threatened to block the development of the state's *smychka* with the peasantry. This outcome, Lenin had declared a number of times, would thwart the construction of socialism.

Most ominous of all was the private sector's success in the grain *zagotovka*, for as we have noted several times the Bolsheviks attached great importance to accumulating a large grain surplus (and not at high free-market prices). By 1926, newspaper articles appeared frequently with complaints that Nepmen were disrupting the state's grain collection efforts by offering peasants higher prices and taking precious space in freight trains for private grain shipments.[38] The state moved in this period to reduce the private grain trade by cutting off credit to private *zagotovka* operations; limiting the amount of privately owned grain that could be milled in "socialist" facilities; revoking the leases of many large private mills; forbidding state and cooperative agencies to conduct grain transactions with Nepmen; and restricting private grain shipments by rail.

These measures helped reduce the private share of the grain *zagotovka* to the neighborhood of 15 percent by 1926/27. But as the volume of grain marketed by the peasants lagged farther behind demand, the gap between the official and the free-market grain prices widened sharply, prompting more peasants to seek private buyers. By 1928/29 the Nepmen's portion of the *zagotovka* had rebounded to just under one quarter.[39] This rally at the expense of the grain collection effort of the state was undoubtedly one of the factors that prompted Stalin and his allies to launch their momentous collectivization drive and ban the free trade of grain. Only in this way, they no doubt concluded, would the state obtain a steady, reliable source of grain without having to pay free-market prices for it.[40]

Most Nepmen were rather primitive petty traders and artisans, hardly meriting the label of capitalist so often applied to them in the 1920s. Nevertheless, a few private entrepreneurs (generally those with some capital and prewar business experience) operated on a larger scale, not just in permanent shops and factories but also in comparatively sophisticated ventures such as joint-stock companies and credit institutions. Private investors could participate in two basic types of joint-stock enterprises: those in which all shares were privately owned and those, known as mixed companies, where "socialist" organizations held a portion of the shares.[41] To cite two examples of the first type, in June 1922 the state approved a private joint-stock charter for a company named Lim that manufactured sugar products. According to the agreement, Lim was required to pay 25 percent of its profits to the state. Three years later, Nepmen in Krasnodar formed a joint-stock business (Kubzhirprom) through the sale of twenty-five hundred shares of stock at one hundred rubles each. Kubzhirprom's charter permitted it to buy or lease factories for the production of goods from animal fat, conduct its own *zagotovka* operations for raw materials, and open warehouses, branch offices, and stores.[42]

Many private joint-stock companies were actually little more than previously existing enterprises with new names. Much along the lines of a false cooperative, a joint-stock charter often enabled a firm to obtain goods and credit more easily from "socialist" agencies, since the charter indicated that the business had been deemed respectable, even necessary, by the state. In addition, joint-stock undertakings received certain tax privileges, such as exemption from the leveling tax during the first year of business.[43] In Leningrad, for example, a factory that processed liquid gases managed to avoid nationalization during War Communism and continued to function as a private plant following the introduction of NEP. The owners, deciding to take advantage of the privileges available to joint-stock companies, drew up a charter and formed a board of directors. But then they proceeded to buy all the shares of the "new" enterprise and thus controlled it as completely as ever.[44]

Mixed joint-stock ventures were sometimes initiated by state agencies as a means to acquire additional (private) capital for a wide variety of projects. In the Novonikolaevsk region, for instance, the Siberian Revolutionary Committee declared it essential to involve private capital in the completion of the Achinsko-Minusinskaia railroad; to this end Siberia's first mixed joint-stock company was formed in the summer of 1922. At about the same time, the Northwest Economic Committee (headquartered in Petrograd) helped organize a mixed joint-stock undertaking to exploit natural resources along the Murmansk railroad and promote colonization of the region. As a final illustration, a mixed joint-stock fishing enterprise was chartered the following year in Vladivostok. The state fishing agency (Glavryba) contributed half the capital, with Nepmen supplying the rest. Glavryba retained the rights to 60 percent of any additional shares issued and after five years had the option of buying out its private partners.[45] Despite the opportunities, however, most Nepmen with funds to invest in joint-stock companies shied away from the mixed variety.[46] The prospect of intimate state supervision and the fact that the state was supposed to control at least half the shares in mixed enterprises undoubtedly convinced many private entrepreneurs that it would be less risky and more profitable to invest in purely private undertakings.

By the end of 1924, 114 joint-stock businesses had been chartered. Of these, 44 were funded entirely by the state, 38 were mixed (though 95 percent of the capital came from the "socialist" sector), and 32 were

TABLE 14    PRIVATE JOINT-STOCK COMPANIES
IN THE RSFSR

|      | Number Newly Registered | Number Liquidated |
| --- | --- | --- |
| 1923 | 11 | — |
| 1924 | 5 | 6 |
| 1925 | 24 | 2 |
| 1926 | 50 | 6 |
| 1927 | 18 | 25 |
| 1928 | 1 | 29 |

SOURCE: Andrei Fabrichnyi, *Chastnyi kapital na poroge piatiletki* (Moscow, 1930), p. 17.

private. Only 14 of the private firms were actually in operation. Two years later there were 166 joint-stock companies registered in the RSFSR, 89 of which were private.[47] As these figures suggest, the great majority of private joint-stock enterprises sprouted up during the middle of NEP when the business climate was most encouraging. After only five new private joint-stock ventures were registered in 1924, the figure jumped to 23 (one source reports 24) new private undertakings in 1925 and an additional 50 in 1926.[48] In the following years, reflecting the fate of the private sector in general, the number of new private joint-stock companies plummeted (table 14). As early as 1926/27, even before the onslaught of 1928, the profits of private joint-stock enterprises plunged fully 86 percent compared to the previous year.[49]

Holding true to form, the bulk of private joint-stock investment was concentrated in the lines of consumer products that occupied the energies of nearly all Nepmen—food, textiles, haberdashery, leather goods, soap and candles, and metal tools and utensils. In addition, there were a number of firms active in construction work.[50] According to the charters filed by private joint-stock companies, roughly equal numbers of these businesses were involved in trade and manufacturing. But in reality, many of the "industrial" undertakings simply bought and sold items produced elsewhere.[51]

The number of private joint-stock enterprises was never very large (see table 14). During the years from 1923 to 1928 only 185 such firms registered and operated at one time or another in the entire country. Even in the peak year of 1926, the list of private joint-stock companies was well under 100, numbering 80 on October 1.[52] Of the capital invested in all joint-stock ventures ("socialist," mixed, and private), roughly 70 to 80 percent came from the "socialist" sector.[53] Clearly, then, the vast majority of private capital in trade and manufacturing did not flow through the coffers of private joint-stock enterprises.[54]

Private credit organizations proved somewhat more fruitful than stock sales as a source of funds for the Nepmen. These institutions most often took the form of a Society of Mutual Credit (Obshchestvo Vzaimnogo Kredita or OVK), a sort of credit cooperative. OVKs obtained reserves through members' deposits and state loans, and then lent money to members engaged in various business activities. Five months after a decree of January 24, 1922, permitted private individuals to organize savings and loan cooperatives, the first OVK appeared (in Leningrad).[55] In the months that followed, several others opened around the country, though the largest and most active OVKs tended to be found in Moscow, where private capital was most heavily concentrated.[56]

The number of OVKs grew at a pace that reflected official policy on the Nepmen. The increase was least impressive in 1924 when the state adopted harsher measures toward the private sector, and most vigorous in the comparatively tolerant years of 1925 and 1926:[57]

| 1 Oct 1922 | 7 | 1 Apr 1924 | 66 |
|---|---|---|---|
| 1 Jan 1923 | 12 | 1 Jul 1924 | 72 |
| 1 Apr 1923 | 26 | 1 Oct 1924 | 77 |
| 1 Jul 1923 | 30 | 1 Oct 1925 | 182 |
| 1 Oct 1923 | 47 | 1 May 1926 | 267 |
| 1 Jan 1924 | 55 | 1 Oct 1926 | 280 |

During the period from October 1922 to October 1926 the OVKs' membership swelled from 1,250 to 85,415 people. But as one would anticipate, in the following years these institutions withered and died— along with NEP itself. On the one hand the state began to cut back its loans to OVKs, and on the other, the elimination of private entrepreneurs removed not only another source of funds but also most of the OVKs' customers. In fact, as part of the official campaign to root out the last Nepmen, Sovnarkom decreed in November 1929 that surviving OVKs had to provide tax officials with the names of those private businessmen still receiving loans.[58]

The majority of members in OVKs were private traders, followed by private manufacturers, with state agencies playing only a minuscule role. The dominance of private traders is evident in the distribution of OVK members in October 1923:[59]

| | |
|---|---|
| Private traders | 56.5% |
| Private manufacturers | 17.4% |
| Handicraftsmen | 4.0% |
| "Socialist" organizations | 3.7% |
| Peasants | 2.8% |
| Others | 15.6% |

As a general rule, the larger the business, the more likely its owner was to join an OVK.[60] Sizable operations tended to require more credit than did those of petty vendors and craftsmen, and they were also more likely to have sufficient cash for the required minimum deposit. The membership figures imply that the lion's share of the credit extended by OVKs went to private traders and manufacturers, and this was indeed the case. In 1924/25, for example, these two groups received roughly 80 percent of the loans made by OVKs in the RSFSR.[61] But the distribution of these loans differed considerably in Moscow and the provinces. In the capital, with its comparatively heavy concentration of large private enterprises, the most important clients of OVKs were private wholesalers and factory owners. In the provinces, where substantial Nepmen were few and far between, smaller-scale private retailers assumed this distinction.[62]

Records available for the three-year interval from October 1923 to October 1926 indicate a dramatic surge in the volume of money lent to Nepmen by OVKs. From just 4.8 million rubles in October 1923, the total jumped nearly 1000 percent to 51.4 million rubles in October 1926.[63] Of all loans made to private entrepreneurs by OVKs and state banks, the portion provided by OVKs climbed from roughly 10 percent to 50 percent during this period.[64] Many of the loans from OVKs were actually made with government funds. State banks slowly but steadily increased their loans to OVKs and in this way supplied roughly a third of the capital that OVKs loaned to Nepmen over these years.[65]

Interestingly, when given an opportunity to voice their opinions (in surveys and short newspaper columns), Nepmen revealed a preference for loans from state banks rather than from OVKs. The reason given most frequently was that the state charged less interest, though sometimes the complaints included the extreme dearth of funds in OVKs and

TABLE 15    ANNUAL INTEREST RATES ON
LOANS BY OVKS

|            | October 1926 | October 1927 |
|------------|--------------|--------------|
| Moscow     | 51.0%        | 42.0%        |
| Leningrad  | 40.3         | 30.0         |
| Provinces  | 35.4         | 30.4         |

SOURCE: *Materialy po istorii SSSR. VII. Dokumenty po istorii sovetskogo ob-shchestva* (Moscow, 1959), p. 26.

the expense of becoming a member.[66] In 1925/26 and 1926/27 private entrepreneurs paid interest on loans from state banks at annual rates in the teens—no more than half the rates charged by OVKs (table 15). Frequently, there was not sufficient credit from either the state or the OVKs, forcing Nepmen either to operate strictly on a cash basis or turn to independent moneylenders on the so-called free credit market. Here, funds could generally be obtained, but at astronomical interest rates—sometimes, depending on demand and the political and economic climate, as high as several hundred percent annually.[67]

The formation of joint-stock companies and OVKs signaled a considerable increase in the sophistication of private economic ventures compared to the early months of NEP. But to reiterate, these initiatives remained exceptions in the private sector. Most private entrepreneurs were small-scale traders and manufacturers without the surplus capital or expertise to invest in joint-stock undertakings or OVKs. This, combined with a comparatively hostile government and uncertainty over long-term business prospects, kept such institutions well below their prewar levels of development. Shortly before the Revolution, for example, there were 1,177 OVKs with far more capital than their successors during NEP. Similarly, around the turn of the century, private joint-stock companies were over ten times as numerous as in 1926.[68]

These contrasts are another manifestation of the generalization that private enterprises were much more likely to be simple and small-scale during NEP than before the Revolution. As noted in chapter 4, nearly two thirds of private trading operations before the war were permanent shops, whereas in 1925 only about one quarter of all private traders worked in such facilities. The reasons for this (such as a greater need to be mobile and inconspicuous, difficulties in obtaining goods and credit from the state, the new tax decrees, and uncertainty over the future) stemmed from the Bolsheviks' ambivalent bargain-with-the-devil attitude (and policies) toward the Nepmen. Even in the heyday of 1925/26, when the state offensive at the end of the decade could hardly have been anticipated, taxation and other regulations must have led veteran private entrepreneurs to recall the prerevolutionary years as the golden age.

# An Epilogue and
# an Assessment

Under a system of private trade and in the normal conditions of
the capitalist economy, the consumer, provided he has money, can
procure whatever he wants whenever he wants it. In these matters,
the socialist apparatus of distribution must be at least as good
as that of private trade. But in view of the high degree of
centralization, there is considerable risk that the socialist apparatus
will degenerate into a cumbrous and dilatory machine in which a
great many articles will rot before they reach the consumer.

—*The ABC of Communism*

It is necessary to recognize clearly that the creation of two markets—
legal and illegal—would do more harm to the national economy
than would the "recognition" of private capital.

—Ia. M. Gol'bert

Soviet historians employ the phrase "liquidation of the new bourgeoisie" to characterize the state's treatment of the Nepmen at the end of the
1920s, and as we have seen, the ranks of private entrepreneurs dwindled
precipitously in these years. But a question remains, particularly in the
absence of a mass emigration of the Nepmen.[1] What became of them
after they were forced to close shop? Most often the term *liquidation*
conjures up images of arrest, imprisonment, and even execution. Though
the information on this point is skimpy, it is clear that some Nepmen
suffered these fates. As a general rule, large-scale entrepreneurs and anyone charged with operating surreptitiously (without a license, in a disguised business, by bribing state officials) were the prime candidates for
such punishment. But as the official interpretation of "speculation"
broadened by the end of the decade to include nearly all private trade,
no merchant could consider himself immune from arrest by a zealous
policeman.

It is nearly impossible to estimate how many Nepmen were arrested, sent to labor camps, or shot. As we have seen, a considerable number were hauled into prisons and tortured in an effort to discover any foreign currencies and precious metals they might have hidden away. But official records detailing the number of these victims are, of course, unavailable. Many non-Soviet sources report frequent arrests of Nepmen. *Sotsialisticheskii vestnik,* for example, received a report from Moscow that by 1930 "the majority of private entrepreneurs have been arrested and exiled, forced by torture to surrender all their property." A Russian-American, describing the state's crackdown in 1927–28, observed:

> Again, as in 1924, the victims of the terror were not as yet the Trotskyites, but the so-called *Lishentsi,* a newly coined name for Nepmen. . . .
> At the October terminal I stood for hours watching Chekists load victims on a freight train. Though many of them were well-to-do Nepmen, they were brought to the station stripped of nearly all their belongings. Administrative arrest carried with it confiscation of all property, including what the brutal Chekists considered "excess" food and clothing.
> [Although there was still snow on the ground], the prisoners were being packed into unheated boxcars which would likely become death traps as the train moved deeper into the frost-bound Siberian wastes.[2]

Soviet sources create a different impression. A survey in 1929 of the new occupations of 148 former private traders in Rostov-on-the-Don recorded that only 7.4 percent of these people had been arrested. The same year a similar study of 34,000 former Nepmen in twelve large cities (including Moscow, Leningrad, and Kiev) and a number of other regions reported that 4.5 percent had been convicted of various crimes.[3] Certainly the large majority of Nepmen—petty traders and artisans— were not arrested, but the figures cited above are undoubtedly on the low side. Both surveys were unable to determine the new activities of approximately 40 percent of the former Nepmen under consideration, and some of these people may well have vanished into the labor camps. Further, it is quite possible that these data do not include people detained (but not necessarily arrested), such as persons suspected of possessing foreign currencies and precious metals.

In any case, whatever the actual percentage, most Nepmen did not fall into the hands of the police, and thus we are still faced with the question of their new activities after quitting businesses that had become unprofitable or unsafe, or both. Many of these people—estimates for various regions range from 12 to 30 percent—took up small-scale handicraft work. Such a move from the category of "nonlabor element" to that of "producer" was common at the end of NEP, because it meant reduced taxes and less harassment from the state. Similar considerations prompted other Nepmen, especially those who still had ties to the countryside and nowhere else to go, to work the land. By the beginning of the 1930s, for instance, the Crimean Jewish agricultural colonies were dominated by former private traders driven from commerce. Some ex-Nepmen managed to secure work in state agencies, and still others retired to live with relatives.[4]

People squeezed out of business might also move into black market activity and other forms of concealed entrepreneurial endeavor. These undertakings, many of which had been officially permitted only a year or two earlier, included *zagotovka* operations, trade, moneylending, and currency speculation.[5] As noted previously, investigations at the end of the decade of the new "careers" of former Nepmen were generally unable to account for 40 percent or more of these individuals.[6] Some were doubtless involved in illicit economic activity. It was possible, for example, to conduct furtive petty trade by blending in with the peasant vendors who were allowed to hawk their goods in market squares during the 1930s.[7] Many artisans, too, some of whom had only recently been merchants, conducted trade under the cover of this still-legal occupation. Just as in previous years, false producers' and consumers' cooperatives sprang up, partly to take advantage of the privileges bestowed on such organizations by the state, but now more than ever to mask what had become illegal private trade.[8] Thus some entrepreneurs did not quit the field and continued at least sporadic covert trading and other activities. Chronic shortages and an inefficient state distribution system continued to provide sufficient opportunity and demand for remnants of the Nepmen who were bold, greedy, or desperate enough to conduct business on the black market. Such transactions recalled those of War Communism and marked a return to illicit undertakings as the sphere of legal private enterprise shrank after 1930 essentially to collective farm trade and some handicrafts. Since then, illegal and semilegal economic activity has swollen to enormous proportions in the Soviet Union. The seemingly limitless array of endeavors in this vast "second economy" ranges from long-familiar black market sales of state and privately produced goods to moonlighting by state employees (often with state tools, raw materials, vehicles) and to private dating services and marriage brokers.[9] Ironically, many of the tasks formerly performed by the Nepmen are undertaken by the "second economy" today, over half

a century after the party proclaimed that private entrepreneurs had
ceased to provide useful services to consumers.

As we have seen, the Nepmen played a number of significant economic roles, but nowhere else were they as important as in retail trade.
Soviet consumers everywhere, especially during the first years of NEP
but also throughout the decade, relied on private traders for a large
percentage of their purchases. In a letter to the editor of *Torgovo-
promyshlennaia gazeta* at the end of 1924, a provincial Nepman contended that the local cooperatives were so poorly stocked that "if it were
not for private trade, the population of the province would be left without the most essential goods, such as wheat flour, yeast, wooden spoons,
peasant horse harnesses, and many other things." [10] This was not a claim
applicable only to the most out-of-the-way villages, for even in Moscow,
where the state and cooperative trade network was comparatively dense,
consumers bought over half their goods from private traders in 1925. [11]
In fact, household-budget studies conducted throughout the country in
1925 and 1926 indicate that the very backbone of the Soviet state—government officials and the proletariat—made 36 to 40 percent of their
purchases from Nepmen, and a similar study in Kiev revealed that as
late as 1928/29 these people obtained 44 percent of their food from private traders (51 percent in 1927/28). [12]

The Soviet urban population was heavily dependent on the Nepmen
for two of the most basic necessities—food and clothing. Muscovites,
for example, bought approximately 70 percent of their bread from private traders in 1924, and reports from various regions indicate that
Nepmen were generally most dominant in the trade of dairy products, eggs, meat, fruits, and vegetables, often accounting for 80 percent or more of total retail sales even toward the end of NEP. [13] In the
marketing of manufactured consumer goods, the Nepmen's share of
retail sales was usually largest for haberdashery, textiles, common hard-
ware and other metal products, and leather goods. Urban private traders around the country frequently conducted at least half the sales of
these products, and out in provincial towns their market share was
sometimes over 90 percent. [14] In such localities Nepmen were often the
population's only source of many essential items, and when they were
forced out of business at the end of NEP, aptly termed "trade deserts"
multiplied rapidly.

Given the relatively small number of state and cooperative stores in the countryside, it is not surprising that the Nepmen played an important role here as well, a development that particularly alarmed many Bolsheviks. As we have seen, Lenin argued that the working class had to cement an alliance (*smychka*) with the peasantry (and drive private trade out of the countryside) by supplying the peasants, mainly through cooperatives, with essential manufactured products in return for the peasants' grain. But this plan (or hope), reiterated frequently by party leaders and in the press, enjoyed modest success at best. According to data collected by the Central Statistical Bureau for the middle of NEP, slightly less than 60 percent of the manufactured goods (such as agricultural and construction tools, clothing, footwear, dishes, soap, and processed food products) bought by peasants were sold to them by private traders. Other studies of purchases made by peasants on shopping trips in local bazaars and larger cities and towns in the period from 1925 to 1927 support the data from the Central Statistical Bureau.[15] In other words, the peasants seemed as inclined to form a *smychka* with the Nepmen as with the proletariat.

The Nepmen's success raises another question: How were they able to carve out such a considerable share of the market, even in cities that had large numbers of state and cooperative stores? After all, the prices charged by the Nepmen were often substantially higher than the prices in "socialist" stores. Furthermore, a variety of observers reported that many "ordinary" (i.e., non-Bolshevik) Russians regarded private entrepreneurs, especially the larger-scale operators, with keen distaste. It is difficult to offer generalizations with any confidence concerning popular attitudes toward the Nepmen. But clearly some Russians considered private traders to be greedy, unscrupulous speculators fattening themselves on the country's misery by selling scarce commodities at exorbitant prices. In particular, many people resented the ostentatious flaunting of wealth by some of the more prosperous entrepreneurs.

The state encouraged a negative view of the Nepmen at every opportunity—in movies, literature, posters, cartoons, parades, and schools—no doubt with some effect on the population.[16] Before long, in any event, Nepmen became the butt of many unflattering popular jokes and folk verses (*chastushki*). More ominously, the stereotypical, odious private trader was often assumed to be Jewish, and thus anti-Semitism and popular aversion to the Nepmen fed on each other. The Nepmen therefore found themselves the object not only of pressure from the state but also of animosity from a portion of the population.[17] Eugene Lyons was probably not overstating the case a great deal when he commented:

It [the "new bourgeoisie"] was a class existing by sufferance, despised and insulted by the population and oppressed by the government. It became a curious burlesque on capitalism, self-conscious, shifty, intimidated, and ludicrous. It had money, comforts and other physical advantages, yet remained a pariah element, the butt of popular humor and the target of official discrimination.[18]

Given all this, one might wonder why so many consumers patronized private traders well past the introduction of NEP. The question was posed by the Kiev correspondent of *Torgovo-promyshlennaia gazeta*, who offered the following reasons for the Nepmen's success: (1) people have to waste time standing in lines at the cooperatives, one at the cashier's stand and one at the counter; (2) customers may examine the merchandise and pick out what they want in private shops, but must buy "in the dark" in the cooperatives; (3) being more numerous, private traders are sometimes much closer than the cooperatives and are sometimes willing to sell "out the back door," when by law shops are supposed to be closed; (4) many private traders offer long-term credit with no collateral; (5) private traders attract customers with their solicitousness; and (6) private shops have a better supply of desirable and essential goods than do the cooperatives.[19]

This compendium of the Nepmen's strengths and the "socialist" sector's weaknesses is supported by reports from around the country. We have already seen that the state trade network was much less widespread than the network in the private sector, but as the correspondent in Kiev indicated, it was not simply a question of numbers. The Nepmen were more flexible in adapting to consumer demand and more resourceful in obtaining scarce goods. They had a knack for sniffing out a supply of desirable goods in a particular locality and then acquiring these wares one way or another for shipment to other regions. In contrast, state and cooperative trade agencies were often plagued by inefficiency, indifference, waste, corruption, and a ponderous supply chain.[20]

For these reasons the selection of merchandise in private shops and markets was generally superior to that in "socialist" stores. There were numerous reports, particularly from the provinces, of shortages and even the complete absence of common consumer goods in the cooperatives and state stores, while the local private traders stocked them in abundance (though most often at higher prices).[21] It was usually not a matter of the state and cooperative stores being completely empty, but rather of their offering wares that few people wanted. This situation was sometimes the result of what were called compulsory assortments, that is, shipments of undesirable goods unloaded by factories, trusts, and central state and cooperative supply agencies on individual stores, particularly those out in the countryside. Given the shortage of so many kinds of consumer goods, suppliers had plenty of leverage to compel stores to accept large batches of unmarketable merchandise along with desirable products. The result, which did not escape the attention of Soviet cartoonists, was that rural cooperatives were forced now and then to offer the peasantry expensive high-heeled shoes, elegant women's hats, perfume, umbrellas, and fancy chamber pots. One village cooperative's complaint that it had been sent cigar cases, mirrors, and playing cards was answered by the declaration that it was necessary to spread enlightenment in the villages.[22]

Even when state and cooperative stores had desirable goods, customers were often plagued by lackadaisical, rude, and sometimes even dishonest clerks. A cooperative journal conceded this point, complaining that nearly everyone "has many examples from personal experience illustrating the negative characteristics of cooperative workers." The writer continued, "These examples and complaints create the impression that such cooperative workers are degenerates of some sort, a kind of special race. And worst of all, the examples adduced by consumers are not malicious slander and invention, but the most authentic reality." In another discussion of the cooperatives, one participant remarked:

> Our cooperative workers are often indifferent to everything that goes beyond the horizon of the eight-hour day or that touches their "dignity." How should it be possible for him to give himself any trouble for a customer or to move a little more quickly behind the counter? He is a complete contrast to the sellers in the private shops, who are always obliging, courteous and busy; he is always crusty, indolent and bad-tempered.[23]

Shoppers in state and cooperative stores around the country also complained that the quality of food products was often poor and that they were not permitted to look over the merchandise and select the item or cut they wanted (which one could do in a private shop). The correspondent of *Torgovo-promyshlennaia gazeta* in Tver', for example, reported that the cooperative shops there seemed to operate on the principle of "take what I give you." Consumers also complained that cooperatives sometimes sold various products at different times during the day, which increased the amount of time one had to spend shopping and standing in the lines that were irritating fixtures inside and outside state and cooperative stores. Shopping forays into the "socialist" sector were also frustrating because one could not be sure from day to day if many common products would be in stock.[24] In the face of such lackluster competition, then, it is hardly surprising that the Nepmen were able to attract numerous customers.

But despite the problems plaguing state and cooperative trade, many consumers patronized these stores, as the ubiquitous lines there (called tails) indicated. During the course of NEP the "socialist" sector gained an increasingly large share of retail trade, so that by the end of 1926, the number of private traders and the volume of their trade began to decline in absolute as well as percentage terms. This trend is generally explained in the works of Soviet historians primarily as a consequence of the economic superiority of state and cooperative trade over private trade. I. Ia. Trifonov, for example, argues that "the socialist sector in trade defeated the new bourgeoisie thanks to its economic advantages, and not at all as the result of administrative pressure."[25]

Certainly there were state and cooperative stores that competed effectively with the Nepmen by offering useful products at low prices.[26] Many private entrepreneurs were undoubtedly driven out of business mainly for this reason. It is sometimes difficult, however, to be certain what constitutes fair *economic* competition. If the state denies goods and credit to a Nepman (or grants them only on burdensome terms) and taxes him at a much higher rate than "socialist" enterprises, and if as a result the Nepman cannot compete with state and cooperative stores, can this be considered a consequence of the superiority of "socialist" trade? It was certainly not by chance that the Nepmen's rapid decline coincided with increased pressure from the state. This, rather than economic obsolescence or inferiority, is the key to the Nepmen's demise. Anyone familiar with Soviet shops today (or the cartoons in the Soviet satirical journal *Krokodil*) is aware that many of the problems that hampered state and cooperative trade in the 1920s have yet to be overcome. State trade has *still* not proven itself superior in every way to private trade, which is apparent from the immense "second economy" and the crowds of shoppers in the collective farm markets (*rynki*) where people can sell their own produce and meat at prices higher than those in state stores.

In the heady days of revolutionary struggle, the Bolsheviks did not anticipate the need to tolerate "capitalist" elements for an extended period after the "socialist" revolution. This did not seem a matter for concern, because the party expected its revolution to trigger other socialist revolutions in the more developed countries of the West. Then, according to the scenario, these more advanced countries would supply materiel and expertise to help revive Russia's economy and construct the industrial foundation for socialism. As revolution failed to spread westward, however, this hope became untenable, and the Bolsheviks were forced to rely on Russia's own resources and people to rebuild the shattered economy. By 1921, Lenin was arguing (much more comprehensively than in the spring of 1918) that Russia would require, first of all, a considerable period of time to prepare itself for socialism and, second, the services of the "bourgeoisie."

This general point—that a lengthy transition period, including private economic activity, would be necessary between the "socialist revolution" and the actual attainment of socialism—has been made by communist revolutionaries in other economically backward and ravaged countries, most notably China. Unlike many Bolsheviks during War Communism, Mao and other Chinese Communist leaders did not seriously entertain the hope of plunging immediately into socialism upon assuming power. In an important essay titled "On the People's Democratic Dictatorship," written in June 1949, a few months before the proclamation of the People's Republic (and sounding much like Lenin in 1921–22), Mao stated the need to cooperate with the bourgeoisie in order to rebuild the economy.

> To counter imperialist oppression and to raise her backward economy to a higher level, China must utilize all the factors of urban and rural capitalism that are beneficial and not harmful to the national economy and the people's livelihood; and we must unite with the national bourgeoisie in common struggle. Our present policy is to regulate capitalism, not to destroy it.[27]

The spectacle of a legal and flourishing private sector, however, proved so unpalatable to many in both the Soviet and Chinese Communist parties that harsh campaigns were launched against private entrepreneurs after what turned out to be rather short transition periods (the crackdown in China coming in the mid-1950s).[28] In neither country, though, did the "socialist" sector of the economy manage to provide all the goods and services formerly offered by private entrepreneurs, and in the decades thereafter party policy toward the remaining legal private economic activity (mainly kitchen-garden commerce) fluctuated between sharp disfavor and comparative leniency. Such policy changes have been most evident recently in China and reflect continuing disagreement in the party on the question of whether private enterprise should be extirpated or harnessed. At present, with the ascendancy of Teng Hsiao-p'ing and the "experts" at the expense of the "reds" in the party, private trade has experienced a revival strikingly similar to that during the Soviet New Economic Policy of the 1920s. Not surprisingly, though, some Chinese officials are dismayed by Teng's encouragement of a "market system." Certain senior party members have warned of the spread of "money worship" and corruption, and officials in various localities continue to harass private entrepreneurs.[29]

The leaders of some Eastern European socialist states seem quite willing to accept a considerable private sector for the foreseeable future. Here there is a mutual dependence between the public and private sectors, with neither struggling seriously to eliminate the other. In Hungary, for instance, the state often rents out its smaller, less profitable retail stores and restaurants to private businessmen, who are generally able to run them more effectively. Besides freeing the state of some marginal operations and permitting more private enterprise, this policy helps ensure continued service to consumers in localities where it otherwise might have been reduced.[30] Referring not just to rented businesses, a Hungarian economist with a seat on the Central Committee remarked: "We will never be able to replace this private sector entirely. It has become an integral part of our economy."[31]

Although a similar acceptance of *permanent* participation by the Nepmen in the Soviet economy was anathema to the Bolsheviks in the 1920s, it was clear to all that private entrepreneurs, for better or for worse, played an important role in the economy. Nor was it only consumers who depended on the Nepmen. As we have seen, many state enterprises and agencies relied, at least in part, on private *zagotovka* agents, middlemen-contractors, and retail distributors. This interdependence was much more widespread in the first half of NEP than in the second, though even at the end of the decade some state concerns used (now more discreetly) the services of private entrepreneurs. Further, as supporters of the "new trade practice" contended, the development of private trade (besides providing more tax revenues) effected a division of labor with the state, permitting the state to concentrate more of its personnel and resources on the primary goal of industrialization. Much the same argument was advanced in some Soviet economic journals in support of small-scale private manufacturing of consumer goods, which, it was noted, freed the state to focus its attention on heavy industry.

But this was a minority view in the party. To many Bolsheviks, impatient with Bukharin's gradualism, the presence of private entrepreneurs seemed incompatible with an all-out industrialization campaign and served as an irritating daily reminder that the Revolution had yet to be completed. In 1929 the ideological and economic menace that many party members saw in the Nepmen far outweighed anything that could be said in their favor. At the Fifth All-Union Congress of Soviets (May 1929), for example, a delegate from the Moscow Commodity Exchange suggested that Nepmen loyal to the state be used in industry. He was interrupted by laughter from the floor and cries of "There are no loyal *chastniki* [private entrepreneurs]."[32] Such sentiment in the party, combined with Stalin's political dexterity, vanquished those Bolsheviks—the Right Opposition—who favored a less turbulent construction of socialism and a long-term toleration of the private sector. With the fall of the Right, the Nepmen found themselves the victims of an official campaign every bit as relentless as that directed against private entrepreneurs during War Communism.

The portion of Soviet society (other than the entrepreneurs themselves) most directly hurt by the "liquidation" of the Nepmen was not the government or the party but Soviet consumers. This was not because of any altruism of the Nepmen but because of the shortcomings and lack of resources in the "socialist" consumer goods sector. The Bolsheviks had always been most keenly perceptive of the greed and other abuses that could accompany private trade (and industry) and felt confident that all of this would be eradicated with the coming of socialism. In theory, socialist trade seemed far more desirable—a public service supplying goods at the lowest possible prices—compared to the anarchy of unscrupulous "speculators" extorting the highest prices the market could bear. But in practice, as we have seen, the problems besetting state and cooperative trade prevented it from eliminating its rival in the private sector. Consumers were (and still are) often faced with the choice of either buying a scarce item at a high price from a private entrepreneur or not finding it (or only finding it at the end of a long wait in line) in a state store.

The inability of the state to satisfy consumer demand has left private entrepreneurs ample opportunity for profit, from the black market of War Communism to the "second economy" today. This economic activity has presented the party with a thorny dilemma ever since the Revolution, the same dilemma with which the Chinese Communist party is now grappling. Private business transactions, although ideologically grating on the one hand, have, on the other, proved an effective means of stimulating the production and distribution of essential commodities. Little wonder, then, that in the years after 1917 the state's policies toward the private sector have fluctuated between concern for ideological purity and emphasis on economic expediency. Today, once again, Mikhail Gorbachev is recruiting private enterprise to breathe life into the Soviet economy. Recalling the dawn of NEP, thousands of new ventures have sprung forth, now bearing the name "cooperative." Terms such as "capitalist"—applied by Lenin to the Nepman—are no longer officially acceptable for legal private undertakings. Nearly three-quarters of a century after the Revolution, the time has passed for "building communism with bourgeois hands." But, sanitized in their cooperative labels, the new entrepreneurs have produced a range of responses powerfully echoing debate in the 1920s. Critics associate cooperatives with high prices, profiteering, exploitation, and the appearance of gaudy new millionaires, while defenders stress the need to encourage private endeavor in order to boost productivity above the dismal level endemic in the state sector. A recent column in the *Moscow News* exudes the practical spirit of NEP. "Today we invite people to form cooperatives, tomorrow we blast them to hell. As a result, we are unable to feed ourselves." [33] At the same time, the Party First Secretary in Krasnodar Territory voiced sentiments dominant at Party meetings in 1929. "Cooperatives are a social evil, a malignant tumor. Let us combat this evil in a united front. . . . We can't remain inactive when people are protesting against this vandalism and shamelessness." [34]

Currently, with little but deepening hardship to show for Gorbachev's economic policies, hostility toward cooperatives appears widespread. The new private entrepreneurs, commonly viewed as fattening themselves on an economy of scarcity, have drawn strong disapproval in public opinion polls and speeches in the Supreme Soviet. Predictably, both foes and promoters of cooperatives enlist the past to support their views. Critics often seek to "rehabilitate" accomplishments of the Stalinist command economy, or attack "speculators" by arguing that shops were full before cooperatives appeared. Advocates have defended the unleashing of private initiative by asking: "Hasn't our mistake of abolishing NEP served as a lesson?" [35] There seems little doubt that the Soviet Union's economic disarray, ethnic unrest, and political ferment promise a turbulent interval in which people of diverse outlooks will continue to search the past for guidance. Amidst their cries of peril and promises of reform, it will be interesting to observe what "lessons" they choose to derive from NEP.

# Notes

## INTRODUCTION

1. V. I. Lenin, *Polnoe sobranie sochinenii,* 5th ed., 55 vols. (Moscow, 1958–65) (hereafter cited as Lenin, *PSS*), 36:176–178 (emphasis in the original).

2. Ibid., 36:158–159, 179.

3. Ibid., 36:311. See also 36:305, 310.

4. For additional examples of Lenin's arguments on this need for the bourgeoisie (from his pamphlets and speeches during the next two years), see ibid., 38:54, 58; 39:314; 40:218.

5. *The Marx-Engels Reader,* ed. Robert C. Tucker (New York, 1972), p. 339.

6. Lenin, *PSS,* 11:37.

7. Ibid., 11:43–44.

8. Ibid., 31:151.

9. Ibid., 32:233.

10. Ibid., 34:155.

11. E. H. Carr, *The Bolshevik Revolution,* 3 vols. (London, 1950–53; reprint, Harmondsworth, 1973), 2:14, n. 7.

12. Lenin, *PSS,* 37:417–418. For similar remarks (in a speech and an article) in 1919 and 1920, see ibid., 39:121; 41:108. On occasion Lenin demanded that "speculators" be apprehended and shot on the spot. See ibid., 35:311–312.

13. See, for example, speeches, articles, and pamphlets in ibid., 37:415–416; 38:61–62; 39:168–169; 39:407.

14. See speeches, articles, and pamphlets in ibid., 38:64–65; 39:170; 39:315; 39:357–358; 39:408.

15. Ibid., 38:374.

16. Ibid., 39:122–123 (speech at a Moscow conference of representatives from factory committees, trade unions, and a cooperative in July 1919); 39:154 (a letter in *Pravda* and *Izvestiia,* August 28, 1919).

17. Ibid., 39:153.

18. *Sobranie uzakonenii i rasporiazhenii. 1917–1949* (Moscow, 1920–50) (hereafter cited as *SU*), 1917–1918, No. 5, art. 73; *SU,* 1917–1918, No. 10, art. 150; *SU,* 1917–1918, No. 29, art. 385; Maurice Dobb, *Soviet Economic Development Since 1917* (New York–London, 1966), p. 84.

19. *SU,* 1917–1918, No. 47, art. 559.

20. Carr, *Bolshevik Revolution*, 2:103–104.

21. *SU*, 1920, No. 93, art. 512.

22. V. M. Selunskaia, ed., *Izmeneniia sotsial'noi struktury sovetskogo obshchestva. oktiabr' 1917–1920* (Moscow, 1976), p. 259; I. Ia. Trifonov, *Klassy i klassovaia bor'ba v SSSR v nachale nepa*, Vol. 2, *Podgotovka ekonomicheskogo nastupleniia na novuiu burzhuaziiu* (Leningrad, 1969), p. 44; and Alec Nove, *An Economic History of the U.S.S.R.* (London, 1969; reprint, Harmondsworth, 1972), pp. 69–70. For more on the state's inability to control artisans, see Thomas F. Remington, "Democracy and Development in Bolshevik Socialism, 1917–1921" (Ph.D. diss., Yale University, 1978), pp. 282–285.

23. Lenin, *PSS*, 36:505, 510.

24. *SU*, 1917–1918, No. 83, art. 879.

25. *SU*, 1917–1918, No. 84, art. 884; *Na novykh putiakh. Itogi novoi ekonomicheskoi politiki 1921–1922 g.g.* (Moscow, 1923), *vypusk* I, p. 385.

26. Victor Serge, *Memoirs of a Revolutionary 1901–1941* (London, 1967; reprint, 1975), pp. 79, 115 (emphasis in the original). See also Philip Gibbs, *Since Then* (London, 1930), p. 335; Pitirim A. Sorokin, *Hunger as a Factor in Human Affairs* (Gainesville, Fla., 1975), p. xxxiv. Thomas Remington reports that a witticism of the day was "The nationalization of trade means that the whole nation is trading." Remington, "Democracy and Development," p. 278.

27. *Planovoe khoziaistvo*, 1927, No. 11, pp. 95–96; M. M. Zhirmunskii, *Chastnyi torgovyi kapital v narodnom khoziaistve SSSR* (Moscow, 1927), p. 39; Trifonov, *Klassy*, 2:45; and L. N. Kritsman, "Geroicheskii period velikoi russkoi revoliutsii (opyt analiza t. n. voennogo kommunizma)," *Vestnik kommunisticheskoi akademii*, 1924, No. 9, p. 118.

28. Serge, *Memoirs*, p. 74; Carr, *Bolshevik Revolution*, 2:242, 245; Selunskaia, *Izmeneniia*, p. 255; and Kritsman, "Geroicheskii period," p. 119. On the Moscow Soviet's grudging acceptance of some private trade in November 1920, see Remington, "Democracy and Development," p. 281.

29. *Mestnoe khoziaistvo* (Kiev), 1925, No. 3 (December), p. 71; Carr, *Bolshevik Revolution*, 2:242; and Kritsman, "Geroicheskii period," p. 121.

30. Serge, *Memoirs*, pp. 115–116.

31. V. P. Dmitrenko, *Torgovaia politika sovetskogo gosudarstva posle perekhoda k NEPu 1921–1924 gg.* (Moscow, 1971), p. 142; Ilya Ehrenburg, *First Years of Revolution, 1918–21* (London, 1962), p. 143; and Carr, *Bolshevik Revolution*, 2:243–244.

32. M. M. Zhirmunskii, *Chastnyi kapital v tovarooborote* (Moscow, 1924), pp. 3–4.

33. Serge, *Memoirs*, p. 71.

34. *Dela i dni*, 1920, *kniga pervaia*, p. 495; Sorokin, *Hunger*, p. 196.

35. *Dela i dni*, 1920, *kniga pervaia*, p. 495; Patrick G. Friel, "Theater and Revolution: The Struggle for Theatrical Autonomy in Soviet Russia (1917–1920)" (Ph.D. diss., University of North Carolina at Chapel Hill, 1977), p. 135; and Sorokin, *Hunger*, pp. 111–112, 140, 230–231.

36. Quoted in Friel, "Theater and Revolution," p. 196.

37. Ibid., pp. 190–191.

38. Angelica Balabanoff, *My Life as a Rebel* (New York, 1938), p. 204. After three years of such privation, Ilya Ehrenburg and his wife had difficulty adjusting at once to the relative abundance of food in Latvia when they left Russia briefly at the beginning of 1921. "I do not know whether the portions [in a restaurant in Riga] were so large or whether we had become unused to eating, but I could not manage even half my beefsteak. I felt rather sad: here was the piece of meat I had dreamt of for so long, and I could not eat it." Ehrenburg, *First Years of Revolution*, p. 181.

39. Murray Feshbach, "The Soviet Union: Population Trends and Dilemmas," *Population Bulletin* 37 (August 1982): 6–7; *Dela i dni*, 1920, *kniga pervaia*, p. 496.

40. Seth Singleton, "The Tambov Revolt (1920–1921)," *Slavic Review* 25 (September 1966): 498–499; Ehrenburg, *First Years of Revolution*, p. 176.

41. Lenin, *PSS*, 44:159.

42. Ibid., 44:415. In an article published in *Pravda* on November 6–7, 1921, Lenin wrote that Russia, "one of the most backward capitalist countries, tried in one stroke to organize and put into practice the *new* link [direct commodity exchange orchestrated by

the state] between industry and agriculture, but could not accomplish this by 'direct assault' [during War Communism] and now [during NEP] must accomplish it with slow, gradual, careful 'siege' operations." Ibid., 44:226–227.

43. Ibid., 44:203–204.

44. "We had no alternative besides total and rapid monopoly, going as far as seizing all surplus stocks without any compensation. We could not handle this task in any other way." Ibid., 43:79.

45. "We overdid nationalization of trade and industry and shutting down local exchange. Was this a mistake? Without doubt. In this respect we have done much that was simply wrong." Lenin added that the civil war forced the party to take certain wartime economic measures. "But it should not be concealed in our agitation and propaganda that we went farther than was theoretically and politically necessary." Ibid., 43:63–64. For a discussion of the views of some Western scholars, see Paul C. Roberts, "'War Communism': A Re-examination," *Slavic Review* 29 (June 1970): 238–261.

46. Nove, *Economic History,* pp. 79–80.

## CHAPTER 1

1. F. I. Dan, *Dva goda skitanii* (Berlin, 1922), p. 253; Alexander Berkman, *The Bolshevik Myth (Diary 1920–1922)* (New York, 1925), pp. 304–305.

2. Alexandre Barmine, *One Who Survived: The Life Story of a Russian Under the Soviets* (New York, 1945), p. 125; V. A. Arkhipov and L. F. Morozov, *Bor'ba protiv kapitalisticheskikh elementov v promyshlennosti i torgovle. 20-e—nachalo 30-kh godov* (Moscow, 1978), p. 61; Iu. S. Kondurushkin, *Chastnyi kapital pered sovetskim sudom* (Moscow-Leningrad, 1927), p. 26; Anton Karlgren, *Bolshevist Russia* (London, 1927), p. 126; and Victor Serge, *Memoirs of a Revolutionary 1901–1941* (London, 1967; reprint, 1975), pp. 147, 196.

3. V. I. Lenin, *Polnoe sobranie sochinenii,* 5th ed., 55 vols. (Moscow, 1958–65) (hereafter cited as Lenin, *PSS*), 44:220.

4. *Desiatyi s"ezd RKP(b). Mart 1921 goda: stenograficheskii otchet* (Moscow, 1963), p. 406; Lenin, *PSS,* 43:64, 70; 44:310.

5. V. P. Dmitrenko, *Torgovaia politika sovetskogo gosudarstva posle perekhoda k NEPu 1921–1924 gg.* (Moscow, 1971), p. 31; Lenin, *PSS,* 43:62–63, 147–148.

6. L. N. Kritsman, *Tri goda novoi ekonomicheskoi politiki* (Moscow, 1924), p. 27; V. A. Tsybul'skii, "Tovaroobmen mezhdu gorodom i derevnei v pervye mesiatsy nepa," *Istoriia SSSR,* 1968, No. 4, pp. 31–41; Arkhipov and Morozov, *Bor'ba,* p. 26; I. Ia. Trifonov, *Klassy i klassovaia bor'ba v SSSR v nachale nepa,* Vol. 2, *Podgotovka ekonomicheskogo nastupleniia na novuiu burzhuaziiu* (Leningrad, 1969), p. 194; and *Pravda,* August 16, 1921, p. 1.

7. Lenin, *PSS,* 44:207–208, 214–215.

8. Ibid., 43:229; 44:161.

9. Ibid., 43:233, 354. See also pp. 220–221, 270–271, and 309.

10. Ibid., 45:82, 98.

11. Ibid., 43:232 (emphasis in the original).

12. Ibid., 44:167.

13. *KPSS v rezoliutsiiakh i resheniiakh s"ezdov, konferentsii i plenumov TsK,* 8th ed. (Moscow, 1970–) (hereafter cited as *KPSS*), 2:257; *Resheniia partii i pravitel'stva po khoziaistvennym voprosam* (Moscow, 1967–), 1:212–214. A decree from the Council of People's Commissars (Sovnarkom) on March 28 set the 1921/22 grain tax at somewhat over half the previously established requisition target, in part to ensure the peasants a surplus to trade. *Sobranie uzakonenii i rasporiazhenii. 1917–1949* (Moscow, 1920–50) (hereafter cited as *SU*), 1921, No. 26, art. 148. For similar decrees concerning other agricultural products, see *SU,* 1921, No. 38, art. 204; *SU,* 1921, No. 48, art. 235 and art. 239. Sovnarkom issued another decree on March 28 (*SU,* 1921, No. 26, art. 149) calling for the rapid implementation of VTsIK's decree of March 21 and providing some details on how and in what regions this was to be done.

14. *Resheniia partii i pravitel'stva po khoziaistvennym voprosam,* 1:233–234; *SU,* 1921, No. 57, art. 356. During 1922, decrees were issued throughout the land by local officials specifying the hours that trade could be conducted, when the lunch break was to be, what types of trade could be conducted on holidays, what places would be designated for markets and bazaars, what sanitation measures were to be observed, and so on. *Na novykh putiakh. Itogi novoi ekonomicheskoi politiki 1921–1922 g.g.* (Moscow, 1923), *vypusk* I, p. 416.

15. *SU,* 1921, No. 59, art. 403; *Pravda,* August 12, 1921, p. 1.

16. *SU,* 1921, No. 60, art. 410; *Zakony o chastnom kapitale. Sbornik zakonov, instruktsii, prikazov i raz"iasnenii,* comp. B. S. Mal'tsman and B. E. Ratner (Moscow, 1928), pp. 247–248. Another decree indicates that private individuals were publishing books in the late summer of 1921, without interference from the authorities. *SU,* 1921, No. 61, art. 430.

17. *Ekonomicheskaia zhizn' SSSR. Khronika sobytii i faktov 1917–1965,* 2 vols. (Moscow, 1967), 1:103; *SU,* 1922, No. 6, art. 58; *SU,* 1922, No. 12, art. 110; *SU,* 1922, No. 28, art. 318; *SU,* 1922, No. 34, art. 399; *SU,* 1922, No. 41, art. 488; *SU,* 1922, No. 71, art. 905; and *Torgovo-promyshlennaia gazeta* (hereafter cited as *TPG*), 1922, No. 69 (June 2), p. 2. See also *Resheniia partii i pravitel'stva po khoziaistvennym voprosam,* 1:313–315; *Na novykh putiakh, vypusk* I, p. 402.

18. *Resheniia partii i pravitel'stva po khoziaistvennym voprosam,* 1:232–233; *SU,* 1921, No. 48, art. 240; *SU,* 1921, No. 53, art. 313; *Zakony o chastnom kapitale,* pp. 182–183; and *KPSS,* 2:269. Sovnarkom announced that producers' cooperatives would be given privileged treatment with regard to state orders, supplies, and credit in order to encourage independent artisans to join. Most artisans, however, remained outside these cooperatives throughout NEP. See *Zakony o chastnom kapitale,* pp. 186–187 for a decree of December 10, 1921, that affirmed the May 17 denationalization decree.

19. *KPSS,* 2:305; *SU,* 1921, No. 63, art. 458; *SU,* 1921, No. 68, art. 527; and *SU,* 1921, No. 72, art. 576 and art. 577.

20. *Zakony o chastnom kapitale,* pp. 6–7, 19–20. The entire Civil Code may be found in *SU,* 1922, No. 71, art. 904. Similar codes were adopted by the other republics. Nepmen renting or leasing a state-owned factory were required to insure it fully, keep it repaired, and get production up to the level agreed upon in the lease. If the lease did not specify production level and a time limit by which it was to be reached, the lease was invalid. *Zakony o chastnom kapitale,* p. 22. For more on the number of workers permitted in private factories, see *Ekonomicheskoe obozrenie,* 1926, August, p. 119; *Zakony o chastnom kapitale,* pp. 183, 253; *Finansy i narodnoe khoziaistvo,* 1927, No. 19, pp. 29–30; *TPG,* 1923, No. 140 (June 26), p. 1; and *Torgovo-promyshlennyi vestnik,* 1923, No. 7–8, p. 3.

21. Lenin, *PSS,* 43:159.

22. Ibid., 43:277. See also 43:160, 313–314; 45:266.

23. Ibid., 43:25; 44:163.

24. Ibid., 45:387–388. See also 44:160, 164; 45:77–78, 81.

25. Ibid., 44:160; 45:86.

26. Ibid., 43:27, 329. In the same vein, Lenin told the Third All-Russian Food Conference in June 1921: "I would like to remind you of the decision of the last [Tenth] Party Conference that dealt specifically with the question of the New Economic Policy. The Party Conference was urgently convened in order to convince all comrades completely that this policy, as was noted at the Conference, has been adopted seriously and for a long time, and to prevent any wavering on this score in the future." Ibid., 43:353–354.

27. Ibid., 43:330. On another occasion at the Tenth Party Conference Lenin stated that NEP had been adopted for "a long period, measured in years." The following month he guessed that it would take "at least ten years" to restore the country's industrial base. Ibid., 43:333, 357. By the end of 1921, Lenin appeared to think that NEP could very well last twenty-five years or more. "Either you learn to work at a different tempo," he lectured the Ninth All-Russian Congress of Soviets in December, "reckoning the task in terms of decades, not months, and relying on the masses that are worn out and cannot perform their daily work at a revolutionary-heroic tempo—either you learn this or you should be

called geese." In one of his last works, titled "On Cooperation" and written in January 1923, Lenin again seemed to be thinking in terms of more than one decade. In order to reach socialism, he wrote, the population would have to understand the advantages of the cooperatives and want to participate. For this, a "whole historical epoch," lasting "one or two decades," would be needed. Without this epoch of "cultural development," he stressed, "we will not achieve our goal." Presumably, then, Lenin anticipated that private trade would exist for "one or two decades," until consumers were convinced of the superiority of the cooperative system. Ibid., 44:325; 45:372.

28. Ibid., 45:8, 83–84 (emphasis in the original). For more on NEP as a retreat, see ibid., 44:206–208, 229; 45:87, 92, 302.

29. Ibid., 44:311.

30. I. V. Stalin, *Sochineniia*, 13 vols. (Moscow, 1946–52), 12:171.

31. Lenin, *PSS*, 44:159–160; *Desiatyi s"ezd*, p. 407.

32. Lenin, *PSS*, 45:117–118.

33. "State capitalism," Lenin declared at the Eleventh Party Congress, "is capitalism which we will be able to restrict, for which we can set up limits." Or, as he proclaimed on another occasion, the state must try "to control the capitalists with an appropriate bridle, in order to direct capitalism into the state channel and create a capitalism subordinate to the state and serving it." Ibid., 44:161; 45:85. See also 43:221–223.

34. The best source for Lenin's concept of state capitalism in 1918 is his essay "'Left-Wing' Childishness and the Petty Bourgeois Mentality" in ibid., 36:283–314.

35. *Zakony o chastnom kapitale*, pp. 7, 165–166, 168, 187–190; *SU*, 1923, No. 24, art. 285; *Direktivy KPSS i sovetskogo pravitel'stva po khoziaistvennym voprosam. 1917–1957 gody*, 4 vols. (Moscow, 1957–58), 1:371–372; *Ekonomicheskaia zhizn' SSSR*, 1:115; and J. Leyda, *Kino. A History of the Russian and Soviet Film* (London, 1960), p. 167. A decree of July 10, 1923, added more teeth to some of the statutes in the Criminal Code concerning economic activity. According to the revised version of article 137, for example, "malicious" (*zlostnyi*) raising of prices by buying up goods or withholding them from the market was punished with imprisonment for not less than six months and loss of part of one's property if only one person was involved. If a number of people worked together in this way to raise prices, the punishment was imprisonment for not less than two years, confiscation of all property, and loss of the right to trade. *SU*, 1923, No. 48, art. 479.

36. *SU*, 1921, No. 56, art. 354; *SU*, 1922, No. 16, art. 162; Dmitrenko, *Torgovaia politika*, p. 156; *Torgovaia gazeta*, 1922, No. 8 (February 9), p. 3; and Trifonov, *Klassy*, 2:188.

37. *SU*, 1921, No. 56, art. 354. Small cooperatives and cartels were exempt from this tax. The others were given a number of tax breaks during NEP as the state tried to entice producers, traders, and consumers out of the private sector. In July 1922, for example, Sovnarkom reduced the business tax on cooperatives by 50 percent if they sold to members only, and by 25 percent if they sold to the general public. *SU*, 1922, No. 45, art. 559.

38. *SU*, 1922, No. 17, art. 180; *SU*, 1923, No. 5, art. 88 and 89; V. P. D'iachenko, *Istoriia finansov SSSR (1917–1950 gg.)* (Moscow, 1978), pp. 117–119; and Dmitrenko, *Torgovaia politika*, p. 160.

39. *SU*, 1922, No. 76, art. 940; Dmitrenko, *Torgovaia politika*, p. 158; and D'iachenko, *Istoriia finansov*, pp. 119–120.

40. *SU*, 1921, No. 80, art. 693; *SU*, 1923, No. 4, art. 77; Dmitrenko, *Torgovaia politika*, pp. 158, 160–162; I. Ia. Trifonov, *Likvidatsiia ekspluatatorskikh klassov v SSSR* (Moscow, 1975), p. 204; and E. H. Carr, *The Bolshevik Revolution*, 3 vols. (London, 1950–53; reprint, Harmondsworth, 1973), 2:354 (text and footnote).

41. Trifonov, *Klassy*, 2:177–178; Dmitrenko, *Torgovaia politika*, p. 157.

42. *SU*, 1922, No. 22, art. 244; *SU*, 1922, No. 34, art. 400; and *SU*, 1923, No. 100, art. 998; Trifonov, *Klassy*, 2:82, 176–177; and Dmitrenko, *Torgovaia politika*, pp. 94–95.

43. Lenin, *PSS*, 44:322–323, 328–329, 337, 397.

44. Ibid., 44:337.

45. See, for example, *TPG*, 1922, No. 69 (June 2), p. 1; 1922, No. 119 (August 2), p. 1; *Ekonomicheskoe stroitel'stvo*, 1923, No. 6–7, p. 83.

46. *TPG*, 1923, No. 113 (May 24), p. 2. For more complaints from Nepmen concerning the state's unclear and unstable policy toward the private sector, see *Torgovye izvestiia*, 1925, No. 87 (November 10), p. 2; 1926, No. 98 (September 9), p. 2; *TPG*, 1923, No. 86 (April 20), p. 2; 1923, No. 113 (May 24), p. 2; and G. P. Paduchev, *Chastnyi torgovets pri novoi ekonomicheskoi politike (po dannym biudzhetnogo obsledovaniia)* (Voronezh, 1926), p. 63.

47. Lenin, *PSS*, 43:237; *SU*, 1921, No. 55, art. 346.

48. Ilya Ehrenburg, *Memoirs: 1921–1941* (New York, 1966), p. 68.

49. Lenin, *PSS*, 52:217–218; Dmitrenko, *Torgovaia politika*, pp. 58–59; and *Izvestiia*, May 17, 1921, p. 2.

50. *SU*, 1921, No. 49, art. 256; Dmitrenko, *Torgovaia politika*, pp. 151–153. An article in *Ekonomicheskaia zhizn'* warned local officials not to be too eager to ban private trade during campaigns to collect the tax in kind. *Ekonomicheskaia zhizn'*, 1922, No. 196 (September 2), p. 1. Another article in the same paper pointed out that bans on private trade had been ordered in various regions in 1921 but had not proven effective. *Ekonomicheskaia zhizn'*, 1922, No. 186 (August 19), p. 1.

51. Dmitrenko, *Torgovaia politika*, p. 155.

52. *TPG*, 1923, No. 70 (March 29), p. 4; Dmitrenko, *Torgovaia politika*, pp. 153–154.

53. *Torgovaia gazeta*, 1922, No. 31 (March 30), p. 4; 1922, No. 42 (April 27), p. 2.

54. *Ekonomicheskaia zhizn'*, 1922, No. 205 (September 13), p. 2; *Torgovaia gazeta*, 1922, No. 42 (April 27), p. 2; and *Na novykh putiakh, vypusk* I, p. 417.

55. *Torgovaia gazeta*, 1922, No. 42 (April 27), p. 2; Paduchev, *Chastnyi torgovets*, p. 53.

56. *Ekonomicheskoe obozrenie*, 1926, March, pp. 150, 153.

57. *Torgovaia gazeta*, 1922, No. 35 (April 6), p. 3; *Na novykh putiakh, vypusk* I, pp. 414–415.

58. Frank Alfred Golder and Lincoln Hutchinson, *On the Trail of the Russian Famine* (Stanford, 1927), pp. 227–228.

59. Dmitrenko, *Torgovaia politika*, pp. 151, 153; A. M. Ginzburg, ed., *Chastnyi kapital v narodnom khoziaistve SSSR. Materialy kommissii VSNKh SSSR* (Moscow-Leningrad, 1927), p. 294; *Zakony o chastnoi promyshlennosti*, comp. A. E. Vorms and S. V. Mints (Moscow, 1924), pp. 26–27; *SU*, 1921, No. 79, art. 684; D. I. Mishanin, "Arenda gosudarstvennykh predpriiatii chastnymi predprinimateliami, kak odna iz form gosudarstvennogo kapitalizma v ekonomike perekhodnogo perioda ot kapitalizma k sotsializmu v SSSR," in E. A. Messerle and D. I. Mishanin, *Metodicheskoe posobie po politekonomii* (Alma-Ata, 1961), p. 64; and Carr, *Bolshevik Revolution*, 2:300.

CHAPTER 2

1. *Torgovye izvestiia*, 1926, No. 98 (September 9), p. 2. There is a similar complaint on this page from another private firm.

2. Ibid., 1925, No. 87 (November 10), p. 2. For additional reports on the Nepmen's unhappiness with fluctuating state policies (generally in the realm of taxation and the supply of goods), see *Torgovo-promyshlennaia gazeta* (hereafter cited as *TPG*), 1923, No. 86 (April 20), p. 2; 1923, No. 113 (May 24), p. 2; G. P. Paduchev, *Chastnyi torgovets pri novoi ekonomicheskoi politike (po dannym biudzhetnogo obsledovaniia)* (Voronezh, 1926), p. 63.

3. A. M. Ginzburg, ed., *Chastnyi kapital v narodnom khoziaistve SSSR. Materialy kommissii VSNKh SSSR* (Moscow-Leningrad, 1927), p. 112. The author of an article on private credit institutions wrote: "The position of these institutions and the [state's] policy concerning them have been extremely unsteady for the last five years of their postrevolutionary existence, reflecting the frequent change of the Soviet government's entire policy toward private capital." F. Lifshits, "Osnovnye linii kredita i kreditnoi politiki za 1917–1927 gg," in *Finansovaia politika sovetskoi vlasti za 10 let. Sbornik statei* (Moscow, 1928), p. 82. See also Ts. M. Kron, *Chastnaia torgovlia v SSSR* (Moscow, 1926), p. 4.

4. Paul Scheffer, *Seven Years in Soviet Russia* (New York, 1932), p. 174. Scheffer's figure of 300,000 may be too high (depending on what he means by "private enterprises"), but his general characterization of the period is reliable.

5. William Reswick, *I Dreamt Revolution* (Chicago, 1952), pp. 58–59, 61.

6. Walter Duranty, *I Write as I Please* (New York, 1935), pp. 210–211; Walter Duranty, *Duranty Reports Russia* (New York, 1934), pp. 152–153; Anton Karlgren, *Bolshevist Russia* (London, 1927), pp. 144–145. David Dallin labeled this policy change "a new course and partial abolition of NEP." *Sotsialisticheskii vestnik* (Berlin), 1924, No. 10, pp. 6–7. See also 1924, No. 2, pp. 6–7; 1924, No. 19, p. 12.

7. Ginzburg, *Chastnyi kapital*, pp. 171–172.

8. S. O. Zagorskii, *K sotsializmu ili k kapitalizmu?* (Paris, 1927), pp. 125–126; I. V. Stalin, *Sochineniia*, 13 vols. (Moscow, 1946–52), 6:244.

9. Duranty, *I Write*, pp. 145–147; Duranty, *Duranty Reports*, p. 108; Reswick, *I Dreamt*, pp. 53, 56; F. A. Mackenzie, *Russia Before Dawn* (London, 1923), p. 212; Anna Louise Strong, *The First Time in History* (New York, 1924), pp. 23, 33; Edwin W. Hullinger, *The Reforging of Russia* (New York, 1925), pp. 65, 69, 278, 326–327, 334–335; Richard Eaton, *Under the Red Flag* (New York, 1924), p. 39; Markoosha Fischer, *My Lives in Russia* (New York, 1944), p. 10; Pitirim A. Sorokin, *Leaves from a Russian Diary—and Thirty Years After* (Boston, 1950), p. 271; Allan Monkhouse, *Moscow, 1911–1933* (Boston, 1934), pp. 134–135; Iu. S. Kondurushkin, *Chastnyi kapital pered sovetskim sudom* (Moscow-Leningrad, 1927), p. 40; and *Torgovo-promyshlennyi vestnik*, 1923, No. 4 (June 9), p. 9. For some photographs of the annual *"Derbi"* (for trotters) in Moscow, see *Illiustrirovannaia Rossiia* (Paris), 1926, No. 33, p. 4; 1927, No. 33, p. 5; 1928, No. 33, p. 9. For a description of a wild party thrown by a wealthy Nepman, see Reswick, *I Dreamt*, pp. 54–56. "He [the Nepman] and his beautiful mistress, the daughter of a former governor general of Petrograd, had purchased from the government a well-preserved mansion and were entertaining on a scale reminiscent of Tsarist days." NEP's night life figured prominently in many literary works of the period. For a sampling, see Valentin Kataev, *Embezzlers* (Ann Arbor, 1975), pp. 166–167, 171, 194–196; Vladimir Lidin, *The Price of Life* (Westport, Conn., 1973), pp. 119–122, 191–194, 212–215, 219–226; Anatoly Marienhoff, *Cynics* (Westport, Conn., 1973), pp. 146, 174–180; and Boris Lavrenyov, "The Heavenly Cap," in *The Fatal Eggs and Other Soviet Satire* (New York, 1965; reprint, 1968), p. 175.

10. Duranty, *I Write*, pp. 145–146.

11. Frank Alfred Golder and Lincoln Hutchinson, *On the Trail of the Russian Famine* (Stanford, 1927), p. 159.

12. Duranty, *I Write*, p. 209; *Sotsialisticheskii vestnik* (Berlin), 1924, No. 2, p. 7.

13. Alexander Berkman, *The Bolshevik Myth (Diary 1920–1922)* (New York, 1925), pp. 304–305.

14. Victor Serge, *Memoirs of a Revolutionary 1901–1941* (London, 1967; reprint, 1975), pp. 198–199.

15. Reswick, *I Dreamt*, pp. 59, 61.

16. L. N. Kritsman, *Tri goda novoi ekonomicheskoi politiki* (Moscow, 1924), p. 34. During the summer of 1924, *Torgovo-promyshlennaia gazeta* ran numerous articles on the campaign to eliminate private wholesalers.

17. Ginzburg, *Chastnyi kapital*, pp. 171–172; I. Ia. Trifonov, *Klassy i klassovaia bor'ba v SSSR v nachale nepa*, Vol. 2, *Podgotovka ekonomicheskogo nastupleniia na novuiu burzhuaziiu* (Leningrad, 1969), pp. 160–162; *Ekonomicheskoe obozrenie*, 1925, March, pp. 278–279, and April, p. 198; and S. L. Fridman, *Chastnyi kapital na denezhnom rynke* (Moscow, 1925), pp. 30, 32, 33, 46.

18. I. Mingulin, *Puti razvitiia chastnogo kapitala* (Moscow-Leningrad, 1927), pp. 59–61; Kron, *Chastnaia torgovlia*, p. 120; M. M. Zhirmunskii, *Chastnyi kapital v tovarooborote* (Moscow, 1924), p. 166; *Ekonomicheskoe obozrenie*, 1926, March, p. 142; 1926, August, p. 93; *TPG*, 1924, No. 112 (May 20), p. 3; 1924, No. 126 (June 5), p. 2; 1924, No. 156 (July 12), p. 1; and Paduchev, *Chastnyi torgovets*, p. 66.

19. Trifonov, *Klassy*, 2:191; Fridman, *Chastnyi kapital na denezhnom rynke*, p. 95; Duranty, *I Write*, p. 236; Kron, *Chastnaia torgovlia*, p. 108; *Mestnoe khoziaistvo* (Kiev),

1925, No. 3 (December), p. 74; and Ginzburg, *Chastnyi kapital*, pp. 192–193. For the tax decrees themselves see, for example, *Sobranie zakonov i rasporiazhenii raboche-krest'ianskogo pravitel'stva SSSR. 1924–1949* (Moscow, 1925–50) (hereafter cited as *SZ*), 1924, No. 20, art. 196 (new income tax decree); *SZ*, 1924, No. 8, art. 82 (an additional tax on the trade of luxury goods); and *Sobranie uzakonenii i rasporiazhenii. 1917–1949* (Moscow, 1920–50) (hereafter cited as *SU*), 1924, No. 63, art. 636 (an additional tax on the living space of "nonlabor elements," a category made up largely of private entrepreneurs).

20.  Komvnutorg (which became Narkomvnutorg in the spring of 1924) was given the power to set price ceilings for certain goods in private as well as state and cooperative shops, and all traders were required to post price lists of goods designated by Komvnutorg. *SU*, 1924, No. 35, art. 332 and art. 338; *Direktivy KPSS i sovetskogo pravitel'stva po khoziaistvennym voprosam. 1917–1957 gody*, 4 vols. (Moscow, 1957–58), 1:451–458; *Khoziaistvo Sev.-Zap. kraia*, 1924, No. 8 (November), p. 148; and *KPSS v rezoliutsiiakh i resheniiakh s"ezdov, konferentsii i plenumov TsK*, 8th ed. (Moscow, 1970–) (hereafter cited as *KPSS*), 2:531.

21.  *Sotsialisticheskii vestnik* (Berlin), 1924, No. 19, p. 12; *Torgovye izvestiia*, 1925, No. 14 (May 9), p. 2.

22.  *Sotsialisticheskii vestnik* (Berlin), 1924, No. 2, p. 8.

23.  *Ekonomicheskoe obozrenie*, 1926, August, p. 89; Ginzburg, *Chastnyi kapital*, pp. 111–112; I. A. Bialyi and A. I. Litvin, *Chastnyi kapital v g. Irkutske* (Irkutsk, 1929), pp. 29–30; and *Torgovye izvestiia*, 1925, No. 41 (July 25), p. 6.

24.  For more on Bukharin's rise to power, see Stephen S. Cohen, *Bukharin and the Bolshevik Revolution: A Political Biography 1888–1938* (New York, 1973; reprint, 1975).

25.  See, for example, Alexander Erlich, *The Soviet Industrialization Debate, 1924–1928* (Cambridge, Mass., 1960); Alec Nove, *An Economic History of the U.S.S.R.* (London, 1969; reprint, Harmondsworth, 1972); Cohen, *Bukharin*; Nicholas Spulber, ed., *Foundations of Soviet Strategy for Economic Growth: Selected Soviet Essays, 1924–1930* (Bloomington, 1964); Nicholas Spulber, *Soviet Strategy for Economic Growth* (Bloomington, 1964); and Moshe Lewin, *Political Undercurrents in Soviet Economic Debates* (Princeton, 1974).

26.  N. I. Bukharin, *Put' k sotsializmu i raboche-krest'ianskii soiuz*, 2d ed. (Moscow-Leningrad, 1925), pp. 54–55, 64; N. I. Bukharin, *Tekushchii moment i osnovy nashei politiki* (Moscow, 1925), pp. 13, 16.

27.  Cohen, *Bukharin*, pp. 179–180.

28.  N. Valentinov, *Doktrina pravogo kommunizma, 1924–1926 gody v istorii sovetskogo gosudarstva* (Munich, 1962), p. 23; *Krasnaia nov'*, 1925, No. 4, p. 266; and Bukharin, *Put' k sotsializmu*, pp. 51–52. In 1924 Bukharin wrote: "Earlier [during the years of revolution and War Communism] the class struggle had for us, in the first place, a military-political shock character; now it has a peaceful-economic-organic [*mirno-khoziaistvenno-organicheskaia*] physiognomy." *Bol'shevik*, 1924, No. 2, p. 6. For Bukharin's "enrich yourself" slogan, see *Bol'shevik*, 1925, No. 9–10, p. 5.

29.  Bukharin, *Put' k sotsializmu*, pp. 52–53; N. I. Bukharin, "Lenin kak marksist," in *Put' k sotsializmu v Rossii. Izbrannye proizvedeniia N. I. Bukharina*, ed. Sidney Heitman (New York, 1967), pp. 238–239.

30.  Bukharin, *Put' k sotsializmu*, pp. 25–27, 65; Cohen, *Bukharin*, p. 199. Bukharin expressed confidence that the "socialist" sector of the economy would eventually leave consumers no doubt that it was superior to the private sector.

31.  Cohen, *Bukharin*, p. 215.

32.  Stalin, *Sochineniia*, 7:359.

33.  *XIV s"ezd vsesoiuznoi kommunisticheskoi partii (b). 18–31 dekabria 1925 g.: stenograficheskii otchet* (Moscow, 1926), pp. 41, 47–48, 958–959.

34.  The first important party meeting in 1925 was a Central Committee Plenum in April, whose resolution on rural economic policy called for a "decisive elimination of the survivals of 'War Communism' in the countryside—for example, the cessation of struggle by administrative means against private trade, the kulaks, etc.—[measures that were] con-

tradictory to the development of market relations permitted under NEP." A few pages later the Plenum announced "the lightening of the present tax burden [on rural private trade] and the removal of administrative obstacles to private trade in the countryside in order, by proper and exclusively economic measures, to include its work in the general chain of Soviet trade." Similar sentiments appeared in resolutions adopted by the Fourteenth Party Conference in April, the Third All-Union Congress of Soviets in May, and the Fourteenth Party Congress at the end of the year. The Congress of Soviets, for example, warned against the adoption of "any sort of administrative measures" in the countryside and shortly thereafter declared that taxes on private traders "must be set at a level that will not cause a reduction in the volume of trade." *KPSS*, 3:160, 166, 174–175, 191; *S"ezdy sovetov soiuza SSR, soiuznykh i avtonomnykh sovetskikh sotsialisticheskikh respublik. Sbornik dokumentov v semi tomakh, 1917–1937 g.g.*, 7 vols. (Moscow, 1959–65), 3:83, 87; *Resheniia partii i pravitel'stva po khoziaistvennym voprosam* (Moscow, 1967–), 1:483; and *XIV s"ezd*, p. 962.

35. The title of the lead article in *Sotsialisticheskii vestnik* (Berlin), 1925, No. 10, is "Neo-NEP." The phrase *novaia torgovaia praktika* was employed frequently in Soviet newspapers such as *Torgovye izvestiia* and *Ekonomicheskaia zhizn'* during the spring and summer of 1925.

36. See, for example, *Torgovlia, promyshlennost' i finansy*, 1925, No. 7–8, pp. 190, 196–198; *Ekonomicheskii vestnik Zakavkaz'ia* (Tiflis), 1925, No. 1, pp. 15–16; and *Ekonomicheskaia zhizn'*, 1925, No. 1 (January 1), p. 2.

37. *Torgovlia, promyshlennost' i finansy*, 1925, No. 7–8, pp. 190–191, 198, 205; *Torgovye izvestiia*, 1925, No. 4 (April 9), p. 3; 1925, No. 41 (July 25), p. 6; *Severo-Kavkazskii krai* (Rostov-on-the-Don), 1925, No. 4–5, pp. 110–112; *Viatsko-Vetluzhskii krai* (Viatka), 1926, No. 1, pp. 52–54; and *Ekonomicheskii vestnik Zakavkaz'ia* (Tiflis), 1926, No. 6, pp. 34–35. Foreigners in Russia, including John Maynard Keynes, noted this policy change in 1925. See, for example, J. M. Keynes, *A Short View of Russia* (London, 1925), p. 18; Karlgren, *Bolshevist Russia*, pp. 145–146.

38. Quoted in Karlgren, *Bolshevist Russia*, p. 146.

39. *TPG*, 1925, No. 5 (January 7), p. 2.

40. *Torgovye izvestiia*, 1925, No. 1 (April 2), p. 1. Naturally, Sheinman's opinions were evident in various Narkomvnutorg reports in 1925, one of which stated: "The struggle to eliminate private trading capital from rural trade must be carried out on a purely economic basis. Administrative action, especially tax pressure, should not be used in any circumstances." Trifonov, *Klassy*, 2:215. For views of other state officials along these lines, see *Torgovlia, promyshlennost' i finansy*, 1925, No. 7–8, p. 197; 1925, No. 9, p. 221; *Torgovye izvestiia*, 1925, No. 6 (April 14), p. 2; *TPG*, 1925, No. 5 (January 7), p. 2; and F. E. Dzerzhinskii, *Izbrannye stat'i i rechi* (Moscow, 1947), p. 191. Several chairmen of provincial branches of VSNKh, responding to a survey distributed by the newspaper *Ekonomicheskaia zhizn'* at the end of 1924, favored a larger role for Nepmen in trade in order to free more state funds for industrial development. *Ekonomicheskaia zhizn'*, 1924, No. 354 (December 7), p. 3.

41. *Torgovye izvestiia*, 1925, No. 2 (April 4), p. 6; Judah Zelitch, *Soviet Administration of Criminal Law* (Philadelphia, 1931), pp. 365–366. See also *Torgovye izvestiia*, 1925, No. 38 (July 18), p. 6.

42. Ia. M. Gol'bert, ed., *Novaia torgovaia praktika* (Moscow, 1925), p. 54.

43. *Torgovye izvestiia*, 1925, No. 11 (April 30), p. 3; 1925, No. 12 (May 5), p. 3; 1925, No. 14 (May 9), p. 2; 1925, No. 15 (May 12), p. 3. Similar meetings between Nepmen and state officials were held in other locations as well. See, for example, *Sotsialisticheskii vestnik* (Berlin), 1925, No. 22, p. 1; 1926, No. 6, p. 1; *Ekonomicheskaia zhizn'*, 1924, No. 353 (December 6), p. 4. When given an opportunity to express their views in the press, private traders called most often for the same reforms. See the six articles in *Ekonomicheskaia zhizn'*, 1925, No. 47 (February 26), p. 3; 1925, No. 49 (February 28), p. 3.

44. *Torgovye izvestiia*, 1925, No. 9 (April 25), pp. 1, 6; 1925, No. 27 (June 13), p. 4; 1925, No. 76 (October 15), p. 6; Ginzburg, *Chastnyi kapital*, pp. 185, 193; and Kron, *Chastnaia torgovlia*, p. 108.

45. *SZ*, 1925, No. 16, art. 122; *SZ*, 1925, No. 25, art. 168; *SZ*, 1925, No. 32, art. 213; *SZ*, 1925, No. 38, art. 285; *SZ*, 1925, No. 65, art. 481; *SZ*, 1926, No. 3, art. 16; *SZ*, 1926, No. 6, arts. 37, 38, 39, 42; *SU*, 1926, No. 10, art. 73; *Ekonomicheskoe obozrenie*, 1927, May, p. 177; and V. A. Arkhipov and L. F. Morozov, *Bor'ba protiv kapitalisticheskikh elementov v promyshlennosti i torgovle. 20-e—nachalo 30-kh godov* (Moscow, 1978), p. 124. There were some new taxes during this period, such as a special levy on the amount of living space occupied by urban Nepmen who were subject to the income tax (in order to raise money for workers' housing). *SZ*, 1925, No. 26, art. 178. But for nearly all Nepmen the tax reductions mentioned above more than offset the new taxes.

46. Iu. Larin, *Chastnyi kapital v SSSR* (Moscow-Leningrad, 1927), pp. 273–274; Vasil'kov, *Chastnyi kapital v khoziaistve orlovskoi gubernii. (Issledovatel'skaia rabota Gubplana pod rukovodstvom i redaktsiei Vasil'kova)* (Orel, 1928), p. 93.

47. Larin, *Chastnyi kapital*, p. 279.

48. *Ekonomicheskoe obozrenie*, 1926, August, p. 109; and Arkhipov and Morozov, *Bor'ba*, p. 193. See also V. P. D'iachenko, *Istoriia finansov SSSR (1917–1950 gg.)* (Moscow, 1978), p. 187.

49. Mingulin, *Puti razvitiia*, pp. 59–61; *Ekonomicheskoe obozrenie*, 1926, March, p. 143; *Torgovye izvestiia*, 1925, No. 12 (May 5), p. 3; 1925, No. 27 (June 13), p. 6; and *Narodnoe khoziaistvo Srednei Azii* (Tashkent), 1927, No. 5, p. 59.

50. Societies of Mutual Credit were lending institutions with varying combinations of state and private capital. Some were managed by private individuals, some by state officials, and others by state and private financiers together. The bulk of the Nepmen's credit (over 75 percent) came directly from state banks, not through Societies of Mutual Credit. More information on these organizations is provided in chapter 7. On the flow of state credit to the private sector, see Ginzburg, *Chastnyi kapital*, p. 172; Mingulin, *Puti razvitiia*, p. 63; *Ekonomicheskoe obozrenie*, 1927, March, pp. 132–133; A. Zalkind, ed., *Chastnaia torgovlia Soiuza SSR* (Moscow, 1927), p. 100; *Torgovlia, promyshlennost' i finansy*, 1925, No. 9, p. 221; and *Torgovye izvestiia*, 1925, No. 27 (June 13), p. 6; 1925, No. 53 (August 22), p. 2; 1925, No. 76 (October 15), p. 6.

51. For instance, there were numerous reports from local markets of tax reductions in 1925 arresting the decline of private trade. See, for example, *Mestnoe khoziaistvo* (Kiev), 1925, No. 3 (December), pp. 74–75; *Torgovye izvestiia*, 1925, No. 28 (June 25), p. 5; 1925, No. 34 (July 9), p. 6; 1925, No. 82 (October 29), p. 4. The revival of private trade in 1925 will be examined more closely in Part II.


CHAPTER 3

1. *XIV s"ezd vsesoiuznoi kommunisticheskoi partii(b). 18–31 dekabria 1925 g.: stenograficheskii otchet* (Moscow, 1926), p. 252.

2. *The Challenge of the Left Opposition (1926–27)*, ed. Naomi Allen and George Saunders (New York, 1980), pp. 307–308, 379. See also pp. 79, 96, 103–104, 134, 230, 234–235, 302–304, 341–342.

3. *KPSS v rezoliutsiiakh i resheniiakh s"ezdov, konferentsii i plenumov TsK*, 8th ed. (Moscow, 1970–) (hereafter cited as *KPSS*), 3:442 (emphasis in the original); *S"ezdy sovetov soiuza SSR, soiuznykh i avtonomnykh sovetskikh sotsialisticheskikh respublik. Sbornik dokumentov v semi tomakh, 1917–1937 g.g.* (Moscow, 1959–65), 4 (part 1): 95.

4. *S"ezdy sovetov*, 4 (part 1): 92. That summer, a Joint Plenum of the Party Central Committee (CC) and Central Control Commission (CCC) rejected the Left Opposition's call for "the supertaxation of private trade, which would lead to its rapid liquidation before state and cooperative trade would be ready to control the whole market. The CC and CCC consider that these suggestions [of the Left Opposition] are aimed, in essence, at the abolition of the New Economic Policy, established by the party under the leadership of Lenin." *KPSS*, 3:485–486. Ironically, as the CC and CCC issued this resolution, the party was on the eve of adopting just such a taxation policy.

5. Stephen S. Cohen, *Bukharin and the Bolshevik Revolution: A Political Biography 1888–1938* (New York, 1973; reprint, 1975), pp. 243–247.

6. *KPSS*, 3:379, 442–443.

7. *Challenge*, ed. Allen and Saunders, pp. 464–465.

8. *KPSS*, 3:509, 516; 4:18, 35, 43.

9. *Piatnadtsatyi s"ezd VKP(b). Dekabr' 1927 goda: stenograficheskii otchet*, 2 vols. (Moscow, 1961), 1:66.

10. See, for example, Robert C. Tucker, *Stalin as Revolutionary, 1879–1929* (New York, 1974); Moshe Lewin, *Russian Peasants and Soviet Power: A Study of Collectivization* (London, 1968; reprint, New York, 1975); Cohen, *Bukharin;* and Alec Nove, *An Economic History of the U.S.S.R.* (London, 1969; reprint, Harmondsworth, 1972).

11. Victor Kravchenko, *I Chose Freedom* (New York, 1946), p. 50.

12. *Piatnadtsatyi s"ezd*, 1:70; I. V. Stalin, *Sochineniia*, 13 vols. (Moscow, 1946–52), 11:46, 170–172.

13. Stalin, *Sochineniia*, 12:15, 37; 13:207–208.

14. *KPSS*, 4:32, 108–109, 249. See also *S"ezdy sovetov*, 3:155, 4 (part 1): 114–115; *Shestnadtsataia konferentsiia VKP(b). Aprel' 1929 goda: stenograficheskii otchet* (Moscow, 1962), pp. 193, 195–196; and *KPSS*, 4:412.

15. Stalin, *Sochineniia*, 11:167, 231. See also pp. 226, 270.

16. Ibid., 11:231.

17. Ibid., 11:318–319.

18. Ibid., 12:44–45. Stalin's charges were reiterated by his supporters at party meetings and approved in numerous party resolutions. See, for example, *Shestnadtsataia konferentsiia*, pp. 70, 171, 197, 232, 399; *XVI s"ezd vsesoiuznoi kommunisticheskoi partii(b): stenograficheskii otchet* (Moscow-Leningrad, 1931), pp. 155–156, 257; and *KPSS*, 4:183, 189, 197, 410, 447.

19. Cohen, *Bukharin*, pp. 147–148, 159.

20. Stalin, *Sochineniia*, 12:29–30, 32.

21. Ibid., 12:32, 35. See also p. 305.

22. Cohen, *Bukharin*, pp. 334–335. At the Sixteenth Party Congress in the summer of 1930, Rykov again "confessed" that the Right Opposition had been wrong and that its policies "objectively aided, not the attack on the petty bourgeoisie, but the opposite." *XVI s"ezd*, pp. 148–151.

23. *Torgovo-promyshlennaia gazeta* (hereafter cited as *TPG*), 1927, No. 174 (August 3), p. 2; 1927, No. 249 (October 30), p. 3; 1927, No. 276 (December 2), p. 5; 1928, No. 192 (August 19), p. 4; 1928, No. 293 (December 18), p. 4; *Ekonomicheskaia zhizn'*, 1927, No. 236 (October 15), p. 3.

24. I. Ia. Trifonov, *Ocherki istorii klassovoi bor'by v SSSR v gody NEPa (1921–1937)* (Moscow, 1960), p. 84; *Mestnoe khoziaistvo* (Kiev), 1925, No. 3 (December), p. 86; and *Torgovye izvestiia*, 1925, No. 1 (April 2), p. 5; 1925, No. 9 (April 25), p. 1; 1925, No. 20 (May 23), p. 1; 1925, No. 27 (June 13), p. 4.

25. *Finansy i narodnoe khoziaistvo*, 1929, No. 3, p. 16.

26. *Materialy po istorii SSSR. VII. Dokumenty po istorii sovetskogo obshchestva* (Moscow, 1959), p. 110; Vasil'kov, *Chastnyi kapital v khoziaistve orlovskoi gubernii. (Issledovatel'skaia rabota Gubplana pod rukovodstvom i redaktsiei Vasil'kova)* (Orel, 1928), pp. 93, 95.

27. *Sobranie zakonov i rasporiazhenii raboche-krest'ianskogo pravitel'stva SSSR. 1924–1949* (Moscow, 1925–50) (hereafter cited as *SZ*), 1926, No. 42, art. 307; *SZ*, 1927, No. 25, art. 273; *Zakony o chastnom kapitale. Sbornik zakonov, instruktsii, prikazov i raz"iasnenii*, comp. B. S. Mal'tsman and B. E. Ratner (Moscow, 1928), pp. 316–323; L. F. Morozov, *Reshaiushchii etap bor'by s nepmanskoi burzhuaziei (1926–1929)* (Moscow, 1960), p. 44; and *Materialy. VII.*, p. 111. Approximately 90 percent of the total superprofit tax revenue was paid by private traders (as opposed to private manufacturers), because the tax was only levied on those branches of industry (leather and wool products, vegetable oil, and flour) where, in Narkomfin's opinion, Nepmen played a harmful, speculative role. Morozov, *Reshaiushchii etap*, pp. 44–45.

184 Notes to Pages 70–74

28. *SZ,* 1926, No. 63, art. 474; *SZ,* 1926, No. 64, art. 484; *Finansy i narodnoe khoziaistvo,* 1927, No. 37, pp. 22–23; 1929, No. 3, p. 16; Morozov, *Reshaiushchii etap,* pp. 43–45; and I. Mingulin, *Puti razvitiia chastnogo kapitala* (Moscow-Leningrad, 1927), pp. 125–126.

29. *Finansy i narodnoe khoziaistvo,* 1927, No. 37, pp. 22–23; V. P. D'iachenko, *Istoriia finansov SSSR (1917–1950 gg.)* (Moscow, 1978), p. 187.

30. *Zakony o chastnom kapitale,* p. 324; *SZ,* 1926, No. 44, art. 312; *SZ,* 1927, No. 6, art. 57; *SZ,* 1927, No. 16, art. 172; Morozov, *Reshaiushchii etap,* p. 45; and F. S. Pavlov, "Oktiabr'skaia revoliutsiia i istoricheskii opyt KPSS v likvidatsii srednei i melkoi promyshlennoi i torgovoi burzhuazii v perekhodnyi period k sotsializmu," in *Velikaia oktiabr'skaia sotsialisticheskaia revoliutsiia i stroitel'stvo kommunizma* (Dnepropetrovsk, 1967), p. 72.

31. Morozov, *Reshaiushchii etap,* p. 73; I. Ia. Trifonov, *Likvidatsiia ekspluatatorskikh klassov v SSSR* (Moscow, 1975), pp. 216, 234; *TPG,* 1927, No. 191 (August 24), p. 4; *Torgovye izvestiia,* 1926, No. 47 (April 29), p. 2; *Zakony o chastnom kapitale,* pp. 10, 144–145, 156–157; and N. Riauzov, *Vytesnenie chastnogo posrednika iz tovarooborota* (Moscow, 1930), pp. 35–36.

32. Trifonov, *Likvidatsiia,* pp. 216, 231; Morozov, *Reshaiushchii etap,* pp. 42, 73; *TPG,* 1927, No. 20 (January 26), p. 2; and *Materialy. VII.,* pp. 23, 34–35.

33. *Ekonomicheskaia zhizn',* 1927, No. 9 (January 12), p. 2; *Pravda,* September 1, 1926, p. 4; Vasil'kov, *Chastnyi kapital,* pp. 29, 31; A. M. Ginzburg, ed., *Chastnyi kapital v narodnom khoziaistve SSSR. Materialy kommissii VSNKh SSSR* (Moscow-Leningrad, 1927), pp. 265–266; Morozov, *Reshaiushchii etap,* p. 61; *Sovetskaia torgovlia,* 1927, No. 5, p. 14; and S. F. Kuchurin, *Zheleznodorozhnye gruzovye tarify* (Moscow, 1950), p. 25. Some local officials harassed private grain traders in 1925, even though this was not yet official policy. See, for example, *Torgovye izvestiia,* 1925, No. 2 (April 4), p. 5.

34. *Sovetskaia torgovlia,* 1927, No. 5, p. 14; 1927, No. 7, pp. 8, 15; V. A. Arkhipov and L. F. Morozov, *Bor'ba protiv kapitalisticheskikh elementov v promyshlennosti i torgovle. 20-e—nachalo 30-kh godov* (Moscow, 1978), pp. 136, 190; A. Zalkind, ed., *Chastnaia torgovlia Soiuza SSR* (Moscow, 1927), p. 67; *Severo-Kavkazskii krai* (Rostov-on-the-Don), 1926, No. 3, pp. 61–63; *TPG,* 1927, No. 121 (May 31), p. 6; and *Torgovye izvestiia,* 1926, No. 111 (October 9), p. 2. Though the new railway regulations were aimed primarily at private grain trade, they also applied to private shipments of other products. Here, too, the effect of these measures is hard to gauge with much precision.

35. Paul Scheffer, *Seven Years in Soviet Russia* (New York, 1932), pp. 55, 208. Theodore Dreiser, who spent eleven weeks in the Soviet Union during the winter of 1927–28 (including stays in Moscow, Leningrad, Rostov-on-the-Don, Odessa, Sevastopol', and Baku), was struck by the number of private traders he saw arrested "all over Russia." Theodore Dreiser, *Dreiser Looks at Russia* (New York, 1928), p. 233.

36. H. J. Greenwall, *Mirrors of Moscow* (London, 1929), p. 112. See also Arkhipov and Morozov, *Bor'ba,* pp. 195, 207; Arthur Feiler, *The Russian Experiment* (New York, 1930), p. 61; William C. White, *These Russians* (New York, 1931), p. 68; and E. Ashmead-Bartlett, *The Riddle of Russia* (London, 1929), pp. 159, 173–174.

37. Maurice Hindus, *Humanity Uprooted* (New York, 1929), p. 59; *TPG,* 1928, No. 15 (January 18), p. 5; 1928, No. 27 (February 1), p. 4; 1928, No. 166 (July 19), p. 2; and *SZ,* 1929, No. 4, art. 31.

38. Lewin, *Russian Peasants,* pp. 225, 389; Walter Duranty, *Duranty Reports Russia* (New York, 1934), p. 156; White, *These Russians,* p. 325; *Ekonomicheskoe obozrenie,* 1928, No. 4, p. 171; *Sotsialisticheskii vestnik* (Berlin), 1928, No. 8–9, p. 31; and Eugene Lyons, *Assignment in Utopia* (New York, 1937), p. 99. Railway freight rates for private shipments were raised yet again in 1930. In June 1929 the Commissariat of Transportation (NKPS) was granted the right to "forbid and restrict" private shipments via rail and water of goods specified by the Council of Labor and Defense (STO). A decree of February 1930 permitted NKPS to "forbid and restrict" the transportation of any kind of private freight via the railways or waterways. This decree was abolished a month later by a third decree that transferred the decision concerning such prohibitions to STO. Kuchurin,

*Zheleznodorozhnye gruzovye tarify*, p. 25; *SZ*, 1929, No. 39, art. 350; *SZ*, 1930, No. 14, art. 150; and *SZ*, 1930, No. 21, art. 236.

39. Eugene Lyons, *Moscow Carrousel* (New York, 1935), p. 327; Lyons, *Assignment*, pp. 81–82; *Sotsialisticheskii vestnik* (Berlin), 1930, No. 1, p. 14; Aleksandr I. Solzhenitsyn, *The Gulag Archipelago 1918–1956: An Experiment in Literary Investigation*, 3 vols. (New York, 1974–78), 1:52; Duranty, *Duranty Reports*, p. 384; White, *These Russians*, pp. 67, 75; *TPG*, 1928, No. 246 (October 21), p. 6; E. H. Carr and R. W. Davies, *Foundations of a Planned Economy, 1926–1929*, 2 vols. (London, 1969), 1 (part 2): 671; and *Finansy i narodnoe khoziaistvo*, 1930, No. 1, p. 20.

40. Concerning the income tax, see *SZ*, 1928, No. 1, art. 2; *SZ*, 1928, No. 58, art. 515; *SZ*, 1928, No. 58, art. 520; *SZ*, 1929, No. 48, art. 435; *SZ*, 1929, No. 68, art. 639; *SZ*, 1929, No. 71, art. 678; *SZ*, 1930, No. 46, art. 482; and Morozov, *Reshaiushchii etap*, p. 72.
Concerning the business tax, see *SZ*, 1928, No. 50, art. 443; *SZ*, 1930, No. 3, art. 32; *SZ*, 1930, No. 5, art. 53; *SZ*, 1930, No. 46, art. 481; D'iachenko, *Istoriia finansov*, pp. 188–189; and *Finansy i narodnoe khoziaistvo*, 1929, No. 12, pp. 11–12.
The old inheritance-tax decree of January 1926 was replaced in February 1929 by a law that approximately doubled the tax for Nepmen on gifts or inheritances up to 100,000 rubles. *SZ*, 1929, No. 8, art. 78.

41. *Finansy i narodnoe khoziaistvo*, 1930, No. 27, p. 25. For additional data on the Nepmen's growing tax burden during these years, see *Finansy i narodnoe khoziaistvo*, 1928, No. 39, p. 3; 1929, No. 28, p. 26; 1930, No. 1, pp. 20–21; 1930, No. 27, p. 24; and D'iachenko, *Istoriia finansov*, pp. 185–186.

42. Walter Duranty, *I Write as I Please* (New York, 1935), pp. 275–277.

43. *Istoriia sovetskoi konstitutsii (v dokumentakh) 1917–1956* (Moscow, 1957), p. 155. Other people not permitted to vote included monks and priests, former tsarist police officials, and the mentally ill or retarded.

44. Ibid., pp. 296–297, 331, 355–356, 526, 543–544, 585, 602, 651–652.

45. I. Ia. Trifonov, *Klassy i klassovaia bor'ba v SSSR v nachale nepa*, Vol. 2, *Podgotovka ekonomicheskogo nastupleniia na novuiu burzhuaziiu* (Leningrad, 1969), pp. 75–76; White, *These Russians*, pp. 66–68, 78; William H. Chamberlin, *Soviet Russia: A Living Record and a History* (Boston, 1931), pp. 108–109; *Ekonomicheskoe obozrenie*, 1927, May, p. 172; John Johnson, *Russia in the Grip of Bolshevism* (New York, 1931), pp. 104–105; Carr and Davies, *Foundations*, 1 (part 2): 701; Lyons, *Assignment*, pp. 175–76; Theodor Seibert, *Red Russia* (London, 1932), p. 315; *Sotsialisticheskii vestnik* (Berlin), 1930, No. 1, p. 14; *SZ*, 1929, No. 3, art. 23; and *Illiustrirovannaia Rossiia* (Paris), 1929, No. 9, p. 5.

46. Morozov, *Reshaiushchii etap*, pp. 98–99; White, *These Russians*, pp. 75–76; *Sotsialisticheskii vestnik* (Berlin), 1930, No. 1, p. 14; Seibert, *Red Russia*, pp. 314–315; Negley Farson, *Black Bread and Red Coffins* (New York, 1930), pp. 14–15; Duranty, *Duranty Reports*, p. 385; and Lyons, *Assignment*, p. 176.

47. *Ekonomicheskoe obozrenie*, 1927, May, p. 172; Anton Karlgren, *Bolshevist Russia* (London, 1927), p. 308; *Sobranie uzakonenii i rasporiazhenii. 1917–1949* (Moscow, 1920–50) (hereafter cited as *SU*), 1927, No. 13, art. 88; *Biulleten' tverskogo okruzhnogo ispolnitel'nogo komiteta* (Tver'), 1929, No. 15, pp. 10–12; Spektator [M. I. Nachimson], *Russkii "Termidor"* (Kharbin, 1927), p. 100; White, *These Russians*, pp. 23, 50; *Sotsialisticheskii vestnik* (Berlin), 1929, No. 4, p. 13; and Markoosha Fischer, *My Lives in Russia* (New York, 1944), p. 38.

48. *Sotsialisticheskii vestnik* (Berlin), 1930, No. 2, p. 16; Hindus, *Humanity Uprooted*, pp. 61–62. The daily papers carried many announcements of the following sort: "I, Ivan Ivanovich Ivanov, of (age) and (address) hereby sever all relations with my parents of (address)." Lyons, *Moscow Carrousel*, p. 86; Fischer, *My Lives*, p. 38.

49. *Finansy i narodnoe khoziaistvo*, 1930, No. 12, pp. 4–5; 1930, No. 14, p. 22; 1930, No. 17, p. 26; Seibert, *Red Russia*, p. 363; *Sotsialisticheskii vestnik* (Berlin), 1929, No. 21, p. 7; 1930, No. 4, pp. 12–13; and Calvin B. Hoover, *The Economic Life of Soviet Russia* (New York, 1931), p. 209.

50. Solzhenitsyn, *Gulag,* 1 : 52–53; Alexandre Barmine, *One Who Survived: The Life Story of a Russian Under the Soviets* (New York, 1945), p. 174; and Lyons, *Assignment,* pp. 455–457. For details on the methods used by the GPU to extort gold, see Vladimir V. Tchernavin, *I Speak for the Silent* (Boston–New York, 1935), pp. 200–209.

51. Lyons, *Assignment,* p. 286.

52. Hoover, *Economic Life,* p. 151; Eve Garrette Grady, *Seeing Red: Behind the Scenes in Russia Today* (New York, 1931), pp. 159, 171–172.

53. Walter A. Rukeyser, *Working for the Soviets: An American Engineer in Russia* (New York, 1932), p. 217; Calvin B. Hoover, "The Fate of the New Economic Policy of the Soviet Union," *Economic Journal* 40 (June 1930): 186–187. Maurice Hindus recorded similar impressions of Moscow in June 1930: "I made the rounds of the restaurants. The socialist offensive of the previous winter had swept the private ones out of existence. All were now under Soviet cooperative control. On the much-abbreviated menus which I scanned, I found that everything smacking of luxury had been removed." Until recently, he added, there had been many private food peddlers in the streets. "Now, save for an occasional man or woman offering questionable sausage, stale bread or dried fish, these food vendors have vanished." Maurice Hindus, *Red Bread* (New York, 1931), pp. 72, 74.

54. Hoover, "The Fate," pp. 187–188; Arkhipov and Morozov, *Bor'ba,* p. 217; *SZ,* 1930, No. 10, art. 120; *SZ,* 1930, No. 18, art. 209; and Seibert, *Red Russia,* pp. 268–269.

55. *Finansy i narodnoe khoziaistvo,* 1929, No. 7, p. 16; *KPSS,* 4 : 203; Andrei Fabrichnyi, *Chastnyi kapital na poroge piatiletki* (Moscow, 1930), pp. 24, 27; and *Tverskoi krai* (Tver'), 1928, No. 4–5, pp. 85–88.

56. For some examples, see *TPG,* 1928, No. 177 (August 1), p. 4; 1928, No. 267 (November 17), p. 4; 1928, No. 269 (November 20), p. 4.

57. *KPSS,* 4 : 396–397; Hoover, "The Fate," p. 191. For other eyewitness descriptions of private trade (almost exclusively by peasants) after 1930, see J. G. Lockhart, *Babel Visited: A Churchman in Soviet Russia* (Milwaukee, 1933), p. 114; George A. Burrell, *An American Engineer Looks at Russia* (Boston, 1932), pp. 103–104; Ella Winter, *Red Virtue: Human Relationships in the New Russia* (New York, 1933), p. 14; and Fischer, *My Lives,* p. 105.

58. Stalin, *Sochineniia,* 12 : 43, 306–307.

59. *Resheniia partii i pravitel'stva po khoziaistvennym voprosam* (Moscow, 1967–), 2 : 388–389; *SZ,* 1934, No. 3, art. 22; *SZ,* 1934, No. 3, art. 23; *SZ,* 1934, No. 3, art. 24; *SZ,* 1935, No. 1, art. 3; and *SZ,* 1935, No. 4, art. 29. For references to small-scale private traders and handicraftsmen in tax decrees of the 1930s, see, for example, *SZ,* 1933, No. 5, art. 31; *SZ,* 1934, No. 5, art. 38; *SZ,* 1934, No. 27, art. 211b; *SZ,* 1935, No. 4, art. 31; and *SZ,* 1936, No. 2, art. 18.

60. *SZ,* 1932, No. 65, art. 375; *SU,* 1932, No. 87, art. 385. Speaking at a Plenum of the CC and CCC in January 1933, Stalin declared: "In the most recent period we have been able to throw private traders, merchants, and middlemen of all sorts completely out of trade. Of course this does not exclude the possibility that private traders and speculators may again appear in trade according to the law of atavism, taking advantage of an especially favorable field for them—collective farm trade. Furthermore, the collective farmers themselves are not adverse to engaging in speculation, which of course does them no honor. But to combat these unhealthy developments the Soviet government has recently issued measures for the suppression of speculation and the punishment of speculators. You know, of course, that this law does not suffer from softness. You understand, of course, that such a law did not and could not exist during the first stage of NEP." Stalin, *Sochineniia,* 13 : 204.

61. Stalin, *Sochineniia,* 13 : 220–221.

62. It is interesting to note that Trotsky, then in exile, regarded free collective-farm trade as necessary and observed its partial resemblance to NEP: "All-round collectivization . . . extraordinarily lowered the labour incentives available to the peasantry. . . . The answer to this threat was the legalization of trade. In other words . . . it was necessary partially to restore the NEP, or the free market, which was abolished too soon and too definitively." Quoted in Richard B. Day, *Leon Trotsky and the Politics of Economic Isolation* (Cambridge, 1973), p. 182.

## CHAPTER 4

1. V. I. Lenin, *Polnoe sobranie sochinenii*, 5th ed., 55 vols. (Moscow, 1958–65), 44:207–208, 214–215.

2. Armand Hammer, *The Quest of the Romanoff Treasure* (New York, 1932), pp. 55–56.

3. Walter Duranty, *Duranty Reports Russia* (New York, 1934), pp. 88–89.

4. F. A. Mackenzie, *Russia Before Dawn* (London, 1923), p. 207. For other accounts of the revival of private trade, see Edwin Ware Hullinger, *The Reforging of Russia* (New York, 1925), pp. 70–71; Michael S. Farbman, *Bolshevism in Retreat* (London, 1923), pp. 295–296; Walter Duranty, *I Write as I Please* (New York, 1935), pp. 139–140; Pitirim A. Sorokin, *Leaves from a Russian Diary—and Thirty Years After* (Boston, 1950), p. 270; Paul Scheffer, *Seven Years in Soviet Russia* (New York, 1932), p. 3; Mackenzie, *Russia Before Dawn*, pp. 24, 54, 57; Emma Goldman, *My Further Disillusionment in Russia* (Garden City, N.Y., 1924), pp. 78–79; Victor Serge, *Memoirs of a Revolutionary 1901–1941* (London, 1967; reprint, 1975), p. 147; Ilya Ehrenburg, *Memoirs: 1921–1941* (New York, 1966), p. 66; and I. Ia. Trifonov, *Klassy i klassovaia bor'ba v SSSR v nachale nepa*, Vol. 2, *Podgotovka ekonomicheskogo nastupleniia na novuiu burzhuaziiu* (Leningrad, 1969), p. 49.

5. A. M. Ginzburg, ed., *Chastnyi kapital v narodnom khoziaistve SSSR. Materialy kommissii VSNKh SSSR* (Moscow-Leningrad, 1927), pp. 41, 69; V. M. Selunskaia, ed., *Izmeneniia sotsial'noi struktury sovetskogo obshchestva. 1921-seredina 30-kh godov* (Moscow, 1979), p. 114; Spektator [Miron Isaakovich Nachimson], *Russkii "Termidor"* (Kharbin, 1927), pp. 106–107; E. H. Carr and R. W. Davies, *Foundations of a Planned Economy, 1926–1929*, 2 vols. (London, 1969), 1 (part 2): 663; Trifonov, *Klassy*, 2:49, 68; *Torgovo-promyshlennaia gazeta* (hereafter cited as *TPG*), 1922, No. 215 (November 25), p. 5; and I. Mingulin, *Puti razvitiia chastnogo kapitala* (Moscow-Leningrad, 1927), p. 86. Many people, especially small-scale artisans, engaged in both manufacturing and trade.

6. M. M. Zhirmunskii, *Chastnyi kapital v tovarooborote* (Moscow, 1924), pp. 7, 133; N. Riauzov, *Vytesnenie chastnogo posrednika iz tovarooborota* (Moscow, 1930), p. 30; *Materialy po istorii SSSR. VII. Dokumenty po istorii sovetskogo obshchestva* (Moscow, 1959), pp. 146–149; Alexander Wicksteed, *Life Under the Soviets* (London, 1928), p. 2; Scheffer, *Seven Years*, p. 4; K. Borisov, *75 dnei v SSSR. Vpechatleniia* (Berlin, 1924), p. 13; *Nash krai* (Astrakhan'), 1926, No. 8, p. 27; *TPG*, 1923, No. 261 (November 18), p. 4; 1924, No. 13 (January 16), p. 5; 1924, No. 102 (May 8), p. 4; *Torgovye izvestiia*, 1925, No. 19 (May 21), p. 6; 1925, No. 25 (June 6), p. 4; and F. I. Dan, *Dva goda skitanii* (Berlin, 1922), p. 255.

7. *Sobranie uzakonenii i rasporiazhenii. 1917–1949* (Moscow, 1920–50) (hereafter cited as *SU*), 1921, No. 56, art. 354; *SU*, 1922, No. 17, art. 180; *SU*, 1923, No. 5, art. 89; and *Sobranie zakonov i rasporiazhenii raboche-krest'ianskogo pravitel'stva SSSR. 1924–1949* (Moscow, 1924–50) (hereafter cited as *SZ*), 1926, No. 63, art. 474.

8. A tax decree of September 2, 1930, aimed at private businesses, defined a new set of categories devoted primarily to small-scale activity, undoubtedly because virtually all large-scale private entrepreneurs had been driven out of business by this time. *SZ*, 1930, No. 46, art. 481.

9. *Na novykh putiakh. Itogi novoi ekonomicheskoi politiki 1921–1922 g.g.* (Moscow, 1923), *vypusk* I, p. 175; *Ekonomicheskaia zhizn'*, 1921, No. 287 (December 21), p. 2; 1922, No. 92 (April 27), p. 4; I. A. Gladkov, ed., *Sovetskoe narodnoe khoziaistvo v 1921–1925 gg.* (Moscow, 1960), p. 449; *Ekonomicheskoe obozrenie*, 1925, April, p. 190; P. C. Hiebert and Orie O. Miller, *Feeding the Hungry: Russian Famine 1919–1925* (Scottdale, Pa., 1929), p. 114; Mackenzie, *Russia Before Dawn*, p. 18; and Ts. M. Kron, *Chastnaia torgovlia v SSSR* (Moscow, 1926), p. 10.

10. *Promyshlennost' i torgovlia*, 1922, No. 3, pp. 24–25; *Nashe khoziaistvo* (Vladimir), 1923, No. 7–9, pp. 42–43; V. P. Dmitrenko, *Torgovaia politika sovetskogo gosudarstva posle perekhoda k NEPu 1921–1924 gg.* (Moscow, 1971), pp. 143, 145; V. A. Arkhipov and L. F. Morozov, *Bor'ba protiv kapitalisticheskikh elementov v promyshlen-*

*nosti i torgovle. 20-e—nachalo 30-kh godov* (Moscow, 1978), p. 39; *Ekonomicheskaia zhizn'*, 1921, No. 287 (December 21), p. 2; and *Mesiachnye obzory narodnogo khoziaistva*, 1922, March, p. 68; 1922, April, p. 60. For photographs of "primitive" traders (including some children) in 1921, see Mackenzie, *Russia Before Dawn*, picture facing p. 82; Anthony Cash, *The Russian Revolution* (London, 1967), p. 112.

11. Hiebert and Miller, *Feeding the Hungry*, p. 207.

12. Mackenzie, *Russia Before Dawn*, p. 192.

13. Dmitrenko, *Torgovaia politika*, pp. 57–58; Trifonov, *Klassy*, 2:47; and Arkhipov and Morozov, *Bor'ba*, p. 27.

14. *Izvestiia*, May 17, 1921, p. 2.

15. Frank Alfred Golder and Lincoln Hutchinson, *On the Trail of the Russian Famine* (Stanford, 1927), p. 204. See also p. 83.

16. William C. White, *These Russians* (New York, 1931), p. 32; Victor Kravchenko, *I Chose Freedom* (New York, 1946), pp. 31–32. For more on bagging, see Hiebert and Miller, *Feeding the Hungry*, p. 115; Duranty, *Duranty Reports*, p. 39.

17. Mackenzie, *Russia Before Dawn*, pp. 228–229. See also Golder and Hutchinson, *On the Trail*, p. 163.

18. *Finansy i narodnoe khoziaistvo*, 1926, No. 2, p. 25. See also *TPG*, 1922, No. 93 (July 2), p. 5; *Torgovaia gazeta*, 1922, No. 7, p. 4; and Farbman, *Bolshevism*, p. 283.

19. *TPG*, 1924, No. 120 (May 29), p. 4; Zhirmunskii, *Chastnyi kapital*, p. 7; A. Zalkind, ed., *Chastnaia torgovlia Soiuza SSR* (Moscow, 1927), p. 157; Mackenzie, *Russia Before Dawn*, p. 22; and Golder and Hutchinson, *On the Trail*, p. 227.

20. Iu. S. Kondurushkin, *Chastnyi kapital pered sovetskim sudom* (Moscow-Leningrad, 1927), p. 59; *Mestnoe khoziaistvo* (Kiev), 1924, No. 6 (March), pp. 18–19; *TPG*, 1923, No. 45 (February 27), p. 2; 1923, No. 261 (November 18), p. 4; *Na novykh putiakh*, *vypusk* I, p. 183; and Scheffer, *Seven Years*, p. 4. For photographs of permanent shops, see E. M. Newman, *Seeing Russia* (New York, 1928), pp. 200, 202.

21. *Na novykh putiakh*, *vypusk* I, pp. 187, 236.

22. Zhirmunskii, *Chastnyi kapital*, p. 36; *Na novykh putiakh*, *vypusk* I, p. 179; and *TPG*, 1922, No. 122 (August 5), p. 3; 1922, No. 244 (December 28), p. 6.

23. S. O. Zagorskii, *K sotsializmu ili k kapitalizmu?* (Paris, 1927), p. 127. For additional data illustrating these trends, see *Ekonomicheskoe obozrenie*, 1925, May, p. 68; *Nashe khoziaistvo* (Vladimir), 1923, No. 7–9, pp. 42–43, 51; *Na novykh putiakh, vypusk* I, pp. 178–179, 184; and Gladkov, *Sovetskoe narodnoe khoziaistvo*, pp. 451–452.

24. Trifonov, *Klassy*, 2:51; *Torgovaia gazeta*, 1922, No. 7, p. 4; and *TPG*, 1922, No. 58 (May 19), p. 3; 1922, No. 67 (May 31), p. 3; 1922, No. 144 (September 2), p. 5; 1922, No. 172 (October 5), p. 4.

25. *Ekonomicheskaia zhizn'*, 1922, No. 92 (April 27), p. 4; Dmitrenko, *Torgovaia politika*, pp. 147–148; *TPG*, 1922, No. 198 (November 4), p. 4; G. P. Paduchev, *Chastnyi torgovets pri novoi ekonomicheskoi politike (po dannym biudzhetnogo obsledovaniia)* (Voronezh, 1926), pp. 96–97, 99; and *Voprosy torgovli*, 1929, No. 15, p. 71.

26. V. Ia. Laverychev, *Krupnaia burzhuaziia v poreformennoi Rossii (1861–1900 gg.)* (Moscow, 1974), p. 71.

27. Kondurushkin, *Chastnyi kapital*, p. 70; Serge, *Memoirs*, p. 201.

28. Trifonov, *Klassy*, 2:71; *Torgovye izvestiia*, 1925, No. 19 (May 21), p. 6; 1925, No. 45 (August 4), p. 6; *TPG*, 1924, No. 78 (April 5), p. 1; *Mestnoe khoziaistvo* (Kiev), 1924, No. 6 (March), p. 70.

29. *Ekonomicheskoe obozrenie*, 1924, No. 6, pp. 46–47; 1925, October, pp. 162–164; Ginzburg, *Chastnyi kapital*, pp. 120–121, 200; and Zalkind, *Chastnaia torgovlia*, pp. 9, 11, 160. Figures for Moscow and a number of the provinces concerning the distribution of private traders in the five trade ranks may be found in *Na novykh putiakh, vypusk* I, p. 184; *Finansy i narodnoe khoziaistvo*, 1928, No. 21, p. 26; *Severo-Kavkazskii krai* (Rostov-on-the-Don), 1925, No. 4–5, p. 107; 1925, No. 10, p. 54; *Ekonomicheskii vestnik Zakavkaz'ia* (Tiflis), 1926, No. 6, p. 22; *Nashe khoziaistvo* (Riazan'), 1924, No. 1, p. 38; and *Khoziaistvo Urala* (Sverdlovsk), 1925, No. 2 (July), p. 55.

30. It should be noted that the number of large shops (primarily businesses in ranks IV and V) was smaller than the number of Nepmen who operated them. As a general rule, the

larger an enterprise, the more likely it was to have more than one owner. This was in part because of the need for considerable quantities of capital in the upper ranks but also because of the Nepmen's desire to avoid hired labor (the presence of which often meant additional taxes and regulation). *Finansy i narodnoe khoziaistvo,* 1927, No. 4, p. 10; *Torgovye izvestiia,* 1925, No. 45 (August 4), p. 6; 1926, No. 1 (January 5), p. 5; 1926, No. 59 (June 1), p. 4; *Mestnoe khoziaistvo* (Kiev), 1924, No. 6 (March), p. 70; and *Mestnoe khoziaistvo Ekaterinoslavshchiny* (Ekaterinoslav), 1924, No. 1 (October-December), p. 34.

31. Ginzburg, *Chastnyi kapital,* p. 203; Zalkind, *Chastnaia torgovlia,* p. 18; and *Materialy. VII.,* p. 90.

32. Zalkind, *Chastnaia torgovlia,* p. 129.

33. Ibid., pp. 31, 36; Ginzburg, *Chastnyi kapital,* p. 125; and *Materialy. VII.,* pp. 124–125. See also *Ekonomicheskoe stroitel'stvo,* 1926, No. 9, p. 19; *Nashe khoziaistvo* (Vladimir), 1923, No. 4–5, p. 63.

34. Wicksteed, *Life Under the Soviets,* pp. 1–2; Hullinger, *Reforging Russia,* p. 253; *Torgovye izvestiia,* 1925, No. 8 (April 23), p. 5; *Torgovo-promyshlennyi vestnik,* 1923, No. 1, p. 9; and *Mestnoe khoziaistvo* (Kiev), 1925, No. 3 (December), p. 77. For photographs of markets in several cities, see *Illiustrirovannaia Rossiia* (Paris), 1924, No. 5, p. 11; 1926, No. 7, p. 1; 1926, No. 11, p. 4; 1926, No. 45, p. 9; 1926, No. 46, p. 4; 1926, No. 50, p. 1; 1927, No. 39, p. 9; 1929, No. 27, p. 5; Newman, *Seeing Russia,* pp. 16, 214, 314; and Cash, *Russian Revolution,* p. 116. For photographs of petty street trade, see *Illiustrirovannaia Rossiia* (Paris), 1927, No. 10, p. 1; 1927, No. 26, p. 20; 1927, No. 37, p. 20; 1928, No. 3, p. 2; Newman, *Seeing Russia,* p. 124.

35. *Torgovye izvestiia,* 1925, No. 66 (September 22), p. 2.

36. Borisov, *75 dnei,* pp. 44–46.

37. Negley Farson, *Black Bread and Red Coffins* (New York, 1930), pp. 240–241. See also Newman, *Seeing Russia,* p. 329.

38. *TPG,* 1923, No. 194 (August 30), p. 3; 1923, No. 195 (August 31), p. 3; 1923, No. 196 (September 1), p. 3; 1923, No. 197 (September 2), p. 5; 1923, No. 208 (September 15), p. 3; *Torgovye izvestiia,* 1925, No. 28 (June 25), p. 5; 1925, No. 88 (November 12), p. 5; and *Mestnoe khoziaistvo* (Kiev), 1925, No. 3 (December), p. 73.

39. *TPG,* 1923, No. 194 (August 30), p. 3. See also *TPG,* 1923, No. 196 (September 1), p. 3; 1923, No. 197 (September 2), p. 5; 1923, No. 208 (September 15), p. 3; and *Torgovye izvestiia,* 1925, No. 28 (June 25), p. 5.

40. *Torgovye izvestiia,* 1925, No. 8 (April 23), p. 5; *Mestnoe khoziaistvo* (Kiev), 1925, No. 3 (December), p. 77; *TPG,* 1923, No. 194 (August 30), p. 3; and *Torgovo-promyshlennyi vestnik,* 1923, No. 15, pp. 11–12; 1923, No. 16, pp. 9–10.

41. *Torgovye izvestiia,* 1925, No. 1 (April 2), p. 2; 1925, No. 107 (December 29), p. 5.

42. *TPG,* 1922, No. 122 (August 5), p. 3; 1924, No. 13 (January 16), p. 5; and *Narodnoe khoziaistvo Srednei Azii* (Tashkent), 1927, No. 5, pp. 43–45; 1927, No. 6–7, pp. 104–105.

43. Karl Borders, *Village Life Under the Soviets* (New York, 1927), p. 93.

44. White, *These Russians,* pp. 271–272.

45. Maurice Hindus, *Broken Earth* (New York, 1926), pp. 121–122. For a photograph of a local fair, see *Illiustrirovannaia Rossiia* (Paris), 1928, No. 45, p. 7.

46. *Na novykh putiakh, vypusk* I, pp. 272, 279; *Obshchestvennoe dvizhenie v Rossii v nachale XX-go veka,* ed. L. Martov, P. Maslov, and A. Potresov, 4 vols. (St. Petersburg, 1909–14), 1:124; *TPG,* 1922, No. 118 (August 1), p. 1; 1924, No. 13 (January 16), p. 5; *Torgovye izvestiia,* 1926, No. 18 (February 16), p. 4; and *Khoziaistvo Urala* (Sverdlovsk), 1925, No. 1 (June), pp. 135–136, 138.

47. Dmitrenko, *Torgovaia politika,* pp. 138–139, 148; Zalkind, *Chastnaia torgovlia,* p. 35; Zhirmunskii, *Chastnyi kapital,* p. 35; Kron, *Chastnaia torgovlia,* p. 11; *Ekonomicheskoe obozrenie,* 1924, No. 6, p. 47; *Nashe khoziaistvo* (Riazan'), 1924, No. 1, p. 38; *Severo-Kavkazskii krai* (Rostov-on-the-Don), 1925, No. 4–5, pp. 96–98; and *Ekonomicheskii vestnik Zakavkaz'ia* (Tiflis), 1926, No. 6, p. 27. Although peasants were more self-sufficient than city dwellers, it would be wrong to suggest that trade was uncom-

mon in the countryside. The comparatively small number of licensed rural traders was joined, as we have seen, by numerous peasants and other people operating beyond the reach of the state's statistical net.

48. Zalkind, *Chastnaia torgovlia*, p. 127. The average rural private trader in rank II had 73 percent of the capital of the average urban private trader in rank II. For rank I the figure was 96 percent.

49. *Sovetskaia torgovlia*, 1926, No. 8, p. 6; *Ekonomicheskoe obozrenie*, 1925, May, p. 69; *Viatsko-Vetluzhskii krai* (Viatka), 1925, No. 2, pp. 65–66; and *Severo-Kavkazskii krai* (Rostov-on-the-Don), 1925, No. 4–5, table between pp. 92 and 93; 1926, No. 4, p. 93.

50. The Commissariat of Finance estimated in 1923 that only about 3 percent of private wholesale trade took place outside the cities, and data for the last quarter of 1922 show that 70 percent of all private wholesale trading was conducted in Moscow alone. L. N. Kritsman, *Tri goda novoi ekonomicheskoi politiki* (Moscow, 1924), p. 23; Zhirmunskii, *Chastnyi kapital*, pp. 107–108; Kron, *Chastnaia torgovlia*, p. 13; *TPG*, 1923, No. 45 (February 27), p. 2; *Torgovye izvestiia*, 1925, No. 76 (October 15), p. 6; and *Vnutrenniaia torgovlia soiuza SSR za X let* (Moscow, 1928), p. 259.

51. Riauzov, *Vytesnenie*, p. 33. Similar figures for rural trade alone in 1925/26 and 1926/27 are available in *Materialy. VII.*, p. 153. As one would expect, over 80 percent of all private traders were located in the RSFSR and the Ukraine in 1926/27. *Voprosy torgovli*, 1929, No. 15, p. 61; *Materialy. VII.*, pp. 80, 126–127. Of the private traders in Central Asia, roughly 80 percent worked in the Uzbek Republic. *Narodnoe khoziaistvo Srednei Azii* (Tashkent), 1927, No. 5, p. 46.

52. Zalkind, *Chastnaia torgovlia*, p. 8; Riauzov, *Vytesnenie*, p. 33. Similar information for rural trade in 1925/26 and 1926/27 is available in *Materialy. VII.*, pp. 123–124, 154–155. Other data for rural trade indicate that private sales per capita were highest in Central Asia (though higher in the Ukraine than in Transcaucasia) and that the largest numbers of private traders per 10,000 citizens were in Central Asia and Transcaucasia. *Materialy. VII.*, pp. 122, 152.

53. Lionel Kochan, ed., *The Jews in Soviet Russia Since 1917*, 3d ed. (Oxford, 1978), pp. 92, 139.

54. Zvi Y. Gitelman, *Jewish Nationality and Soviet Politics: The Jewish Sections of the CPSU, 1917–1930* (Princeton, 1972), pp. 19–20.

55. *Voprosy torgovli*, 1929, No. 15, p. 61. The figures for Transcaucasia and Central Asia were 57 and 32 percent, respectively.

56. Gitelman, *Jewish Nationality*, p. 381.

57. For more on disfranchisement, see the preceding chapter.

58. By October 1927 this figure had fallen to 29 percent. The drop was primarily the result of government efforts to recruit Jews for special agricultural colonies in the Ukraine and the Crimea. Disfranchised Jews who agreed to participate regained their voting rights. Salo W. Baron, *The Russian Jew Under Tsars and Soviets* (New York, 1964), pp. 226–227; Gitelman, *Jewish Nationality*, p. 354. For more on attempts to relocate Jews in agricultural colonies, see Anthony C. Sutton, *Western Technology and Soviet Economic Development 1917 to 1930* (Stanford, 1968), pp. 129–131; Gitelman, *Jewish Nationality*, pp. 384–388, 430, 439–440; Markoosha Fischer, *My Lives in Russia* (New York, 1944), pp. 19, 24; Baron, *The Russian Jew*, pp. 264, 266; Iu. Larin, *Chastnyi kapital v SSSR* (Moscow-Leningrad, 1927), pp. 23–24; and, for numerous photographs of these colonies, Newman, *Seeing Russia*, pp. 6, 23, 31, 34, 53, 86, 128, 130, 349–354.

59. Maurice Hindus, *Humanity Uprooted* (New York, 1929), p. 272. See also Anna Louise Strong, *The First Time in History* (New York, 1924), pp. 183–185; Dorothy Thompson, *The New Russia* (New York, 1928), p. 47.

60. Baron, *The Russian Jew*, p. 250. See also Isaac Deutscher, *Stalin: A Political Biography*, 2d ed. (London, 1966; reprint, New York, 1969), pp. 604–605.

61. Soviet newspaper correspondents, frequently employing the phrase "sales crisis" (*krizis sbyta*), filed numerous reports from around the country on the problems plaguing trade in 1923. *TPG*, 1923, No. 67 (March 25), p. 4; 1923, No. 80 (April 13), p. 4; 1923,

No. 90 (April 25), p. 4; 1923, No. 105 (May 13), p, 5; 1923, No. 207 (September 14), p. 4; 1923, No. 224 (October 4), p. 3; 1923, No. 227 (October 7), p. 6.

62. Ginzburg, *Chastnyi kapital*, p. 200. These figures do not include the free licenses (roughly 25,000) issued to very small-scale traders.

63. Ibid., p. 192.

64. Gladkov, *Sovetskoe narodnoe khoziaistvo*, p. 456.

65. *Sovetskaia torgovlia*, 1926, No. 8, p. 5; Zalkind, *Chastnaia torgovlia*, p. 18; and *Ekonomicheskaia zhizn'*, 1926, No. 158 (July 13), p. 2.

66. *Finansy i narodnoe khoziaistvo*, 1927, No. 25, p. 28; Mingulin, *Puti razvitiia*, p. 133. The data in these and other sources vary somewhat as the result of differences in the number of regions surveyed, the inclusion (or exclusion) of figures concerning free trade licenses for certain categories of artisans and petty traders, and other factors.

67. *Torgovye izvestiia*, 1925, No. 25 (June 6), p. 4.

68. Zalkind, *Chastnaia torgovlia*, p. 13; Ginzburg, *Chastnyi kapital*, p. 200.

69. *Finansy i narodnoe khoziaistvo*, 1927, No. 25, p. 28. These figures include both regular and free licenses.

70. Gladkov, *Sovetskoe narodnoe khoziaistvo*, p. 456. These figures have been adjusted for inflation.

71. *Finansy i narodnoe khoziaistvo*, 1928, No. 4, p. 27. For figures on the waning of private trade in other regions in 1926/27, see L. F. Morozov, *Reshaiushchii etap bor'by s nepmanskoi burzhuaziei (1926–1929)* (Moscow, 1960), pp. 46–47; *Finansy i narodnoe khoziaistvo*, 1927, No. 35, p. 15.

72. *40 let sovetskoi torgovli* (Moscow, 1957), p. 6.

73. Riauzov, *Vytesnenie*, p. 17.

74. *TPG*, 1928, No. 293 (December 18), p. 4; and Morozov, *Reshaiushchii etap*, pp. 73, 76. For additional statistics and reports on the decline of trade in a number of cities and regions, see *Sotsialisticheskii vestnik* (Berlin), 1928, No. 20, p. 13; *TPG*, 1928, No. 261 (November 10), p. 4; 1928, No. 267 (November 17), p. 4; *Finansy i narodnoe khoziaistvo*, 1929, No. 7, p. 16; 1929, No. 17, p. 24; Morozov, *Reshaiushchii etap*, p. 46; Arkhipov and Morozov, *Bor'ba*, p. 216; and *Ekonomicheskaia zhizn'*, 1928, No. 67 (March 20), p. 5; 1928, No. 113 (May 17), p. 5.

75. Wicksteed, *Life Under the Soviets*, pp. 3–4.

76. Eugene Lyons, *Assignment in Utopia* (New York, 1937), p. 86.

77. *Finansy i narodnoe khoziaistvo*, 1928, No. 39, pp. 2–3; 1929, No. 7, p. 16; G. A. Dikhtiar, *Sovetskaia torgovlia v period postroeniia sotsializma* (Moscow, 1961), p. 335.

78. *TPG*, 1927, No. 277 (December 3), p. 2.

79. Ginzburg, *Chastnyi kapital*, pp. 120–121, 200; and Zalkind, *Chastnaia torgovlia*, pp. 9, 160.

80. In some sources the figures differ slightly. Trifonov, *Klassy*, 2:251; Carr and Davies, *Foundations*, 1 (part 2): 962; *Ekonomicheskaia zhizn' SSSR. Khronika sobytii i faktov 1917–1965*, 2 vols. (Moscow, 1967), 1:163, 176, 189, 206, 221; and Riauzov, *Vytesnenie*, pp. 18, 21. Not surprisingly, Nepmen were far less important in wholesale trade. In 1926, the best year for private wholesale trade, retail sales represented approximately 80 percent of all private trade, and the percentage was even higher at the beginning and end of NEP. Less than 5 percent of private rural trade was wholesale. *Materialy. VII.*, pp. 103, 150; Kritsman, *Tri goda*, p. 23; and *Vnutrenniaia torgovlia soiuza SSR*, p. 259. Nepmen accounted for roughly 20 percent of all (state, cooperative, and private) wholesale trade in 1923/24, 10 percent in 1924/25, 9 percent in 1925/26, 5 percent in 1926/27, 2 percent in 1927/28, and 0.4 percent in 1928/29. Carr and Davies, *Foundations*, 1 (part 2): 961; Trifonov, *Klassy*, 2:50, 248; and Riauzov, *Vytesnenie*, p. 18.

Although the private share of retail sales fell throughout the decade, as indicated in the table, this was for years the result of the growing number of state and cooperative stores, not of a decline in the *volume* of private retail trade. With the exception of 1924 (which, we have seen, was marked by heightened pressure on the Nepmen), private retail sales increased every year through 1926. The Nepmen's share of the total number of trade licenses (figures presented earlier in the chapter) was greater than their share of sales, because state and cooperative stores were larger operations than those of the average private entrepreneur.

81. *Finansy i narodnoe khoziaistvo*, 1929, No. 7, p. 16.

82. See, for example, *TPG*, 1928, No. 266 (November 16), p. 6; 1928, No. 293 (December 18), p. 4.

83. For a sampling of reports filed by *TPG*'s correspondents in Saratov, Tver', Poltava, Kiev, Sverdlovsk, Smolensk, and Penza, see ibid., 1927, No. 122 (June 1), p. 4; 1928, No. 225 (September 27), p. 4; 1928, No. 266 (November 16), p. 6; 1928, No. 267 (November 17), p. 4; and 1928, No. 269 (November 20), p. 4. See also *Ekonomicheskaia zhizn'*, 1928, No. 53 (March 2), p. 4; 1928, No. 113 (May 17), p. 5.

84. *TPG*, 1928, No. 177 (August 1), p. 4; 1928, No. 269 (November 20), p. 4.

85. Lyons, *Assignment*, p. 97.

86. Riauzov, *Vytesnenie*, p. 24; Morozov, *Reshaiushchii etap*, pp. 47–48; *TPG*, 1928, No. 177 (August 1), p. 4; 1928, No. 218 (September 19), p. 4; 1928, No. 293 (December 18), p. 4; and *Finansy i narodnoe khoziaistvo*, 1928, No. 39, p. 3.

87. White, *These Russians*, p. 62. See also H. J. Greenwall, *Mirrors of Moscow* (London, 1929), p. 35; Albert Muldavin, *The Red Fog Lifts* (New York, 1931), p. 50.

88. Riauzov, *Vytesnenie*, p. 45.

89. *Sotsialisticheskii vestnik* (Berlin), 1928, No. 8–9, p. 31; 1929, No. 10–11, p. 10; 1929, No. 21, p. 5; *TPG*, 1928, No. 209 (September 8), p. 5; 1928, No. 285 (December 8), p. 4; 1928, No. 293 (December 18), p. 4. The supply of manufactured goods rarely satisfied demand fully during NEP. For numerous articles on a *tovarnyi golod* in 1925, for example, see November and December issues of *Torgovye izvestiia*. The problem at the end of the decade was more severe, however, in part because there were serious shortages of food as well as manufactured products.

90. Freda Utley, *The Dream We Lost* (New York, 1940), p. 86.

91. Anne O'Hare McCormick, *The Hammer and the Scythe* (New York, 1928), p. 24; Calvin B. Hoover, *The Economic Life of Soviet Russia* (New York, 1931), pp. 150–151. A longtime British resident of the Soviet Union wrote that by 1928, "as the licence for street selling costs a good deal and the profits are very meagre, very few of these traders take them out, with the consequence that every now and then you see them flying like the leaves before the wind. If on these occasions you look round carefully you will see in the middle distance a militiaman (i.e., street policeman) from whom they are flying." Wicksteed, *Life Under the Soviets*, p. 17. See also Muldavin, *Red Fog*, pp. 50, 112–113; *Sotsialisticheskii vestnik* (Berlin), 1929, No. 21, p. 7; Greenwall, *Mirrors*, pp. 38–39; and Bernard Edelhertz, *The Russian Paradox: A First-Hand Study of Life Under the Soviets* (New York, 1930), p. 9.

92. Eve Garrette Grady, *Seeing Red: Behind the Scenes in Russia Today* (New York, 1931), pp. 176–177. See also White, *These Russians*, p. 75; *TPG*, 1929, No. 103 (May 9), p. 4; and *Materialy. VII.*, p. 125.

93. Julian Huxley, *A Scientist Among the Soviets* (New York, 1932), pp. 46–48.

94. George A. Burrell, *An American Engineer Looks at Russia* (Boston, 1932), pp. 98, 103. For more on the continuation of private trade after NEP, see *Sotsialisticheskii vestnik* (Berlin), 1930, No. 10, p. 15; 1931, No. 1, p. 14; 1931, No. 17, p. 15; John Scott, *Behind the Urals: An American Worker in Russia's City of Steel* (Bloomington, 1973), pp. 39, 241; Utley, *The Dream We Lost*, p. 79; Maurice Hindus, *Red Bread* (New York, 1931), p. 72; Fischer, *My Lives*, p. 105; Ella Winter, *Red Virtue: Human Relationships in the New Russia* (New York, 19??), p. 14; J. G. Lockhart, *Babel Visited: A Churchman in Soviet Russia* (Milwaukee, 19??), p. 114; and *Illiustrirovannaia Rossiia* (Paris), 1930, No. 23, p. 6. Many observers were struck by the extremely high prices in the markets (prices that reflected the acute shortages of nearly all commodities).

95. Waldo Frank, *Dawn in Russia: The Record of a Journey* (New York, 1932), pp. 12, 79; Fischer, *My Lives*, pp. 128–129.

CHAPTER 5

1. Armand Hammer, *The Quest of the Romanoff Treasure* (New York, 1932), p. 199.
2. S. O. Zagorskii, *K sotsializmu ili k kapitalizmu?* (Paris, 1927), p. 120; Iu. Larin, *Chastnyi kapital v SSSR* (Moscow-Leningrad, 1927), pp. 7, 12, 25–26; E. H. Carr, *The Bolshevik Revolution*, 3 vols. (London, 1950–53; reprint, Harmondsworth, 1973), 2:312; M. M. Zhirmunskii, *Chastnyi kapital v tovarooborote* (Moscow, 1924), pp. 10–11, 23; A. Zalkind, ed., *Chastnaia torgovlia Soiuza SSR* (Moscow, 1927), p. 157; Ts. M. Kron, *Chastnaia torgovlia v SSSR* (Moscow, 1926), pp. 14, 113; *Iugo-Vostok* (Rostov-on-the-Don), 1922, No. 2, p. 164; and *Torgovo-promyshlennaia gazeta* (hereafter cited as *TPG*), 1922, No. 150 (September 9), p. 1.
3. Iu. S. Kondurushkin, *Chastnyi kapital pered sovetskim sudom* (Moscow-Leningrad, 1927), pp. 43–44; and Larin, *Chastnyi kapital*, p. 26.
4. *Na novykh putiakh. Itogi novoi ekonomicheskoi politiki 1921–1922 g.g.* (Moscow, 1923), *vypusk* I, pp. 116–118, 237, 317; *Ekonomicheskoe obozrenie*, 1925, April, p. 192; and *TPG*, 1922, No. 150 (September 9), p. 1.
5. Spektator [Miron Isaakovich Nachimson], *Russkii "Termidor"* (Kharbin, 1927), p. 132; Zhirmunskii, *Chastnyi kapital*, pp. 22, 86; A. M. Ginzburg, ed., *Chastnyi kapital v narodnom khoziaistve SSSR. Materialy kommissii VSNKh SSSR* (Moscow-Leningrad, 1927), pp. 18, 20; *TPG*, 1922, No. 124 (August 8), p. 4; 1922, No. 132 (August 17), p. 3; 1924, No. 79 (April 6), p. 1; *Iugo-Vostok* (Rostov-on-the-Don), 1924, No. 4, p. 64; *Na novykh putiakh*, *vypusk* I, p. 111; and *Sobranie uzakonenii i rasporiazhenii. 1917–1949* (Moscow, 1920–50) (hereafter cited as *SU*), 1923, No. 29, art. 336.
6. Zhirmunskii, *Chastnyi kapital*, p. 24; Ginzburg, *Chastnyi kapital*, p. 19; Kron, *Chastnaia torgovlia*, p. 16; *Torgovye izvestiia*, 1925, No. 76 (October 15), p. 5; *Ekonomicheskii vestnik Zakavkaz'ia* (Tiflis), 1926, No. 2, p. 54; *Severo-Kavkazskii krai* (Rostov-on-the-Don), 1925, No. 4–5, p. 101; and *Ekonomicheskoe obozrenie*, 1925, April, p. 194.
7. Maurice Dobb, *Soviet Economic Development Since 1917* (London–New York, 1966), p. 143; G. A. Dikhtiar, *Sovetskaia torgovlia v period postroeniia sotsializma* (Moscow, 1961), p. 210; V. A. Arkhipov and L. F. Morozov, *Bor'ba protiv kapitalisticheskikh elementov v promyshlennosti i torgovle. 20-e—nachalo 30-kh godov* (Moscow, 1978), p. 65; and Ginzburg, *Chastnyi kapital*, pp. 10, 127–128, 130.
8. Zhirmunskii, *Chastnyi kapital*, pp. 19, 77; Dikhtiar, *Sovetskaia torgovlia*, p. 208.
9. Kron, *Chastnaia torgovlia*, p. 31; *Torgovye izvestiia*, 1925, No. 65 (September 19), p. 1.
10. Kondurushkin, *Chastnyi kapital*, pp. 30–33, 58–59; *Ekonomicheskoe obozrenie*, 1925, April, p. 192; and Zagorskii, *K sotsializmu*, p. 121.
11. Kondurushkin, *Chastnyi kapital*, pp. 42, 100; Arkhipov and Morozov, *Bor'ba*, p. 78.
12. Kondurushkin, *Chastnyi kapital*, pp. 56, 59–60, 186.
13. *TPG*, 1922, No. 70 (June 3), p. 2; 1922, No. 127 (August 11), p. 1; and *SU*, 1923, No. 1, art. 8. Some state officials secretly owned private businesses even at the end of NEP. *Finansy i narodnoe khoziaistvo*, 1929, No. 22, p. 17.
14. Kondurushkin, *Chastnyi kapital*, pp. 3, 53–54, 158–160; Frank Alfred Golder and Lincoln Hutchinson, *On the Trail of the Russian Famine* (Stanford, 1927), pp. 202–203; Larin, *Chastnyi kapital*, p. 10; *Ekonomicheskoe obozrenie*, 1925, April, p. 199; Ilya Ehrenburg, *Memoirs: 1921–1941* (New York, 1966), p. 68; Edwin W. Hullinger, *The Reforging of Russia* (New York, 1925), p. 235; Richard Eaton, *Under the Red Flag* (New York, 1924), p. 116; and I. Ia. Trifonov, *Klassy i klassovaia bor'ba v SSSR v nachale nepa*, Vol. 2, *Podgotovka ekonomicheskogo nastupleniia na novuiu burzhuaziiu* (Leningrad, 1969), pp. 60–61, 164.
15. Walter Duranty, *I Write as I Please* (New York, 1935), pp. 140–144.
16. I. Ia. Trifonov, *Ocherki istorii klassovoi bor'by v SSSR v gody NEPa (1921–1937)* (Moscow, 1960), pp. 78–79; Kondurushkin, *Chastnyi kapital*, pp. 65, 191; and *Zakony o chastnom kapitale. Sbornik zakonov, instruktsii, prikazov i raz"iasnenii*, comp. B. S. Mal'tsman and B. E. Ratner (Moscow, 1928), pp. 143–144.

17. Kondurushkin, *Chastnyi kapital*, pp. 94, 153.

18. *Torgovye izvestiia*, 1925, No. 93 (November 24), p. 5; Trifonov, *Ocherki*, p. 80. See also Ia. Grinval'd, I. Khankin, and I. Chilim, *Klass protiv klassa*. *Ekonomicheskaia kontrrevoliutsiia v Astrakhani* (Saratov, 1930), pp. 113–117; *Torgovye izvestiia*, 1926, No. 44 (April 22), p. 4.

19. *Torgovye izvestiia*, 1925, No. 69 (September 29), p. 2; 1926, No. 52 (May 15), p. 4; Zagorskii, *K sotsializmu*, p. 155; and *Ekonomicheskaia zhizn'*, 1925, No. 246 (October 27), p. 4.

20. Andrei Fabrichnyi, *Chastnyi kapital na poroge piatiletki* (Moscow, 1930), pp. 31, 37; Zagorskii, *K sotsializmu*, p. 152; Trifonov, *Klassy*, 2:218, 240; Kondurushkin, *Chastnyi kapital*, p. 146; Zhirmunskii, *Chastnyi kapital*, p. 167; *Zakony o chastnom kapitale*, pp. 143–144, 153; L. Kolesnikov, *Litso klassovogo vraga* (Moscow-Leningrad, 1928), pp. 32–33; I. Mingulin, *Puti razvitiia chastnogo kapitala* (Moscow-Leningrad, 1927), p. 66; *TPG*, 1926, No. 225 (October 1), p. 6; 1927, No. 21 (January 27), p. 3; 1928, No. 106 (May 9), p. 6; 1929, No. 97 (April 27), p. 6; *Torgovye izvestiia*, 1926, No. 99 (September 11), p. 4; *Finansy i narodnoe khoziaistvo*, 1930, No. 3, p. 19; and *Ekonomicheskaia zhizn'*, 1922, No. 250 (November 4), p. 2; 1924, No. 237 (July 19), p. 4; 1925, No. 252 (November 3), p. 4; 1926, No. 173 (July 30), p. 4.

21. L. F. Morozov, *Reshaiushchii etap bor'by s nepmanskoi burzhuaziei* (1926–1929) (Moscow, 1960), pp. 74–75; Arkhipov and Morozov, *Bor'ba*, p. 191; *Torgovye izvestiia*, 1926, No. 32 (March 25), p. 3; and *Ekonomicheskaia zhizn'*, 1925, No. 257 (November 11), p. 3.

22. Trifonov, *Klassy*, 2:219.

23. Kron, *Chastnaia torgovlia*, p. 119; Morozov, *Reshaiushchii etap*, p. 51; Zagorskii, *K sotsializmu*, pp. 149, 154; Larin, *Chastnyi kapital*, p. 32; and N. Riauzov, *Vytesnenie chastnogo posrednika iz tovarooborota* (Moscow, 1930), p. 35.

24. *TPG*, 1927, No. 210 (September 15), p. 6; *Torgovye izvestiia*, 1925, No. 90 (November 17), p. 2; 1926, No. 32 (March 25), p. 4.

25. *TPG*, 1928, No. 55 (March 4), p. 6; 1928, No. 267 (November 17), p. 4; Theodor Seibert, *Red Russia* (London, 1932), p. 339; and William C. White, *These Russians* (New York, 1931), p. 76.

26. Kondurushkin, *Chastnyi kapital*, pp. 123–124; Ginzburg, *Chastnyi kapital*, p. 14; and Victor Serge, *Memoirs of a Revolutionary 1901–1941* (London, 1967; reprint, 1975), p. 200.

27. Kondurushkin, *Chastnyi kapital*, p. 132; Larin, *Chastnyi kapital*, p. 116.

28. Ginzburg, *Chastnyi kapital*, p. 14.

29. Riauzov, *Vytesnenie*, p. 35. See also *Mestnoe khoziaistvo* (Kiev), 1924, No. 6 (March), p. 72.

30. *Kooperativnoe stroitel'stvo*, 1926, No. 14, p. 47; Zhirmunskii, *Chastnyi kapital*, p. 100; *TPG*, 1922, No. 127 (August 11), p. 2; 1923, No. 190 (August 25), p. 4; 1928, No. 225 (September 27), p. 4; Kron, *Chastnaia torgovlia*, p. 34; and *Materialy po istorii SSSR. VII. Dokumenty po istorii sovetskogo obshchestva* (Moscow, 1959), p. 150.

31. Zalkind, *Chastnaia torgovlia*, pp. 66–67, 147; Ginzburg, *Chastnyi kapital*, p. 30; Zhirmunskii, *Chastnyi kapital*, p. 96; Spektator, *Russkii "Termidor"*, pp. 133–134; Bernard Edelhertz, *The Russian Paradox: A First-Hand Study of Life Under the Soviets* (New York, 1930), p. 9; White, *These Russians*, pp. 68, 324, 337; Paul Scheffer, *Seven Years in Soviet Russia* (New York, 1932), p. 55; Karl Borders, *Village Life Under the Soviets* (New York, 1927), pp. 102–103; and *Ekonomicheskaia zhizn'*, 1924, No. 306 (October 10), p. 4.

32. Kron, *Chastnaia torgovlia*, pp. 79–80. See also *Na novykh putiakh, vypusk I*, p. 186; *Torgovye izvestiia*, 1925, No. 91 (November 19), p. 2; 1925, No. 92 (November 21), p. 5; and Zagorskii, *K sotsializmu*, p. 151.

33. Ginzburg, *Chastnyi kapital*, p. 240; Fabrichnyi, *Chastnyi kapital*, p. 35; Zagorskii, *K sotsializmu*, p. 243; and *TPG*, 1929, No. 8 (January 10), p. 4.

34. Spektator, *Russkii "Termidor"*, p. 130; E. H. Carr and R. W. Davies, *Foundations of a Planned Economy*, 1926–1929, 2 vols. (London, 1969), 1 (part 2): 670; *Ekono-*

*micheskoe obozrenie*, 1926, August, p. 96; *TPG*, 1927, No. 276 (December 2), p. 5; and *Torgovye izvestiia*, 1926, No. 6 (January 16), p. 5.

35. I. A. Bialyi and A. I. Litvin, *Chastnyi kapital v g. Irkutske* (Irkutsk, 1929), pp. 31–34, 36–37.

36. *TPG*, 1928, No. 267 (November 17), p. 4. See also Riauzov, *Vytesnenie*, p. 31; Mingulin, *Puti razvitiia*, p. 116; and *TPG*, 1927, No. 31 (February 8), p. 2; 1927, No. 147 (July 2), p. 4.

37. *Torgovye izvestiia*, 1925, No. 85 (November 5), p. 5; *TPG*, 1924, No. 91 (April 20), p. 5; *Severo-Kavkazskii krai* (Rostov-on-the-Don), 1925, No. 1, p. 99; *Ekonomicheskii vestnik Zakavkaz'ia* (Tiflis), 1926, No. 6, p. 29; and Larin, *Chastnyi kapital*, p. 41. Victor Kravchenko served in a Red Army unit assigned to combat smuggling along the Soviet Union's border with Persia. His account creates the impression that smugglers found the border something less than airtight. Victor Kravchenko, *I Chose Freedom* (New York, 1946), pp. 47–49.

Most contraband was imported, not exported. Among the items that were smuggled *out*, foreign currencies and precious metals and stones predominated, followed by commodities such as flax, wool, and furs. *Sovetskaia torgovlia*, 1927, No. 7, pp. 15–16; *Na novykh putiakh*, vypusk I, pp. 220, 223; *Ekonomicheskoe obozrenie*, 1925, November, p. 188; and V. P. Dmitrenko, *Torgovaia politika sovetskogo gosudarstva posle perekhoda k NEPu 1921–1924 gg.* (Moscow, 1971), p. 85.

38. For various estimates on the volume of contraband, see Ginzburg, *Chastnyi kapital*, p. 16; Kondurushkin, *Chastnyi kapital*, p. 133; Fabrichnyi, *Chastnyi kapital*, p. 34; and Larin, *Chastnyi kapital*, p. 36.

39. *Torgovaia gazeta*, 1922, No. 37 (April 11), p. 4; *TPG*, 1922, No. 126 (August 10), p. 5; and Dmitrenko, *Torgovaia politika*, p. 85.

40. *TPG*, 1924, No. 75 (April 2), p. 1.

41. Dmitrenko, *Torgovaia politika*, p. 85.

42. *TPG*, 1922, No. 150 (September 9), p. 1; 1923, No. 194 (August 30), p. 2; 1924, No. 75 (April 2), p. 1; 1924, No. 91 (April 20), p. 5; *Sovetskaia torgovlia*, 1927, No. 7, p. 16; *Ekonomicheskoe obozrenie*, 1925, November, p. 187; *Ekonomicheskaia zhizn'*, 1928, No. 68 (March 21), p. 3; Kondurushkin, *Chastnyi kapital*, pp. 135–136; and Larin, *Chastnyi kapital*, pp. 36–37.

43. *Torgovye izvestiia*, 1925, No. 85 (November 5), p. 5; *Ekonomicheskoe obozrenie*, 1925, November, pp. 186, 190–191; Kondurushkin, *Chastnyi kapital*, p. 135; and Larin, *Chastnyi kapital*, p. 37. For descriptions of tricks used by smugglers to conceal their goods, see *TPG*, 1924, No. 25 (February 1), p. 5; *Torgovye izvestiia*, 1925, No. 85 (November 5), p. 5.

44. *TPG*, 1923, No. 294 (December 30), p. 2; 1924, No. 113 (May 21), p. 3; Larin, *Chastnyi kapital*, p. 39; Zagorskii, *K sotsializmu*, p. 161; Kondurushkin, *Chastnyi kapital*, p. 45; and Arkhipov and Morozov, *Bor'ba*, pp. 191–192.

45. Kondurushkin, *Chastnyi kapital*, pp. 136–137; *Torgovaia gazeta*, 1922, No. 15, p. 5; and *Torgovye izvestiia*, 1925, No. 85 (November 5), p. 5; 1926, No. 10 (January 28), p. 4; 1926, No. 20 (February 20), p. 6; 1926, No. 26 (March 9), p. 4; 1926, No. 27 (March 11), p. 4; 1926, No. 28 (March 16), p. 4.

46. P. C. Hiebert and Orie O. Miller, *Feeding the Hungry: Russian Famine 1919–1925* (Scottdale, Pa., 1929), pp. 161, 209, 267, 278–282; F. A. Mackenzie, *Russia Before Dawn* (London, 1923), p. 157.

47. The food package contained 49 pounds of white flour, 25 pounds of rice, 15 pounds of sugar, 10 pounds of lard or bacon, 3 pounds of tea, and 20 tins of condensed milk. The clothing package contained four and two-thirds yards of wool fabric, four yards of lining for the wool fabric, sixteen yards of muslin, and eight yards of flannelette, as well as buttons and thread.

48. Duranty, *I Write*, p. 149.

49. Kondurushkin, *Chastnyi kapital*, p. 137; *Torgovye izvestiia*, 1926, No. 33 (March 27), p. 4; 1926, No. 87 (August 10), p. 2; *Sovetskaia torgovlia*, 1927, No. 7, p. 17; and *Illiustrirovannaia Rossiia* (Paris), 1926, No. 26, p. 11.

50. E. Ashmead-Bartlett, *The Riddle of Russia* (London, 1929), pp. 207–208.

51. *Torgovye izvestiia*, 1925, No. 5 (April 11), p. 4; Dorothy Thompson, *The New Russia* (New York, 1928), p. 33; Duranty, *I Write*, p. 146; Walter Duranty, *Duranty Reports Russia* (New York, 1934), p. 38; Philip Gibbs, *Since Then* (London, 1930), pp. 335–336, 338; White, *These Russians*, p. 63; Henri Béraud, *The Truth About Moscow* (London, 1926), pp. 47, 121; Kravchenko, *I Chose Freedom*, pp. 66–67; H. J. Greenwall, *Mirrors of Moscow* (London, 1929), p. 39; Hullinger, *Reforging Russia*, pp. 71, 208; and Anne O'Hare McCormick, *The Hammer and the Scythe* (New York, 1928), pp. 34–35. Photographs of "former people" selling their personal possessions may be found in *Illiustrirovannaia Rossiia* (Paris), 1927, No. 44, p. 7; 1929, No. 52, pp. 4–5; 1930, No. 42, p. 5; Thompson, *The New Russia*, page facing p. 32.

52. Thompson, *The New Russia*, p. 34.

## CHAPTER 6

1. *Mestnoe khoziaistvo* (Kiev), 1924, No. 6 (March), pp. 78–79; Markoosha Fischer, *My Lives in Russia* (New York, 1944), p. 39; Walter Duranty, *Duranty Reports Russia* (New York, 1934), p. 107; and Eugene Lyons, *Assignment in Utopia* (New York, 1937), p. 85.

2. V. I. Lenin, *Polnoe sobranie sochinenii*, 5th ed., 55 vols. (Moscow, 1958–65), 45:265.

3. On private manufacturers engaged in trade, see *Promyshlennost' i torgovlia*, 1923, No. 1, p. 14; Salo W. Baron, *The Russian Jew Under Tsars and Soviets* (New York, 1964), p. 251; and Iu. Larin, *Chastnyi kapital v SSSR* (Moscow-Leningrad, 1927), p. 242.

4. Numerous decrees throughout the decade attempted to entice private capital, generally with tax incentives, into several branches of production where the "socialist" sector alone could not meet the country's needs. These activities included mining many different kinds of minerals, pumping oil, producing various construction materials, and constructing housing, as well as producing various consumer goods. See, for example, *Zakony o chastnom kapitale. Sbornik zakonov, instruktsii, prikazov i raz"iasnenii*, comp. B. S. Mal'tsman and B. E. Ratner (Moscow, 1928), pp. 240–241, 246, 268–270, 272–273; *Sobranie zakonov i rasporiazhenii raboche-krest'ianskogo pravitel'stva SSSR. 1924–1949* (Moscow, 1925–50) (hereafter cited as *SZ*), 1927, No. 5, art. 46; *SZ*, 1928, No. 6, art. 49; *SZ*, 1929, No. 9, arts. 85, 89; V. A. Arkhipov and L. F. Morozov, *Bor'ba protiv kapitalisticheskikh elementov v promyshlennosti i torgovle. 20-e—nachalo 30-kh godov* (Moscow, 1978), p. 49; and *Torgovo-promyshlennaia gazeta* (hereafter cited as *TPG*), 1928, No. 254 (October 31), p. 2. These decrees were not strikingly effective, but they do illustrate the party's desire to utilize private manufacturing, even at the end of NEP. Another decree issued in May 1928 stressed the need to increase handicraft production of consumer goods to ease the "goods famine." The state's ultimate goal was not to "liquidate" these private manufacturers but to organize them into producers' cooperatives. *SZ*, 1928, No. 30, art. 267.

5. *Resheniia partii i pravitel'stva po khoziaistvennym voprosam* (Moscow, 1967–), 1:232.

6. *Sobranie uzakonenii i rasporiazhenii. 1917–1949* (Moscow, 1920–50) (hereafter cited as *SU*), 1921, No. 53, art. 323.

7. *SU*, 1921, No. 48, art. 240. For the decree of November 29, 1920, see *SU*, 1920, No. 93, art. 512.

8. A. M. Ginzburg, ed., *Chastnyi kapital v narodnom khoziaistve SSSR. Materialy kommissii VSNKh SSSR* (Moscow-Leningrad, 1927), p. 294; *Zakony o chastnoi promyshlennosti*, comp. A. E. Vorms and S. V. Mints (Moscow, 1924), pp. 26–27; and *SU*, 1921, No. 79, art. 684. See *SU*, 1921, No. 72, art. 583, for yet another restatement by VTsIK of the main point of the May 17 decree. Official interpretations and explanations of these denationalization decrees continued to appear for a number of years after 1921. See, for example, *Zakony o chastnom kapitale*, p. 187.

9. E. H. Carr, *The Bolshevik Revolution*, 3 vols. (London, 1950–53; reprint, Har-

mondsworth, 1973), 2:300; V. M. Kopalkin, *Chastnaia promyshlennost' SSSR* (Moscow-Leningrad, 1927), p. 13; I. Ia. Trifonov, *Klassy i klassovaia bor'ba v SSSR v nachale nepa*, Vol. 2, *Podgotovka ekonomicheskogo nastupleniia na novuiu burzhuaziiu* (Leningrad, 1969), p. 72; and *Torgovaia gazeta*, 1922, No. 8, p. 3.

10. Carr, *Bolshevik Revolution*, 2:300; *SU*, 1921, No. 53, art. 313; and *Zakony o chastnom kapitale*, pp. 196–201. Private leaseholders were also permitted to import raw materials and equipment for "their" factories. *Torgovaia gazeta*, 1922, No. 37, p. 2. Very few engaged in such sophisticated and costly activity, however. For an announcement that a cement factory is available for lease, see *Ekonomicheskaia zhizn'*, 1925, No. 200 (September 3), p. 6.

11. *Ekonomicheskoe obozrenie*, 1923, No. 2, p. 13; D. I. Mishanin, "Arenda gosudarstvennykh predpriiatii chastnymi predprinimateliami, kak odna iz form gosudarstvennogo kapitalizma v ekonomike perekhodnogo perioda ot kapitalizma k sotsializmu v SSSR," in E. A. Messerle and D. I. Mishanin, *Metodicheskoe posobie po politekonomii* (Alma-Ata, 1961), pp. 26, 38, 45.

12. *Ekonomicheskoe obozrenie*, 1923, No. 2, pp. 13–14, 24.

13. Estimates for 1921, 1922, and 1923 may be found in Mishanin, "Arenda," pp. 26, 44; *Na novykh putiakh. Itogi novoi ekonomicheskoi politiki 1921–1922 g.g.* (Moscow, 1923), *vypusk* III, pp. 74–75; Kopalkin, *Chastnaia promyshlennost'*, pp. 15–16; and Trifonov, *Klassy*, 2:69.

14. *Ekonomicheskoe stroitel'stvo*, 1925, No. 1, pp. 93–94; *Promyshlennost' Ukrainy* (Khar'kov), 1924, No. 19, pp. 53–54; *Iugo-Vostok* (Rostov-on-the-Don), 1924, No. 1–2, p. 142; and *TPG*, 1922, No. 221 (December 2), p. 6. For additional reports from the provinces, as well as from Moscow and Petrograd, see *Promyshlennost' i torgovlia*, 1922, No. 1, p. 30; *Nashe khoziaistvo* (Vladimir), 1927, No. 4–5, p. 23; *Torgovaia gazeta*, 1922, No. 7, p. 4; Trifonov, *Klassy*, 2:72; *TPG*, 1922, No. 82 (June 18), p. 4; 1922, No. 96 (July 6), p. 4; 1922, No. 153 (September 13), p. 4; 1922, No. 209 (November 18), p. 4.

15. Iu. S. Kondurushkin, *Chastnyi kapital pered sovetskim sudom* (Moscow-Leningrad, 1927), p. 64; Trifonov, *Klassy*, 2:73; and Mishanin, "Arenda," p. 26.

16. Kopalkin, *Chastnaia promyshlennost'*, pp. 15–16; Arkhipov and Morozov, *Bor'ba*, pp. 49, 125; and Mishanin, "Arenda," p. 45. Although most privately leased factories were small, this was not always the case. Local officials in Vladimir, for example, leased an embroidery factory with more than three hundred workers to a private entrepreneur. *Nashe khoziaistvo* (Vladimir), 1927, No. 4–5, p. 23.

17. *Na novykh putiakh, vypusk* III, pp. 71–72; Mishanin, "Arenda," pp. 26, 56–57; and *Ekonomicheskoe obozrenie*, 1923, No. 2, pp. 17–18.

18. Mishanin, "Arenda," pp. 30–31, 33–36, 58–59; Kopalkin, *Chastnaia promyshlennost'*, pp. 17–18. In 1921 the state recommended that the only factories leased be those requiring repairs before they could be operated. This stipulation was widely ignored, however, which is evident from the fact that fully three fourths of all factories leased by the end of 1922 were ready for production. *Ekonomicheskoe obozrenie*, 1923, No. 2, pp. 16–17.

19. *Na novykh putiakh, vypusk* III, p. 76; *Iugo-Vostok* (Rostov-on-the-Don), 1924, No. 1–2, p. 142; *Ekonomicheskoe obozrenie*, 1923, No. 2, pp. 20, 22–23, 25; Mishanin, "Arenda," pp. 34–35; and Kopalkin, *Chastnaia promyshlennost'*, pp. 17–18.

20. Ginzburg, *Chastnyi kapital*, p. 290; *Ekonomicheskoe obozrenie*, 1923, No. 2, p. 24; Mishanin, "Arenda," pp. 61, 63; and *TPG*, 1922, No. 118 (August 1), p. 5.

21. *Ekonomicheskoe obozrenie*, 1923, No. 2, p. 19; *Iugo-Vostok* (Rostov-on-the-Don), 1924, No. 1–2, p. 142; and Mishanin, "Arenda," pp. 32, 64.

22. *SU*, 1921, No. 56, art. 354.

23. See, for example, *SU*, 1922, No. 16, art. 162; *SU*, 1922, No. 17, art. 180; *SU*, 1923, No. 5, art. 89; *Torgovo-promyshlennyi vestnik*, 1923, No. 16, p. 14; and *SZ*, 1926, No. 63, art. 474.

24. Definitions of census factories differ slightly. See Ginzburg, *Chastnyi kapital*, p. 70; Larin, *Chastnyi kapital*, p. 111. There were some exceptions to any definition. For example, operations of the following types, regardless of the number of workers they em-

ployed, were considered to be in the census category: sugar beet refining; wine, mead, and beer making; cigarette making; yeast processing; oil refining; leather-processing enterprises with over ten tanning vats; brick works with continuous-action kilns; and grain mills with at least five grinding units. For these and other exceptions, see Ginzburg, *Chastnyi kapital*, p. 70.

25. Kopalkin, *Chastnaia promyshlennost'*, p. 16; Ginzburg, *Chastnyi kapital*, p. 38; I. Mingulin, *Puti razvitiia chastnogo kapitala* (Moscow-Leningrad, 1927), p. 102; and I. Ia. Trifonov, *Likvidatsiia ekspluatatorskikh klassov v SSSR* (Moscow, 1975), p. 214.

26. *Ekonomicheskoe obozrenie*, 1926, March, p. 122. See also Mingulin, *Puti razvitiia*, p. 98.

27. These figures can be calculated from the data in Ginzburg, *Chastnyi kapital*, p. 40. See also Vasil'kov, *Chastnyi kapital v khoziaistve orlovskoi gubernii*. (*Issledovatel'skaia rabota Gubplana pod rukovodstvom i redaktsiei Vasil'kova*) (Orel, 1928), p. 47; Mingulin, *Puti razvitiia*, p. 113; and Ginzburg, *Chastnyi kapital*, p. 23. Cooperative census operations were much closer in size to those in the private sector than to state factories.

28. For more on the legal uncertainty, see *Zakony o chastnoi promyshlennosti*, pp. 13, 22–23; Ginzburg, *Chastnyi kapital*, p. 295. For references to private factories with over twenty workers, see *Nashe khoziaistvo* (Vladimir), 1927, No. 4–5, p. 23; Vasil'kov, *Chastnyi kapital*, pp. 47–48; *TPG*, 1923, No. 78 (April 11), p. 3; and Trifonov, *Klassy*, 2:52–53, 68, 74. Some of these factories were privately owned (i.e., not leased).

29. Ginzburg, *Chastnyi kapital*, p. 40; Kopalkin, *Chastnaia promyshlennost'*, p. 23; and Mishanin, "Arenda," p. 64.

30. Trifonov, *Klassy*, 2:52; *Ekonomicheskoe obozrenie*, 1926, March, p. 122; 1926, August, p. 92; E. H. Carr and R. W. Davies, *Foundations of a Planned Economy, 1926–1929*, 2 vols. (London, 1969), 1 (part 2): 950; Ginzburg, *Chastnyi kapital*, pp. 22, 40; and Kopalkin, *Chastnaia promyshlennost'*, p. 23.

31. Ginzburg, *Chastnyi kapital*, p. 40. There are slightly different figures in Kopalkin, *Chastnaia promyshlennost'*, p. 23.

32. When examining statistics on private census production, care should be taken to identify those figures that include the output of a handful of factories (called "concession" factories) leased to foreigners. *Ekonomicheskoe obozrenie*, 1926, March, p. 122; Carr and Davies, *Foundations*, 1 (part 2): 950; and Mingulin, *Puti razvitiia*, pp. 89–90, 98, 114.

33. For reasons that are unclear, the rank I share of licenses dropped to about 60 percent during the first three quarters of 1923, before recovering to approximately 80 percent by the end of the year and remaining at this percentage until the summer of 1925. Ginzburg, *Chastnyi kapital*, p. 201; G. Belkin, *Rabochii vopros v chastnoi promyshlennosti* (Moscow, 1926), p. 108; Trifonov, *Klassy*, 2:68; and *Ekonomicheskoe obozrenie*, 1924, No. 6, p. 44. The definitions of the industrial ranks differed slightly in the various business-tax decrees issued during NEP. A law of February 10, 1922, for example, set the upper limit on rank I operations at four workers. *SU*, 1922, No. 17, art. 180. But most editions of the business-tax table put the limit at three. See *SU*, 1921, No. 56, art. 354; *SU*, 1923, No. 5, art. 89; and *SZ*, 1926, No. 63, art. 474.

34. *Finansy i narodnoe khoziaistvo*, 1927, No. 25, p. 28; 1927, No. 52, p. 26; Ginzburg, *Chastnyi kapital*, p. 201. One source puts the rank I share of licenses at 22 percent for the first half of 1925/26: *Finansy i narodnoe khoziaistvo*, 1927, No. 8, p. 26. This is far out of line with all the other sources. The reason for the disagreement is not apparent.

35. Ginzburg, *Chastnyi kapital*, p. 201; *Ekonomicheskoe obozrenie*, 1924, No. 6, p. 45; Trifonov, *Klassy*, 2:52; and Arkhipov and Morozov, *Bor'ba*, p. 43. If craftsmen without business-tax licenses were included in the statistics, the rural share of private manufacturers would be even more predominant. More information about these people will be presented later in this chapter.

36. *Finansy i narodnoe khoziaistvo*, 1927, No. 46, p. 23; 1927, No. 50, p. 25; 1927, No. 52, p. 26; Ginzburg, *Chastnyi kapital*, p. 201; *Ekonomicheskii vestnik Zakavkaz'ia* (Tiflis), 1926, No. 6, p. 25; *TPG*, 1924, No. 58 (March 11), p. 2; and *Ekonomicheskoe*

*obozrenie*, 1924, No. 6, p. 44. Ranks I and II were defined according to the table in *SU*, 1921, No. 56, art. 354. This definition changed slightly in subsequent decrees. The table in *SZ*, 1926, No. 63, art. 474, was used for rank V in 1927.

37. *Ekonomicheskaia zhizn'*, 1922, No. 209 (September 17), p. 4; Arkhipov and Morozov, *Bor'ba*, p. 43; *Ekonomicheskoe obozrenie*, 1924, No. 6, p. 44; Ginzburg, *Chastnyi kapital*, p. 201 (the figures here do not include Transcaucasia and Uzbekistan); Belkin, *Rabochii vopros*, p. 108; *Finansy i narodnoe khoziaistvo*, 1927, No. 8, p. 26; 1927, No. 25, p. 28; *SZ*, 1925, No. 25, art. 168; *SZ*, 1925, No. 32, art. 213; and *SZ*, 1925, No. 38, art. 285.

38. On the effect of the tax reforms on people in rank I, see Ginzburg, *Chastnyi kapital*, p. 201.

39. In some sources the term *kustari* includes craftsmen in the lowest business-tax "industrial" ranks, but in this work we will understand *kustari* to be only those small-scale producers without business-tax licenses.

40. For some photographs of *kustari* and their workshops, see D. Shapiro, *Kustarnaia promyshlennost' i narodnoe khoziaistvo SSSR* (Moscow-Leningrad, 1928).

41. *Ekonomicheskoe obozrenie*, 1926, August, pp. 92, 96; 1927, June, pp. 119–120; S. O. Zagorskii, *K sotsializmu ili k kapitalizmu?* (Paris, 1927), pp. 226, 229, 231; Mingulin, *Puti razvitiia*, p. 102; Ginzburg, *Chastnyi kapital*, p. 72; Carr and Davies, *Foundations*, 1 (part 1): 390; and I. A. Gladkov, ed., *Sovetskoe narodnoe khoziaistvo v 1921–1925 gg.* (Moscow, 1960), p. 196.

42. *Direktivy KPSS i sovetskogo pravitel'stva po khoziaistvennym voprosam. 1917–1957 gody*, 4 vols. (Moscow, 1957–58), 1:311–314; V. M. Selunskaia, ed., *Izmeneniia sotsial'noi struktury sovetskogo obshchestva. 1921-seredina 30-kh godov* (Moscow, 1979), p. 134; Ginzburg, *Chastnyi kapital*, pp. 12, 84–85, 89; Mingulin, *Puti razvitiia*, pp. 90, 104; Zagorskii, *K sotsializmu*, p. 235; *Ekonomicheskaia zhizn'*, 1925, No. 61 (March 15), p. 2; Arkhipov and Morozov, *Bor'ba*, pp. 50, 205; *Trudy tsentral'nogo statisticheskogo upravleniia*, Vol. 33, *vypusk* I, pp. 86–115; Vol. 33, *vypusk* II, pp. 118–153; Shapiro, *Kustarnaia promyshlennost'*, p. 12; *Ekonomicheskoe obozrenie*, 1926, August, p. 96; and Trifonov, *Likvidatsiia*, p. 222. For statistics from various localities confirming the dominance of the private sector in petty industry see *Tverskoi krai* (Tver'), 1926, No. 1, p. 29; *TPG*, 1924, No. 56 (March 8), p. 1; 1927, No. 276 (December 2), p. 5; 1928, No. 29 (February 3), p. 6; 1928, No. 39 (February 15), p. 3; I. A. Bialyi and A. I. Litvin, *Chastnyi kapital v g. Irkutske* (Irkutsk, 1929), p. 23; A. S. Moskovskii, "Melkaia i kustarno-remeslennaia promyshlennost' Sibiri v kontse vosstanovitel'nogo perioda," in *Bakhrushinskie chteniia* (Novosibirsk, 1974), p. 23; and *Narodnoe khoziaistvo Srednei Azii* (Tashkent), 1927, No. 8–9, p. 78.

43. Mingulin, *Puti razvitiia*, p. 91; Zagorskii, *K sotsializmu*, p. 228; Trifonov, *Klassy*, 2:53, 69; and A. Zolotarev, *Regulirovanie tovarooborota* (Khar'kov, 1926), p. 24.

44. *Ekonomicheskoe obozrenie*, 1924, No. 6, p. 45.

45. *Ekonomicheskoe obozrenie*, 1927, June, p. 117; Mingulin, *Puti razvitiia*, p. 90; *XIV s''ezd vsesoiuznoi kommunisticheskoi partii(b). 18–31 dekabria 1925 g.: stenograficheskii otchet* (Moscow, 1926), p. 33; L. F. Morozov, *Reshaiushchii etap bor'by s nepmanskoi burzhuaziei (1926–1929)* (Moscow, 1960), pp. 12–13; Larin, *Chastnyi kapital*, pp. 118, 121, 127.

46. There were a fair number of private enterprises that produced construction materials such as bricks and nails. But even some of these items were destined for individual consumers, most often peasants.

47. *Promyshlennost' Ukrainy* (Khar'kov), 1924, No. 19, pp. 50–51; Bialyi and Litvin, *Chastnyi kapital*, pp. 5, 58–60; *TPG*, 1922, No. 128 (August 12), p. 3; *Promyshlennost' i torgovlia*, 1923, No. 1, p. 12; *Ekonomicheskoe stroitel'stvo*, 1925, No. 1, p. 95; *Mestnoe khoziaistvo* (Kiev), 1923, No. 3 (December), pp. 55, 58; Vasil'kov, *Chastnyi kapital*, pp. 47, 78; *Severo-Kavkazskii krai* (Rostov-on-the-Don), 1927, No. 10, p. 101; Ginzburg, *Chastnyi kapital*, p. 24; *Nashe khoziaistvo* (Riazan'), 1923, No. 9, pp. 17–18; *Ekonomicheskii vestnik Armenii* (Erevan), 1926, No. 4, p. 126; and *Ekonomicheskii vestnik Zakavkaz'ia* (Tiflis), 1926, No. 6, p. 31. Other types of industry that were fairly important in some regions include brick and glass making, "chemicals" (usually soap and

candles), printing, paper making, jewelry, rope making, and mining of various minerals.

48. *Khoziaistvo Urala* (Sverdlovsk), 1925, No. 2, p. 84. The *New York Times*'s correspondent recorded a similar impression in Samara at the beginning of NEP: "Thus in the market at Samara I have seen peasants buying nails, sandals, metal utensils, sheepskin coats, baskets, etc., which are obviously the work of a single artisan or small group. Even in the famine-stricken villages there was a sale of shoes plaited by cottagers from slips of osier." Duranty, *Duranty Reports*, p. 87.

49. Gladkov, *Sovetskoe narodnoe khoziaistvo*, p. 199. These figures are for petty industry, roughly 80 percent of which was private. The contribution from private census industry may be found in Mingulin, *Puti razvitiia*, p. 101. Some figures for 1923/24 are available in Ginzburg, *Chastnyi kapital*, p. 94.

50. *TPG*, 1923, No. 291 (December 23), p. 3.

51. *Torgovye izvestiia*, 1926, No. 99 (September 11), p. 2; Morozov, *Reshaiushchii etap*, p. 63; *Sovetskaia torgovlia*, 1926, No. 9, p. 9; Trifonov, *Likvidatsiia*, p. 220.

52. Ginzburg, *Chastnyi kapital*, pp. 24–25, 46; Gladkov, *Sovetskoe narodnoe khoziaistvo*, p. 199; and *TPG*, 1923, No. 291 (December 23), p. 3. For some figures on census industry, see *Vestnik statistiki*, 1927, No. 1, pp. 86, 92–95.

53. Morozov, *Reshaiushchii etap*, p. 15; *TPG*, 1923, No. 291 (December 23), p. 3; *Mestnoe khoziaistvo* (Kiev), 1923, No. 3 (December), p. 55; Kopalkin, *Chastnaia promyshlennost'*, p. 26; *Torgovye izvestiia*, 1926, No. 29 (March 18), p. 3; Gladkov, *Sovetskoe narodnoe khoziaistvo*, p. 199; Vasil'kov, *Chastnyi kapital*, pp. 79–80; and *Severo-Kavkazskii krai* (Rostov-on-the-Don), 1926, No. 5, p. 155.

54. Zagorskii, *K sotsializmu*, p. 230; *Ekonomicheskoe obozrenie*, 1927, June, p. 118.

55. *TPG*, 1927, No. 31 (February 8), p. 2; *Materialy po istorii SSSR. VII. Dokumenty po istorii sovetskogo obshchestva* (Moscow, 1959), p. 166; *Sovetskaia torgovlia*, 1927, No. 7, p. 15; 1927, No. 20, p. 8; I. Ia. Trifonov, *Ocherki istorii klassovoi bor'by v SSSR v gody NEPa (1921–1937)* (Moscow, 1960), p. 131; and *Ekonomicheskoe stroitel'stvo*, 1926, No. 9, p. 21.

56. Mingulin, *Puti razvitiia*, pp. 106–107; Shapiro, *Kustarnaia promyshlennost'*, p. 18; Baron, *The Russian Jew*, p. 252; Ginzburg, *Chastnyi kapital*, p. 31; and *Finansovye problemy planovogo khoziaistva*, 1930, No. 7–8, p. 97.

57. Belkin, *Rabochii vopros*, pp. 16–19; Ginzburg, *Chastnyi kapital*, pp. 220–221; and Trifonov, *Klassy*, 2:90, 132.

58. Arkhipov and Morozov, *Bor'ba*, pp. 205–206; Ginzburg, *Chastnyi kapital*, pp. 12, 191, 243; Bialyi and Litvin, *Chastnyi kapital*, pp. 5–6, 17–18; Trifonov, *Ocherki*, p. 127; and *Ekonomicheskoe obozrenie*, 1927, June, pp. 114–115.

59. Ginzburg, *Chastnyi kapital*, pp. 226, 229, 232, 236, 244–245; Belkin, *Rabochii vopros*, pp. 24–27, 101; Trifonov, *Klassy*, 2:69; and Morozov, *Reshaiushchii etap*, p. 84.

60. For some of the decrees that granted tax privileges to producers' cooperatives, see *Zakony o chastnoi promyshlennosti*, pp. 72–74; *SZ*, 1924, No. 26, art. 219; and *SZ*, 1924, No. 28, art. 238.

61. *TPG*, 1927, No. 147 (July 2), p. 4.

62. *Ekonomicheskoe obozrenie*, 1927, June, p. 112. For other examples of false *arteli*, see Andrei Fabrichnyi, *Chastnyi kapital na poroge piatiletki* (Moscow, 1930), p. 39; Larin, *Chastnyi kapital*, p. 115; and *Ekonomicheskoe obozrenie*, 1927, June, p. 111.

63. *Kooperativnoe stroitel'stvo*, 1926, No. 14, pp. 22–23; *Finansy i narodnoe khoziaistvo*, 1927, No. 12, p. 15.

64. Trifonov, *Ocherki*, p. 128; Bialyi and Litvin, *Chastnyi kapital*, p. 17; and *Ekonomicheskoe obozrenie*, 1927, June, pp. 111, 113–114. For more on the numerous false *arteli* at the beginning of NEP, see Belkin, *Rabochii vopros*, pp. 19–20; Ginzburg, *Chastnyi kapital*, pp. 220–222.

65. Trifonov, *Likvidatsiia*, p. 217; Morozov, *Reshaiushchii etap*, pp. 80–81.

66. Trifonov, *Likvidatsiia*, pp. 218–219; Morozov, *Reshaiushchii etap*, p. 80; Mishanin, "Arenda," p. 66; and Arkhipov and Morozov, *Bor'ba*, p. 215. On January 27, 1928, Sovnarkom ordered that leather-processing factories be leased only to state trusts and cooperatives. No new factories of this sort could be built without official permission (gener-

ally given only to state agencies). *Zakony o chastnom kapitale*, p. 266; Morozov, *Reshaiushchii etap*, p. 60.

67. *SZ*, 1928, No. 30, art. 267; *SZ*, 1929, No. 3, art. 28; Fabrichnyi, *Chastnyi kapital*, p. 39; Moshe Lewin, *Russian Peasants and Soviet Power: A Study of Collectivization* (London, 1968; reprint, New York, 1975), p. 280; Trifonov, *Ocherki*, p. 129; and Morozov, *Reshaiushchii etap*, pp. 82–83, 85.

68. *TPG*, 1928, No. 25 (January 29), p. 4.

69. Morozov, *Reshaiushchii etap*, p. 84.

70. For some of these tax decrees, see *SZ*, 1931, No. 31, art. 237; *SZ*, 1931, No. 40, art. 279; and *SZ*, 1932, No. 75, art. 459.

71. Trifonov, *Ocherki*, p. 130.

72. See, for example, *Finansy i narodnoe khoziaistvo*, 1927, No. 19, p. 26; *Ekonomicheskoe obozrenie*, 1926, August, pp. 112–114.

## CHAPTER 7

1. *Sobranie uzakonenii i rasporiazhenii. 1917–1949* (Moscow, 1920–50) (hereafter cited as *SU*), 1923, No. 5, art. 89, *prilozhenie* 2; A. M. Ginzburg, ed., *Chastnyi kapital v narodnom khoziaistve SSSR. Materialy kommissii VSNKh SSSR* (Moscow-Leningrad, 1927), pp. 268–269 (information on private shipping); Anthony C. Sutton, *Western Technology and Soviet Economic Development 1917 to 1930* (Stanford, 1968), p. 256 (private airline); and Anna Louise Strong, *The First Time in History* (New York, 1924), pp. 135–137, 140–141, 148–149 (private landlords).

2. Sheila Fitzpatrick, *The Commissariat of Enlightenment: Soviet Organization of Education and the Arts Under Lunacharsky, October 1917–1921* (Cambridge, 1970), p. 271.

3. See, for example, *Sobranie zakonov i rasporiazhenii raboche-krest'ianskogo pravitel'stva SSSR. 1924–1949* (Moscow, 1925–50) (hereafter cited as *SZ*), 1924, No. 20, art. 196.

4. S. A. Fediukin, *Bor'ba s burzhuaznoi ideologiei v usloviiakh perekhoda k nepu* (Moscow, 1977), pp. 70–71; A. I. Nazarov, *Oktiabr' i kniga* (Moscow, 1968), p. 249.

5. Fitzpatrick, *Commissariat of Enlightenment*, p. 263.

6. *Zakony o chastnom kapitale. Sbornik zakonov, instruktsii, prikazov i raz"iasnenii*, comp. B. S. Mal'tsman and B. E. Ratner (Moscow, 1928), pp. 247–248.

7. *Pechat' i revoliutsiia*, 1922, *kniga* 6, pp. 130–131; Fediukin, *Bor'ba*, p. 73; and Nazarov, *Oktiabr'*, p. 254.

8. *Pechat' i revoliutsiia*, 1922, *kniga* 6, pp. 131–132.

9. Nazarov, *Oktiabr'*, p. 255.

10. E. I. Shamurin, *Sovetskaia kniga za 15 let v tsifrakh* (Moscow, 1933), p. 27.

11. On the literary circles, see Fediukin, *Bor'ba*, p. 75.

12. I. Ia. Trifonov, *Klassy i klassovaia bor'ba v SSSR v nachale nepa*, Vol. 2, *Podgotovka ekonomicheskogo nastupleniia na novuiu burzhuaziiu* (Leningrad, 1969), p. 58. See also Ts. M. Kron, *Chastnaia torgovlia v SSSR* (Moscow, 1926), p. 15.

13. *Ekonomicheskoe obozrenie*, 1925, October, pp. 115–125; G. A. Dikhtiar, *Sovetskaia torgovlia v period postroeniia sotsializma* (Moscow, 1961), pp. 207–208.

14. *Na novykh putiakh. Itogi novoi ekonomicheskoi politiki 1921–1922 g.g.* (Moscow, 1923), *vypusk* I, p. 186; Iu. S. Kondurushkin, *Chastnyi kapital pered sovetskim sudom* (Moscow-Leningrad, 1927), pp. 29–30, 105, 114.

15. V. P. Dmitrenko, *Torgovaia politika sovetskogo gosudarstva posle perekhoda k NEPu 1921–1924 gg.* (Moscow, 1971), p. 185; *Torgovo-promyshlennaia gazeta* (hereafter cited as *TPG*), 1923, No. 1 (January 1), p. 2; and *Na novykh putiakh*, *vypusk* I, p. 235.

16. M. M. Zhirmunskii, *Chastnyi kapital v tovarooborote* (Moscow, 1924), pp. 135–136, 138; Trifonov, *Klassy*, 2:223.

17. *Iugo-Vostok* (Rostov-on-the-Don), 1922, No. 1, p. 55; 1923, No. 2–3, p. 81;

*Ekonomicheskoe stroitel'stvo,* 1923, No. 6–7, p. 89; Zhirmunskii, *Chastnyi kapital,* p. 15; and Kondurushkin, *Chastnyi kapital,* p. 61.

18. *Finansy i promyshlennost',* 1922, No. 3–4, p. 68; Kondurushkin, *Chastnyi kapital,* p. 107. For other examples, see Trifonov, *Klassy,* 2:58, 64.

19. I. Mingulin, *Puti razvitiia chastnogo kapitala* (Moscow-Leningrad, 1927), p. 55; Kondurushkin, *Chastnyi kapital,* p. 46; and Trifonov, *Klassy,* 2:73.

20. See, for example, *Promyshlennost' i torgovlia,* 1923, No. 2, pp. 3–4; *TPG,* 1922, No. 176 (October 10), p. 1; 1922, No. 191 (October 27), p. 3; 1922, No. 192 (October 28), p. 1; 1922, No. 195 (November 1), p. 2. There are similar articles in other issues of *TPG* published in this period.

21. *TPG,* 1922, No. 133 (August 18), p. 4; 1922, No. 190 (October 26), p. 3.

22. Ibid., 1922, No. 228 (December 10), p. 4.

23. *Izvestiia,* March 8, 1923, p. 6. As we will see, Nepmen continued to work legally as middlemen between the "socialist" and private sectors. For additional decrees regulating this activity, see *SZ,* 1925, No. 76, art. 569; *Zakony o chastnom kapitale,* pp. 292–293.

24. *KPSS v rezoliutsiiakh i resheniiakh s"ezdov, konferentsii i plenumov TsK,* 8th ed. (Moscow, 1970–), 4:32.

25. *TPG,* 1923, No. 285 (December 16), p. 2; 1928, No. 220 (September 21), p. 5; *Zakony o chastnom kapitale,* p. 30; and Trifonov, *Klassy,* 2:159.

26. See, for example, *Krokodil,* 1981, No. 29, p. 5.

27. *Ekonomicheskoe stroitel'stvo,* 1923, No. 6–7, p. 90.

28. *Iugo-Vostok* (Rostov-on-the-Don), 1922, No. 1 (November), p. 56. Additional expressions of official distaste for private middlemen may be found in *TPG,* 1922, No. 191 (October 27), p. 3; I. Ia. Trifonov, *Likvidatsiia ekspluatatorskikh klassov v SSSR* (Moscow, 1975), p. 190.

29. *TPG,* 1922, No. 191 (October 27), p. 3; *Ekonomicheskoe obozrenie,* 1925, April, p. 190; *Iugo-Vostok* (Rostov-on-the-Don), 1922, No. 1 (November), p. 55; and I. A. Bialyi and A. I. Litvin, *Chastnyi kapital v g. Irkutske* (Irkutsk, 1929), p. 39.

30. *Na novykh putiakh, vypusk* I, pp. 207–208; Kron, *Chastnaia torgovlia,* pp. 16–17; *TPG,* 1923, No. 231 (October 12), p. 3; and *Trud i khoziaistvo* (Kazan'), 1927, No. 1, p. 84.

31. Estimates differ considerably. See, for example, *Ekonomicheskoe obozrenie,* 1926, August, p. 101; 1928, No. 9, p. 27; *TPG,* 1924, No. 126 (June 5), p. 2; and S. O. Zagorskii, *K sotsializmu ili k kapitalizmu?* (Paris, 1927), p. 150.

32. *Khoziaistvo Sev.-Zap. kraia* (Leningrad), 1924, No. 8, p. 51; Kron, *Chastnaia torgovlia,* p. 37; *Torgovye izvestiia,* 1925, No. 74 (October 10), p. 5; 1926, No. 108 (October 2), p. 4; and Ginzburg, *Chastnyi kapital,* p. 11.

33. *TPG,* 1927, No. 31 (February 8), p. 3; 1928, No. 283 (December 6), p. 4; *Ekonomicheskoe obozrenie,* 1928, No. 4, p. 161; and *Sovetskaia torgovlia,* 1926, No. 10, p. 3; 1927, No. 7, pp. 6–7. For more on the *zagotovka* of various products in different regions, see *Trud i khoziaistvo* (Kazan'), 1927, No. 1, pp. 88–89, 94; *TPG,* 1928, No. 229 (October 2), p. 5; 1928, No. 246 (October 21), p. 6; Vasil'kov, *Chastnyi kapital v khoziaistve orlovskoi gubernii.* (*Issledovatel'skaia rabota Gubplana pod rukovodstvom i redaktsiei Vasil'kova*) (Orel, 1928), p. 33; A. Zlobin, *Gosudarstvennyi, kooperativnyi i chastnyi kapital v tovarooborote sibirskogo kraia* (Novosibirsk, 1927), p. 16; *Tverskoi krai* (Tver'), 1926, No. 7–8, p. 17; and *Finansy i narodnoe khoziaistvo,* 1926, No. 6, p. 27.

34. *Materialy po istorii SSSR. VII. Dokumenty po istorii sovetskogo obshchestva* (Moscow, 1959), p. 150.

35. *Torgovye izvestiia,* 1925, No. 72 (October 6), p. 5.

36. *Sovetskaia torgovlia,* 1926, No. 9, p. 9; 1927, No. 7, p. 7. See also *Na novykh putiakh, vypusk* I, p. 220; Zagorskii, *K sotsializmu,* pp. 123–124, 150.

37. This advantage (along with others) of the private *zagotovka* system has been pointed out in chapter 5. For additional documentation on this point, see *Sovetskaia torgovlia,* 1927, No. 7, pp. 8, 15; *TPG,* 1924, No. 187 (August 20), p. 3; 1928, No. 15 (January 18), p. 5; 1928, No. 206 (September 5), p. 5; *Ekonomicheskoe obozrenie,* 1926, August, p. 118; and *Sotsialisticheskii vestnik* (Berlin), 1929, No. 10–11, p. 11.

38. See, for example, late-summer issues of *Torgovye izvestiia* and *Pravda*.
39. Dikhtiar, *Sovetskaia torgovlia*, p. 271; Moshe Lewin, *Russian Peasants and Soviet Power: A Study of Collectivization* (London, 1968; reprint, New York, 1975), p. 389. A correspondent reported from the Ukraine that free-market grain prices, far above official prices, were severely hampering the state's efforts to buy grain. *TPG*, 1928, No. 209 (September 8), p. 5. The Poltava correspondent sent a similar report concerning the *zagotovka* of hides. *TPG*, 1928, No. 257 (November 3), p. 4.
40. Measures taken against free grain trade have been described in chapter 3. The state also issued decrees banning the private *zagotovka* of furs in many regions. See *Zakony o chastnom kapitale*, pp. 159–160; *SU*, 1927, No. 77, art. 525; *SU*, 1927, No. 87, art. 579; *SU*, 1928, No. 99, art. 626; and *SU*, 1928, No. 101, art. 638. For more on efforts to reduce the private *zagotovka* of hides, see *TPG*, 1928, No. 283 (December 6), p. 4. Private *zagotovka* activity in general was undercut indirectly by the drastic reduction in the number of private retail traders in 1928 and 1929, which left private middlemen with few customers. See (concerning eggs and butter) *Ekonomicheskoe obozrenie*, 1928, No. 4, p. 164.
41. For detailed legal provisions concerning the formation and operation of joint-stock companies, see *Zakony o chastnom kapitale*, pp. 37–57.
42. *Ekonomicheskaia zhizn'*, 1922, No. 145 (July 2), p. 3; *Severo-Kavkazskii krai* (Rostov-on-the-Don), 1925, No. 11–12, pp. 126–127. For other examples, see *Torgovye izvestiia*, 1925, No. 48 (August 11), p. 2; *TPG*, 1923, No. 38 (February 18), p. 2; and *Torgovlia, promyshlennost' i finansy*, 1925, No. 9, p. 232.
43. *Khoziaistvo i upravlenie*, 1927, No. 6, pp. 83, 86. One disadvantage of private joint-stock companies was that they were more prominently in the view of state regulatory and tax agencies than were most ordinary private enterprises.
44. *TPG*, 1928, No. 255 (November 1), p. 4.
45. Ibid., 1922, No. 102 (July 13), p. 3; 1922, No. 120 (August 3), p. 4; 1923, No. 197 (September 2), p. 5.
46. *Torgovye izvestiia*, 1926, No. 76 (July 13), p. 1.
47. Dikhtiar, *Sovetskaia torgovlia*, p. 197; *TPG*, 1927, No. 29 (February 5), p. 2.
48. *Khoziaistvo i upravlenie*, 1927, No. 6, pp. 84, 86; *Materialy. VII.*, p. 36.
49. *Materialy. VII.*, p. 45.
50. *Khoziaistvo i upravlenie*, 1927, No. 6, p. 84; *Torgovye izvestiia*, 1926, No. 76 (July 13), p. 1; and *Materialy. VII.*, pp. 39–40.
51. *Sovetskaia torgovlia*, 1927, No. 15, p. 13; *Materialy. VII.*, p. 37; and *Khoziaistvo i upravlenie*, 1927, No. 6, p. 88.
52. *Materialy. VII.*, p. 36.
53. *Torgovye izvestiia*, 1926, No. 76 (July 13), p. 1; I. A. Gladkov, ed., *Sovetskoe narodnoe khoziaistvo v 1921–1925 gg.* (Moscow, 1960), p. 427.
54. *Khoziaistvo i upravlenie*, 1927, No. 6, p. 87. At least some (and perhaps much) of the private capital invested in joint-stock operations came from foreigners, thus rendering the Nepmen's contribution even less significant. *Ekonomicheskoe stroitel'stvo*, 1925, No. 3, p. 114.
55. *SU*, 1922, No. 12, art. 110; S. L. Fridman, *Chastnyi kapital na denezhnom rynke* (Moscow, 1925), pp. 9–11. There were also a few private banks (operating with some state capital and supervision), the first of which was formed in Rostov-on-the-Don in April.
56. *Nashe khoziaistvo* (Vladimir), 1923, No. 6, p. 65; Trifonov, *Klassy*, 2 : 55; and Fridman, *Chastnyi kapital*, p. 70.
57. Mingulin, *Puti razvitiia*, p. 120; Fridman, *Chastnyi kapital*, p. 69; Zagorskii, *K sotsializmu*, p. 254; and *Ekonomicheskoe obozrenie*, 1926, February, pp. 161–162. Data in some sources differ slightly.
58. *Finansy i narodnoe khoziaistvo*, 1927, No. 41, pp. 16–17; 1929, No. 8, p. 18; *Materialy. VII.*, pp. 30, 35; and *SZ*, 1929, No. 72, art. 690. During the period from October 1, 1926, to October 1, 1927, the state cut its loans to OVKs by 77 percent.
59. *Ekonomicheskoe obozrenie*, 1924, No. 22, p. 46. See also V. V. Ivanovskii, *Chastnyi torgovyi kapital na rynke Saratovskoi gubernii* (Saratov, 1927), p. 55.

60. See, for example, the results of a survey of private traders in Voronezh: G. P. Paduchev, *Chastnyi torgovets pri novoi ekonomicheskoi politike (po dannym biudzhet- nogo obsledovaniia)* (Voronezh, 1926), p. 100.

61. *Ekonomicheskoe obozrenie,* 1926, February, p. 163.

62. Ibid., 1926, August, p. 106; A. Zalkind, ed., *Chastnaia torgovlia Soiuza SSR* (Moscow, 1927), pp. 90, 92; and Ivanovskii, *Chastnyi torgovyi kapital,* p. 54.

63. *Ekonomicheskoe obozrenie,* 1926, February, pp. 161–162; 1927, March, pp. 132–133.

64. For data with which to make these estimates, see Ginzburg, *Chastnyi kapital,* pp. 171–173; *Ekonomicheskoe obozrenie,* 1926, February, pp. 161–162; 1927, March, pp. 132–133; and Mingulin, *Puti razvitiia,* pp. 63, 122. Concerning just the Ukraine, see *Finansy i narodnoe khoziaistvo,* 1927, No. 2, p. 18.

65. The percentages of OVK loans to Nepmen made with funds borrowed from state banks are as follows: October 1, 1924, 23 percent; January 1, 1925, 31 percent; April 1, 1925, 29 percent; July 1, 1925, 34 percent; October 1, 1925, 38 percent; January 1, 1926, 46 percent; April 1, 1926, 33 percent; July 1, 1926, 32 percent; October 1, 1926, 30 percent. These figures can be derived from data in *Ekonomicheskoe obozrenie,* 1927, March, pp. 132–133. Viewed from a different angle, state banks made one fifth of their loans to Nepmen via OVKs in 1925 and one quarter in 1926. Zalkind, *Chastnaia tor- govlia,* p. 100.

66. *Torgovye izvestiia,* 1925, No. 21 (May 26), p. 6; 1925, No. 27 (June 13), p. 4; *Mestnoe khoziaistvo* (Kiev), 1924, No. 6 (March), pp. 74–75; Paduchev, *Chastnyi tor- govets,* pp. 74–75, 77; and Fridman, *Chastnyi kapital,* p. 73.

67. *Finansy i narodnoe khoziaistvo,* 1926, No. 3, p. 18; 1926, No. 8, p. 21; 1927, No. 45, p. 19; Vasil'kov, *Chastnyi kapital,* p. 84; *Mestnoe khoziaistvo* (Kiev), 1924, No. 6 (March), p. 75; and Zagorskii, *K sotsializmu,* pp. 256–257.

68. V. A. Arkhipov and L. F. Morozov, *Bor'ba protiv kapitalisticheskikh elementov v promyshlennosti i torgovle. 20-e—nachalo 30-kh godov* (Moscow, 1978), p. 82; V. Ia. Laverychev, *Krupnaia burzhuaziia v poreformennoi Rossii (1861–1900 gg.)* (Moscow, 1974), p. 20.


EPILOGUE

1. Only a handful of Nepmen emigrated, a venture undoubtedly beyond the means of most petty entrepreneurs (the majority of Nepmen), even assuming that such a course of action appealed to them. Morozov reports two instances of emigration, one in which traders left Turkestan for Iran, and the second involving the journey of a few Nepmen from Kiev to Mexico. L. F. Morozov, *Reshaiushchii etap bor'by s nepmanskoi burzhua- ziei (1926–1929)* (Moscow, 1960), p. 97.

2. *Sotsialisticheskii vestnik* (Berlin), 1930, No. 19, pp. 13–14; William Reswick, *I Dreamt Revolution* (Chicago, 1952), pp. 166–167. See also *Sotsialisticheskii vestnik* (Berlin), 1931, No. 12–13, p. 22; Reswick, *I Dreamt,* pp. 171–174, 217–218; Paul Scheffer, *Seven Years in Soviet Russia* (New York, 1932), p. 208; Calvin B. Hoover, "The Fate of the New Economic Policy of the Soviet Union," *Economic Journal* 40 (June 1930): 191; Walter Duranty, *Duranty Reports Russia* (New York, 1934), p. 211; William H. Chamberlin, *Soviet Russia: A Living Record and a History* (Boston, 1931), p. 196; and Eugene Lyons, *Assignment in Utopia* (New York, 1937), p. 149.

3. *Finansy i narodnoe khoziaistvo,* 1929, No. 26, p. 15; Morozov, *Reshaiushchii etap,* pp. 95–96. See also V. M. Selunskaia, ed., *Izmeneniia sotsial'noi struktury sov- etskogo obshchestva. 1921–seredina 30-kh godov* (Moscow, 1979), p. 130.

4. *Finansy i narodnoe khoziaistvo,* 1928, No. 26, p. 17; 1929, No. 26, p. 15; Mo- rozov, *Reshaiushchii etap,* pp. 95–96; and Salo W. Baron, *The Russian Jew Under Tsars and Soviets* (New York, 1964), p. 264. For more on the move of many Nepmen into handi- craft work at the end of the decade, see *Finansovye problemy planovogo khoziaistva,* 1930, No. 7–8, p. 97; *Finansy i narodnoe khoziaistvo,* 1930, No. 9, p. 13; *Torgovo- promyshlennaia gazeta* (hereafter cited as TPG), 1927, No. 249 (October 30), p. 3;

*Ekonomicheskaia zhizn'*, 1928, No. 53 (March 2), p. 4; Morozov, *Reshaiushchii etap*, p. 73; and William C. White, *These Russians* (New York, 1931), p. 78. For more on former Nepmen finding work in state trade and industrial operations, see *TPG*, 1929, No. 20 (January 25), p. 4; Morozov, *Reshaiushchii etap*, p. 98; Alexander Wicksteed, *Life Under the Soviets* (London, 1928), p. 7; and Eugene Lyons, *Moscow Carrousel* (New York, 1935), pp. 62–64.

5. *Finansy i narodnoe khoziaistvo*, 1928, No. 39, p. 4; 1929, No. 22, p. 17; 1929, No. 34, p. 18; 1930, No. 7, p. 22; 1930, No. 9, pp. 12–13; *TPG*, 1927, No. 249 (October 30), p. 3; 1928, No. 182 (August 8), p. 5; 1928, No. 246 (October 21), p. 6; and *Finansovye problemy planovogo khoziaistva*, 1930, No. 7–8, p. 97.

6. For the results of additional surveys, see *Finansy i narodnoe khoziaistvo*, 1928, No. 26, p. 17; 1929, No. 36, p. 16; 1930, No. 7, p. 22.

7. *Finansovye problemy planovogo khoziaistva*, 1930, No. 7–8, p. 97.

8. *TPG*, 1928, No. 95 (April 24), p. 4; 1928, No. 293 (December 18), p. 4; 1929, No. 8 (January 10), p. 4; *Ekonomicheskaia zhizn'*, 1928, No. 67 (March 20), p. 5; 1928, No. 68 (March 21), p. 3; and *Finansy i narodnoe khoziaistvo*, 1928, No. 39, p. 17; 1929, No. 31, p. 17.

9. Gregory Grossman, "The 'Second Economy' of the USSR," *Problems of Communism*, September–October 1977, pp. 25–40; *New York Times*, September 2, 1982; and Konstantin M. Simis, *USSR: The Corrupt Society* (New York, 1982).

10. *TPG*, 1924, No. 296 (December 31), p. 1.

11. *Ekonomicheskoe stroitel'stvo*, 1926, No. 1, p. 31.

12. *Ekonomicheskoe obozrenie*, 1927, May, p. 160; 1929, No. 1, p. 66; *Finansy i narodnoe khoziaistvo*, 1930, No. 10, p. 19. Other studies of workers' budgets in various regions yielded similar findings. See, for example, A. Zlobin, *Gosudarstvennyi, kooperativnyi i chastnyi kapital v tovarooborote sibirskogo kraia* (Novosibirsk, 1927), p. 10; *Ekonomicheskaia zhizn'*, 1927, No. 236 (October 15), p. 3.

13. *TPG*, 1924, No. 56 (March 8), p. 2; 1927, No. 249 (October 30), p. 3; 1928, No. 266 (November 16), p. 6; 1928, No. 269 (November 20), p. 4; *Tverskoi krai* (Tver'), 1926, No. 6, p. 39; *Sovetskaia torgovlia*, 1927, No. 7, p. 15; *Trud i khoziaistvo* (Kazan'), 1927, No. 1, p. 90; Selunskaia, *Izmeneniia sotsial'noi struktury*, p. 118; A. M. Lezhava, *Vnutrenniaia torgovlia 1923 g.* (Moscow, 1924), p. 12; *Kooperativnoe stroitel'stvo*, 1926, No. 9, pp. 54, 56; *Torgovye izvestiia*, 1925, No. 27 (June 13), p. 6; 1925, No. 34 (July 9), p. 6; *Nash krai* (Astrakhan'), 1926, No. 8, p. 27; and A. Kaktyn', *O podkhode k chastnomu torgovomu kapitalu* (Moscow, 1924), p. 10.

14. *Narodnoe khoziaistvo Srednei Azii* (Tashkent), 1927, No. 5, p. 53; *Torgovye izvestiia*, 1925, No. 34 (July 9), p. 6; *TPG*, 1928, No. 218 (September 19), p. 4; *Nash krai* (Astrakhan'), 1926, No. 8, p. 27; *Kooperativnoe stroitel'stvo*, 1926, No. 14, p. 54; and Kaktyn', *O podkhode*, p. 10.

15. *Torgovlia, promyshlennost' i finansy*, 1925, No. 5–6, p. 161; Vasil'kov, *Chastnyi kapital v khoziaistve orlovskoi gubernii*. (*Issledovatel'skaia rabota Gubplana pod rukovodstvom i redaktsiei Vasil'kova*) (Orel, 1928), p. 19; and *Ekonomicheskoe obozrenie*, 1927, May, p. 160.

16. Maurice Hindus, *Red Bread* (New York, 1931), p. 80; Jay Leyda, *Kino: A History of the Russian and Soviet Film* (London, 1960), p. 256; A. Ruth Fry, *Three Visits to Russia 1922–25* (London, 1942), p. 21; Andrée Viollis, *A Girl in Soviet Russia* (New York, 1929), p. 22; and Anna Louise Strong, *The First Time in History* (New York, 1924), p. 240. The Nepmen were also frequent targets in the Soviet satirical journal *Krokodil*. At a meeting of young Pioneers in the Ukraine, a hat containing written questions was passed among the children. One question read: "What class does a Pioneer never help?" The lad who drew the question had clearly learned his lessons well, for he had no difficulty producing a suitable answer: "Those who exploit the toil of others—rich, bandits, and nepmen." Albert Rhys Williams, *The Russian Land* (New York, 1927), pp. 157–158. For more on children, education, and the Nepmen, see I. Ia. Trifonov, *Klassy i klassovaia bor'ba v SSSR v nachale nepa*, Vol. 2, *Podgotovka ekonomicheskogo nastupleniia na novuiu burzhuaziiu* (Leningrad, 1969), p. 212; Albert Muldavin, *The Red Fog Lifts* (New York, 1931), pp. 40–41, 205; Ella Winter, *Red Virtue: Human Relations in the New Rus-*

*sia* (New York, 1933), pp. 12–13; *Illiustrirovannaia Rossiia* (Paris), 1926, No. 36, p. 11; Dorothy Thompson, *The New Russia* (New York, 1928), p. 231; Anton Karlgren, *Bolshevist Russia* (London, 1927), p. 283; and Lyons, *Moscow Carrousel*, pp. 69–71.

17. Markoosha Fischer, *My Lives in Russia* (New York, 1944), p. 21; Maurice Hindus, *Humanity Uprooted* (New York, 1929), p. 63; Reswick, *I Dreamt*, pp. 105–106; *Mestnoe khoziaistvo* (Kiev), 1924, No. 6 (March), pp. 78–79; Muldavin, *Red Fog*, pp. 82–83; and Duranty, *Duranty Reports*, p. 107. It was not uncommon in these years to encounter repugnant Jewish Nepmen slinking through the pages of Russian belles-lettres. Lionel Kochan, ed., *The Jews in Soviet Russia Since 1917*, 3d ed. (Oxford, 1978), p. 205.

Some foreigners and émigré publications also offered negative characterizations of Nepmen. For example, Theodore Dreiser included a Nepman when describing the types of customers he observed in a Moscow restaurant: "And then next, a really portly Russian, of perhaps the trader or bloodsucker type–fat, red-cheeked, double-chinned, puffy-necked, a really beastlike type. And with him two attractive and yet semi-obese girls or women of not over twenty-six or seven, with a heavy, meaty sensuality radiating from every pore. The white flabby double chins and crinkled necks. The small and yet fat and even puffy hands. The little, shrewd, greedy eyes, half concealed by fat lids." Theodore Dreiser, *Dreiser Looks at Russia* (New York, 1928), p. 225; Frank A. Golder and Lincoln Hutchinson, *On the Trail of the Russian Famine* (Stanford, 1927), p. 150; John Dos Passos, *In All Countries* (New York, 1934), pp. 33, 54; and *Illiustrirovannaia Rossiia* (Paris), 1926, No. 19, p. 9; 1926, No. 29, p. 5.

18. Lyons, *Assignment*, p. 85.

19. *TPG*, 1928, No. 266 (November 16), p. 6.

20. These points are made repeatedly in Soviet periodicals of the 1920s. For a sampling, see *TPG*, 1923, No. 74 (April 3), p. 3; 1923, No. 194 (August 30), p. 3; 1924, No. 37 (February 15), p. 6; 1924, No. 44 (February 23), p. 4; 1924, No. 296 (December 31), p. 1; 1927, No. 180 (August 10), p. 4; 1927, No. 186 (August 18), p. 4; 1927, No. 209 (September 14), p. 4; 1928, No. 269 (November 20), p. 4; *Torgovye izvestiia*, 1925, No. 34 (July 9), p. 6; 1925, No. 36 (July 14), p. 6; 1925, No. 85 (November 5), p. 1; 1926, No. 65 (June 15), p. 4; 1926, No. 103 (September 21), p. 3; 1926, No. 109 (October 5), p. 3; *Severo-Kavkazskii krai* (Rostov-on-the-Don), 1925, No. 4–5, p. 100; *Mestnoe khoziaistvo* (Kiev), 1924, No. 6 (March), p. 73; Lezhava, *Vnutrenniaia torgovlia 1923*, p. 11; *Narodnoe khoziaistvo Srednei Azii* (Tashkent), 1927, No. 6–7, pp. 104–105; *Sovetskaia torgovlia*, 1926, No. 10, p. 4; and *Ekonomicheskii vestnik Zakavkaz'ia* (Tiflis), 1926, No. 3, pp. 78–84.

21. *TPG*, 1923, No. 168 (July 28), p. 3; 1924, No. 44 (February 23), p. 4; 1928, No. 266 (November 16), p. 6; 1929, No. 97 (April 27), p. 6; *Torgovye izvestiia*, 1925, No. 88 (November 12), p. 6; 1926, No. 59 (June 1), p. 4; Lezhava, *Vnutrenniaia torgovlia 1923*, p. 25; *Mestnoe khoziaistvo* (Kiev), 1924, No. 6 (March), p. 73; *Iugo-Vostok* (Rostov-on-the-Don), 1924, No. 5, *prilozhenie*, pp. 17–18; *Severo-Kavkazskii krai* (Rostov-on-the-Don), 1925, No. 4–5, p. 101; *Ekonomicheskaia zhizn'*, 1925, No. 257 (November 11), p. 3; Trifonov, *Klassy*, 2:159–160, 220; and S. O. Zagorskii, *K sotsializmu ili k kapitalizmu?* (Paris, 1927), p. 156.

22. *TPG*, 1928, No. 267 (November 17), p. 4; 1928, No. 283 (December 6), p. 5; 1929, No. 97 (April 27), p. 6; *Torgovye izvestiia*, 1925, No. 80 (October 24), p. 1; Lezhava, *Vnutrenniaia torgovlia 1923*, pp. 25–26; Karlgren, *Bolshevist Russia*, pp. 135–136; Iu. S. Kondrushkin, *Chastnyi kapital pered sovetskim sudom* (Moscow-Leningrad, 1927), p. 144; and *Iugo-Vostok* (Rostov-on-the-Don), 1924, No. 3, pp. 109–112.

Of course state suppliers could also force compulsory assortments on Nepmen. See *Torgovye izvestiia*, 1925, No. 82 (October 29), p. 4; 1925, No. 87 (November 10), p. 2; 1925, No. 98 (December 5), p. 4; G. P. Paduchev, *Chastnyi torgovets pri novoi ekonomicheskoi politike (po dannym biudzhetnogo obsledovaniia)* (Voronezh, 1926), p. 66. But private traders were generally less vulnerable than cooperative and state stores, because they were more resourceful than the officials in the latter concerns and less dependent on state suppliers.

23. *Kooperativnoe stroitel'stvo*, 1926, No. 11, p. 33; Karlgren, *Bolshevist Russia*, pp. 136–137. See also Karl Borders, *Village Life Under the Soviets* (New York, 1927),

pp. 95, 100, 106; *Ekonomicheskaia zhizn'*, 1924, No. 123 (February 28), p. 3; Trifonov, *Klassy*, 2:199; Karlgren, *Bolshevist Russia*, pp. 132–134; and the cartoon in *Pravda*, January 4, 1928, p. 2.

One of the participants at the October 1926 Plenum of the Leningrad Guberniia Party Committee remarked: "Simply drop into a private store to buy something, and then into one of our cooperatives, and what a difference you will notice. Without stretching the point at all, it may be said that the salesman in a private store is equivalent in courtesy, initiative, and sales know-how to two of our cooperative clerks, perhaps even three." V. A. Arkhipov and L. F. Morozov, *Bor'ba protiv kapitalisticheskikh elementov v promyshlennosti i torgovle. 20-e—nachalo 30-kh godov* (Moscow, 1978), p. 186.

24. *TPG*, 1923, No. 262 (November 20), pp. 1–2; 1924, No. 99 (May 4), p. 3; 1928, No. 266 (November 16), p. 6; 1928, No. 267 (November 17), p. 4; 1929, No. 70 (March 27), p. 6; *Torgovye izvestiia*, 1925, No. 34 (July 9), p. 6; *Tverskoi krai* (Tver'), 1925, No. 2, p. 57; Borders, *Village Life*, p. 95; *Severo-Kavkazskii krai* (Rostov-on-the-Don), 1925, No. 4–5, p. 101; *Narodnoe khoziaistvo Srednei Azii* (Tashkent), 1927, No. 6–7, p. 103; and *Iugo-Vostok* (Rostov-on-the-Don), 1923, No. 4, p. 42.

25. Trifonov, *Klassy*, 2:253. See also I. Ia. Trifonov, *Likvidatsiia ekspluatatorskikh klassov v SSSR* (Moscow, 1975), p. 394; Morozov, *Reshaiushchii etap*, p. 100; Arkhipov and Morozov, *Bor'ba*, pp. 229–230; Selunskaia, *Izmeneniia sotsial'noi struktury*, pp. 123–124, 131; and I. A. Gladkov, ed., *Sovetskoe narodnoe khoziaistvo v 1921–1925 gg.* (Moscow, 1960), p. 459.

26. For reports from various cities and regions on the success of some state and co-operative stores, see *TPG*, 1923, No. 156 (July 14), p. 5; 1923, No. 203 (September 9), p. 5; 1924, No. 103 (May 9), p. 4; 1924, No. 131 (June 12), p. 4; 1924, No. 135 (June 18), p. 3; 1924, No. 170 (July 29), p. 4; 1924, No. 176 (August 5), p. 2; 1927, No. 78 (April 7), p. 2; *Iugo-Vostok* (Rostov-on-the-Don), 1924, No. 5, p. 112; and *Khoziaistvo Sev.-Zap. kraia* (Leningrad), 1924, No. 7, p. 51.

27. Mao Tse-Tung, *Selected Works*, 5 vols. (New York, 1954–62), 5:421. The term *national bourgeoisie*, recalling the party's united-front strategy during its years at Yenan, came to mean in practice those private entrepreneurs not linked to Chiang Kai-shek or foreign companies and those not overtly hostile to the Communists for other reasons. Thus the "national bourgeoisie" included most of China's medium-scale and petty "capitalists."

As early as 1945, Mao wrote in "On Coalition Government": "The task of our New Democratic system is . . . to promote the free development of a private capitalist economy that benefits instead of controlling the people's livelihood, and to protect all honestly acquired private property." Quoted in T. J. Hughes and D. E. T. Luard, *The Economic Development of Communist China 1949–1960* (London, 1961), p. 89. In June 1950 Mao told the Party Central Committee: "We should introduce suitable readjustments in industry and commerce and in taxation to improve our relations with the national bourgeoisie rather than aggravate these relations. . . . The national bourgeoisie will eventually cease to exist, but at this stage we should rally them around us and not push them away. We should struggle against them on the one hand and unite with them on the other." Mao Tse-tung, *Selected Works of Mao Tsetung*, 1st ed. (Peking, 1961– ), 5:34–35.

28. In the first years after 1949 the Chinese Communist party not only left most private entrepreneurs unmolested but even encouraged them to expand their businesses. As a result, the private sector played a major role in the Chinese economy. In 1950, for example, private merchants conducted 85 percent of China's retail trade and three quarters of its wholesale trade. During this year private factories accounted for well over a third of total industrial output, excluding handicrafts. If artisan production were included in the calculations, the private share of industrial output would be considerably higher, since virtually all handicraftsmen remained outside cooperatives until the middle of the decade. Jan S. Prybyla, *The Chinese Economy: Problems and Policies* (Columbia, S.C., 1978), p. 168; Alexander Eckstein, *China's Economic Revolution* (Cambridge, 1977), pp. 74, 76; and Maurice Meisner, *Mao's China: A History of the People's Republic* (New York, 1977), pp. 92–93.

Just as in the Soviet Union during NEP, the Chinese Communists labeled their mixed economy "state capitalism," a system in which the state hoped to channel and limit private initiative. For roughly two years the state relied mainly on wage and price ceilings and its role as supplier of raw materials and purchaser of finished products to control the activities of private entrepreneurs. Then, unexpectedly, at the end of 1951 the party launched the "Five Antis" campaign against bribery, tax evasion, theft of state property, fraud, and theft of state economic secrets. This movement (which reached peak intensity in mid-1952) was directed mainly at the "bourgeoisie" and resulted in the investigation of over 450,000 enterprises by early 1953. Employees were called on to denounce employers for the abuses listed above, and mass meetings around the country pilloried the "capitalist" class. Although some businesses were nationalized outright and their owners imprisoned (reports of suicides also reached the West), most of the pressure on the private sector took the form of aggressive tax collecting, heavy fines, and similar financial measures. This pressure forced many private enterprises to reorganize as "joint state-private" undertakings, putting them under de facto state control. Prybyla, *Chinese Economy*, p. 80; Hughes and Luard, *Economic Development*, pp. 90–91; and Meisner, *Mao's China*, p. 96.

By the summer of 1956 virtually all private businesses of any consequence had been reconstituted as "joint state-private" operations, and shortly thereafter most artisans and petty traders were drawn "voluntarily" into cooperatives. Hughes and Luard, *Economic Development*, pp. 95, 97–98; Meisner, *Mao's China*, p. 94; and William G. Rosenberg and Marilyn B. Young, *Transforming Russia and China: Revolutionary Struggle in the Twentieth Century* (New York–Oxford, 1982), p. 233. In 1952–53 former owners (who often stayed on as managers) of the newly transformed "state-private" firms received one quarter of the enterprises' profits. After 1956 this method of compensation was replaced by a fixed annual dividend of 5 percent (later reduced to 3.5 percent) on what the government calculated the former owner's capital investment to have been. These payments, though permitting a comparatively comfortable standard of living in the cities, would not be continued for one's heirs and, in any case, were discontinued during the Cultural Revolution in the latter part of the 1960s. Hughes and Luard, *Economic Development*, pp. 94–95; Eckstein, *China's Economic Revolution*, p. 76; Meisner, *Mao's China*, pp. 93–94; and Prybyla, *Chinese Economy*, p. 81.

29. *New York Times*, September 15, 1984; August 4, 1985.

30. *New Republic*, October 21, 1981, p. 14. Of course there are still "second economies," including black markets, in the Eastern European countries (not to mention the West). *New York Times*, November 2, 1979.

31. *New York Times*, November 2, 1979. "Some old-line Hungarian communists worry that the economic reforms have created a new bourgeoisie." But the concerns of such party members are not determining Hungarian domestic policy at present. *Newsweek*, November 9, 1981, p. 55.

32. Morozov, *Reshaiushchii etap*, p. 81.

33. *Moscow News*, 1989, No. 41, p. 7.

34. Ibid., 1989, No. 39, p. 5.

35. Ibid., 1989, No. 33, p. 7.

# Select Bibliography

This bibliography includes only those works cited in the footnotes.

OFFICIAL PROCEEDINGS, LAWS,
WORKS OF PARTY LEADERS

Bukharin, N. I. *Put' k sotsializmu i raboche-krest'ianskii soiuz.* 2d ed. Moscow-Leningrad, 1925.

———. *Put' k sotsializmu v Rossii. Izbrannye proizvedeniia N. I. Bukharina.* Edited by Sidney Heitman. New York, 1967.

———. *Tekushchii moment i osnovy nashei politiki.* Moscow, 1925.

*The Challenge of the Left Opposition (1926–27).* Edited by Naomi Allen and George Saunders. New York, 1980.

*XIV s"ezd vsesoiuznoi kommunisticheskoi partii(b). 18–31 dekabria 1925 g.: stenograficheskii otchet.* Moscow, 1926.

*Desiatyi s"ezd RKP(b). Mart 1921 goda: stenograficheskii otchet.* Moscow, 1963.

*Direktivy KPSS i sovetskogo pravitel'stva po khoziaistvennym voprosam. 1917–1957 gody.* 4 vols. Moscow, 1957–58.

Dzerzhinskii, F. E. *Izbrannye stat'i i rechi.* Moscow, 1947.

*Istoriia sovetskoi konstitutsii (v dokumentakh) 1917–1956.* Moscow, 1957.

*KPSS v rezoliutsiiakh i resheniiakh s"ezdov, konferentsii i plenumov TsK.* 8th ed. Moscow, 1970–.

Lenin, V. I. *Polnoe sobranie sochinenii.* 5th ed. 55 vols. Moscow, 1958–65.

Mao Tse-tung. *Selected Works.* 5 vols. New York, 1954–62.

———. *Selected Works of Mao Tsetung.* 1st ed. Peking, 1961–.

*The Marx-Engels Reader.* Edited by Robert C. Tucker. New York, 1972.

*Piatnadtsatyi s"ezd VKP(b). Dekabr' 1927 goda: stenograficheskii otchet.* 2 vols. Moscow, 1961.

*Resheniia partii i pravitel'stva po khoziaistvennym voprosam.* Moscow, 1967–.

*S"ezdy sovetov soiuza SSR, soiuznykh i avtonomnykh sovetskikh sotsialisti-cheskikh respublik. Sbornik dokumentov v semi tomakh, 1917–1937 g.g.* 7 vols. Moscow, 1959–65.

*Shestnadtsataia konferentsiia VKP(b). Aprel' 1929 goda: stenograficheskii otchet.* Moscow, 1962.

*XVI s"ezd vsesoiuznoi kommunisticheskoi partii(b): stenograficheskii otchet.* Moscow-Leningrad, 1931.

*Sobranie uzakonenii i rasporiazhenii. 1917–1949.* Moscow, 1920–50.

*Sobranie zakonov i rasporiazhenii raboche-krest'ianskogo pravitel'stva SSSR. 1924–1949.* Moscow, 1925–50.

Stalin, I. V. *Sochineniia.* 13 vols. Moscow, 1946–52.

*Zakony o chastnoi promyshlennosti.* Compiled by A. E. Vorms and S. V. Mints. Moscow, 1924.

*Zakony o chastnom kapitale. Sbornik zakonov, instruktsii, prikazov i raz"ias-nenii.* Compiled by B. S. Mal'tsman and B. E. Ratner. Moscow, 1928.

PERIODICALS PUBLISHED DURING THE 1920s
(published in Moscow unless otherwise indicated)

Soviet newspapers and journals of the 1920s contain hundreds of articles and reports on the Nepmen that were perhaps the single most important source of information for this study. Although the titles of those periodicals that contributed material have been listed, no attempt has been made to specify articles individually.

*Biulleten' tverskogo okruzhnogo ispolnitel'nogo komiteta* (Tver'), 1929–30
*Bol'shevik,* 1924–52.
*Dela i dni* (Petrograd), 1920–22
*Ekonomicheskaia zhizn',* 1918–37
*Ekonomicheskii vestnik Armenii* (Erevan), 1923–29
*Ekonomicheskii vestnik Zakavkaz'ia* (Tiflis), 1924–28
*Ekonomicheskoe obozrenie,* 1923–30
*Ekonomichekoe stroitel'stvo,* 1922–30
*Finansovye problemy planovogo khoziaistva,* 1930
*Finansy i narodnoe khoziaistvo,* 1926–30
*Finansy i promyshlennost'* (Petrograd), 1922–23
*Illiustrirovannaia Rossiia* (Paris), 1924–39
*Iugo-Vostok* (Rostov-on-the-Don), 1922–24
*Izvestiia,* 1917–
*Khoziaistvo i upravlenie,* 1925–27
*Khoziaistvo Sev.-Zap. kraia* (Leningrad), 1924–27
*Khoziaistvo Urala* (Sverdlovsk), 1925–35
*Kooperativnoe stroitel'stvo* (Leningrad), 1926–29
*Krasnaia nov',* 1921–42
*Krokodil,* 1922–
*Mesiachnye obzory narodnogo khoziaistva,* 1922
*Mestnoe khoziaistvo* (Kiev), 1923–26

*Mestnoe khoziaistvo Ekaterinoslavshchiny* (Ekaterinoslav), 1924
*Narodnoe khoziaistvo Srednei Azii* (Tashkent), 1924–30
*Nash krai* (Astrakhan'), 1922–28
*Nashe khoziaistvo* (Riazan'), 1923–26
*Nashe khoziaistvo* (Vladimir), 1921–30
*Pechat' i revoliutsiia*, 1921–30
*Planovoe khoziaistvo*, 1923–
*Pravda*, 1917–
*Promyshlennost' i torgovlia* (Leningrad), 1922–26
*Promyshlennost' Ukrainy* (Khar'kov), 1924
*Severo-Kavkazskii krai* (Rostov-on-the-Don), 1924–33
*Sotsialisticheskii vestnik* (Berlin), 1921–65
*Sovetskaia torgovlia*, 1926–31
*Torgovaia gazeta*, 1922
*Torgovlia, promyshlennost' i finansy* (Leningrad), 1925
*Torgovo-promyshlennaia gazeta*, 1922–29
*Torgovo-promyshlennyi vestnik* (Petrograd), 1923–24
*Torgovye izvestiia*, 1925–26
*Torgovyi biulleten'*, 1921–22
*Trud i khoziaistvo* (Kazan'), 1921–
*Trudy tsentral'nogo statisticheskogo upravleniia*, 1920–27
*Tverskoi krai* (Tver'), 1925–29
*Vestnik kommunisticheskoi akademii*, 1922–35
*Vestnik statistiki*, 1919–29, 1949–
*Viatsko-Vetluzhskii krai* (Viatka), 1925–28
*Voprosy torgovli*, 1927–30

OTHER WORKS

Arkhipov, V. A., and L. F. Morozov. *Bor'ba protiv kapitalisticheskikh elementov v promyshlennosti i torgovle. 20-e—nachalo 30-kh godov.* Moscow, 1978.
Arnold, Arthur Z. *Banks, Credit, and Money in Soviet Russia.* New York, 1937.
Ashmead-Bartlett, E. *The Riddle of Russia.* London, 1929.
Balabanoff, Angelica. *My Life as a Rebel.* New York, 1938.
Barmine, Alexandre. *One Who Survived: The Life Story of a Russian Under the Soviets.* New York, 1945.
Baron, Salo W. *The Russian Jew Under Tsars and Soviets.* New York, 1964.
Belkin, G. *Rabochii vopros v chastnoi promyshlennosti.* Moscow, 1926.
Béraud, Henri. *The Truth About Moscow.* London, 1926.
Berkman, Alexander. *The Bolshevik Myth (Diary 1920–1922).* New York, 1925.
Bialyi, I. A., and A. I. Litvin. *Chastnyi kapital v g. Irkutske.* Irkutsk, 1929.
Borders, Karl. *Village Life Under the Soviets.* New York, 1927.
Borisov, K. *75 dnei v SSSR. Vpechatleniia.* Berlin, 1924.
Burrell, George A. *An American Engineer Looks at Russia.* Boston, 1932.
Carr, E. H. *The Bolshevik Revolution.* 3 vols. London, 1950–53; reprint, Harmondsworth, 1973.

Carr, E. H., and R. W. Davies. *Foundations of a Planned Economy, 1926–1929.* 2 vols. London, 1969.

Cash, Anthony. *The Russian Revolution.* London, 1967.

Chamberlin, William Henry. *Soviet Russia: A Living Record and a History.* Boston, 1931.

Cohen, Stephen S. *Bukharin and the Bolshevik Revolution: A Political Biography 1888–1938.* New York, 1973; reprint, 1975.

Dan, F. I. *Dva goda skitanii.* Berlin, 1922.

Day, Richard B. *Leon Trotsky and the Politics of Economic Isolation.* Cambridge, 1973.

Deutscher, Isaac. *Stalin: A Political Biography.* 2d ed. London, 1966; reprint, New York, 1969.

D'iachenko, V. P. *Istoriia finansov SSSR (1917–1950 gg.).* Moscow, 1978.

Dikhtiar, G. A. *Sovetskaia torgovlia v period postroeniia sotsializma.* Moscow, 1961.

Dmitrenko, V. P. *Torgovaia politika sovetskogo gosudarstva posle perekhoda k NEPu 1921–1924 gg.* Moscow, 1971.

Dobb, Maurice. *Soviet Economic Development Since 1917.* New York–London, 1966.

Dos Passos, John. *In All Countries.* New York, 1934.

Dreiser, Theodore. *Dreiser Looks at Russia.* New York, 1928.

Drobizhev, V. "Likvidatsiia ekspluatatorskikh klassov v SSSR." *Vsesoiuznoe obshchestvo po rasprostraneniiu politicheskikh i nauchnykh znanii.* Ser. 1, 1966, No. 6.

Duranty, Walter. *Duranty Reports Russia.* New York, 1934.

———. *I Write as I Please.* New York, 1935.

Eaton, Richard. *Under the Red Flag.* New York, 1924.

Eckstein, Alexander. *China's Economic Revolution.* Cambridge, 1977.

Edelhertz, Bernard. *The Russian Paradox: A First-Hand Study of Life Under the Soviets.* New York, 1930.

Ehrenburg, Ilya. *First Years of Revolution, 1918–21.* London, 1962.

———. *Memoirs: 1921–1941.* New York, 1966.

*Ekonomicheskaia zhizn' SSSR. Khronika sobytii i faktov 1917–1965.* 2 vols. Moscow, 1967.

Erlich, Alexander. *The Soviet Industrialization Debate, 1924–1928.* Cambridge, Mass., 1960.

Fabrichnyi, Andrei. *Chastnyi kapital na poroge piatiletki.* Moscow, 1930.

Farbman, Michael S. *Bolshevism in Retreat.* London, 1923.

Farson, Negley. *Black Bread and Red Coffins.* New York, 1930.

Fediukin, S. A. *Bor'ba s burzhuaznoi ideologiei v usloviiakh perekhoda k nepu.* Moscow, 1977.

Feiler, Arthur. *The Russian Experiment.* New York, 1930.

Feshbach, Murray. "The Soviet Union: Population Trends and Dilemmas." *Population Bulletin* 37 (August 1982): 1–44.

*Finansovaia politika sovetskoi vlasti za 10 let. Sbornik statei.* Moscow, 1928.

Fischer, Markoosha. *My Lives in Russia.* New York, 1944.

Fitzpatrick, Sheila. *The Commissariat of Enlightenment: Soviet Organization of Education and the Arts Under Lunacharsky, October 1917–1921.* Cambridge, 1970.

*40 let sovetskoi torgovli.* Moscow, 1957.

Frank, Waldo. *Dawn in Russia: The Record of a Journey.* New York, 1932.

Fridman, S. L. *Chastnyi kapital na denezhnom rynke.* Moscow, 1925.

Friel, Patrick George. "Theater and Revolution: The Struggle for Theatrical Autonomy in Soviet Russia (1917–1920)." Ph.D. diss., University of North Carolina at Chapel Hill, 1977.

Fry, A. Ruth. *Three Visits to Russia 1922–25.* London, 1942.

Gibbs, Philip. *Since Then.* London, 1930.

Ginzburg, A. M., ed. *Chastnyi kapital v narodnom khoziaistve SSSR. Materialy kommissii VSNKh SSSR.* Moscow-Leningrad, 1927.

Gitelman, Zvi Y. *Jewish Nationality and Soviet Politics: The Jewish Sections of the CPSU, 1917–1930.* Princeton, 1972.

Gladkov, I. A., ed. *Sovetskoe narodnoe khoziaistvo v 1921–1925 gg.* Moscow, 1960.

Gol'bert, Ia. M., ed. *Novaia torgovaia praktika. (K kharakteristike vnutrennei torgovli v pervoi polovine 1924–25 g.).* Moscow, 1925.

Golder, Frank Alfred, and Lincoln Hutchinson. *On the Trail of the Russian Famine.* Stanford, 1927.

Goldman, Emma. *My Further Disillusionment in Russia.* Garden City, N.Y., 1924.

Grady, Eve Garrette. *Seeing Red: Behind the Scenes in Russia Today.* New York, 1931.

Greenwall, H. J. *Mirrors of Moscow.* London, 1929.

Grinval'd, Ia., I. Khankin, and I. Chilim. *Klass protiv klassa. Ekonomicheskaia kontrrevoliutsiia v Astrakhani.* Saratov, 1930.

Grossman, Gregory. "The 'Second Economy' of the USSR." *Problems of Communism,* September-October 1977, pp. 25–40.

Hammer, Armand. *The Quest of the Romanoff Treasure.* New York, 1932.

Hiebert, P. C., and Orie O. Miller. *Feeding the Hungry: Russian Famine 1919–1925.* Scottdale, Pa., 1929.

Hindus, Maurice. *Broken Earth.* New York, 1926.

———. *Humanity Uprooted.* New York, 1929.

———. *Red Bread.* New York, 1931.

Hoover, Calvin B. *The Economic Life of Soviet Russia.* New York, 1931.

———. "The Fate of the New Economic Policy of the Soviet Union." *Economic Journal* 40 (June 1930): 184–193.

Hughes, T. J., and D. E. T. Luard. *The Economic Development of Communist China 1949–1960.* London, 1961.

Hullinger, Edwin Ware. *The Reforging of Russia.* New York, 1925.

Huxley, Julian. *A Scientist Among the Soviets.* New York, 1932.

Ivanovskii, V. V. *Chastnyi torgovyi kapital na rynke Saratovskoi gubernii.* Saratov, 1927.

Johnson, John. *Russia in the Grip of Bolshevism.* New York, 1931.

Kaktyn', A. *O podkhode k chastnomu torgovomu kapitalu.* Moscow, 1924.

Karlgren, Anton. *Bolshevist Russia.* London, 1927.

Kataev, Valentin. *Embezzlers*. Ann Arbor, 1975.

Keynes, John Maynard. *A Short View of Russia*. London, 1925.

Kochan, Lionel, ed. *The Jews in Soviet Russia Since 1917*. 3d ed. Oxford, 1978.

Kolesnikov, L. *Litso klassovogo vraga*. Moscow-Leningrad, 1928.

Kondurushkin, Iu. S. *Chastnyi kapital pered sovetskim sudom*. Moscow-Leningrad, 1927.

Kopalkin, V. M. *Chastnaia promyshlennost' SSSR*. Moscow-Leningrad, 1927.

Kravchenko, Victor. *I Chose Freedom*. New York, 1946.

Kritsman, L. N. *Tri goda novoi ekonomicheskoi politiki*. Moscow, 1924.

Kron, Ts. M. *Chastnaia torgovlia v SSSR*. Moscow, 1926.

Kuchurin, S. F. *Zheleznodorozhnye gruzovye tarify*. Moscow, 1950.

Larin, Iu. *Chastnyi kapital v SSSR*. Moscow-Leningrad, 1927.

Laverychev, V. Ia. *Krupnaia burzhuaziia v poreformennoi Rossii (1861–1900 gg.)*. Moscow, 1974.

Lavrenyov, Boris. "The Heavenly Cap." In *The Fatal Eggs and Other Soviet Satire*, pp. 151–190. New York, 1965; reprint, 1968.

Lewin, Moshe. *Political Undercurrents in Soviet Economic Debates*. Princeton, 1974.

———. *Russian Peasants and Soviet Power: A Study of Collectivization*. London, 1968; reprint, New York, 1975.

Leyda, Jay. *Kino: A History of the Russian and Soviet Film*. London, 1960.

Lezhava, A. M. *Vnutrenniaia torgovlia 1923 g*. Moscow, 1924.

Lidin, Vladimir. *The Price of Life*. Westport, Conn., 1973.

Lockhart, J. G. *Babel Visited: A Churchman in Soviet Russia*. Milwaukee, 1933.

Lyons, Eugene. *Assignment in Utopia*. New York, 1937.

———. *Moscow Carrousel*. New York, 1935.

Mackenzie, F. A. *Russia Before Dawn*. London, 1923.

Marienhoff, Anatoly. *Cynics*. Westport, Conn., 1973.

*Materialy po istorii SSSR. VII. Dokumenty po istorii sovetskogo obshchestva*. Moscow, 1959.

McCormick, Anne O'Hare. *The Hammer and the Scythe*. New York, 1928.

Meisner, Maurice. *Mao's China: A History of the People's Republic*. New York, 1977.

Mingulin, I. *Puti razvitiia chastnogo kapitala*. Moscow-Leningrad, 1927.

Mishanin, D. I. "Arenda gosudarstvennykh predpriiatii chastnymi predprinimateliami, kak odna iz form gosudarstvennogo kapitalizma v ekonomike perekhodnogo perioda ot kapitalizma k sotsializmu v SSSR." In E. A. Messerle and D. I. Mishanin, *Metodicheskoe posobie po politekonomii*, pp. 15–69. Alma-Ata, 1961.

Monkhouse, Allan. *Moscow, 1911–1933*. Boston, 1934.

Morozov, L. F. *Reshaiushchii etap bor'by s nepmanskoi burzhuaziei (1926–1929)*. Moscow, 1960.

Moskovskii, A. S. "Melkaia i kustarno-remeslennaia promyshlennost' Sibiri v kontse vosstanovitel'nogo perioda." In *Bakhrushinskie chteniia*. Novosibirsk, 1974.

Muldavin, Albert. *The Red Fog Lifts*. New York, 1931.

*Na novykh putiakh. Itogi novoi ekonomicheskoi politiki 1921–1922 g.g.* Moscow, 1923.

Nazarov, A. I. *Oktiabr' i kniga.* Moscow, 1968.

Newman, E. M. *Seeing Russia.* New York, 1928.

Nove, Alec. *An Economic History of the U.S.S.R.* London, 1969; reprint, Harmondsworth, 1972.

*Obshchestvennoe dvizhenie v Rossii v nachale XX-go veka.* Edited by L. Martov, P. Maslov, and A. Potresov. 4. vols. St. Petersburg, 1909–14.

Paduchev, G. P. *Chastnyi torgovets pri novoi ekonomicheskoi politike (po dannym biudzhetnogo obsledovaniia).* Voronezh, 1926.

Pavlov, F. S. "Oktiabr'skaia revoliutsiia i istoricheskii opyt KPSS v likvidatsii srednei i melkoi promyshlennoi i torgovoi burzhuazii v perekhodnyi period k sotsializmu." In *Velikaia oktiabr'skaia sotsialisticheskaia revoliutsiia i stroitel'stvo kommunizma.* Dnepropetrovsk, 1967.

Prybyla, Jan S. *The Chinese Economy: Problems and Policies.* Columbia, S.C., 1978.

Remington, Thomas F. "Democracy and Development in Bolshevik Socialism, 1917–1921." Ph.D. diss., Yale University, 1978.

Reswick, William. *I Dreamt Revolution.* Chicago, 1952.

Riauzov, N. *Vytesnenie chastnogo posrednika iz tovarooborota.* Moscow, 1930.

Roberts, Paul C. "'War Communism': A Re-examination," *Slavic Review* 29 (June 1970): 238–261.

Rosenberg, William G., and Marilyn B. Young. *Transforming Russia and China: Revolutionary Struggle in the Twentieth Century.* New York–Oxford, 1982.

Rukeyser, Walter Arnold. *Working for the Soviets: An American Engineer in Russia.* New York, 1932.

Scheffer, Paul. *Seven Years in Soviet Russia.* New York, 1932.

Scott, John. *Behind the Urals: An American Worker in Russia's City of Steel.* Bloomington, 1973.

Seibert, Theodor. *Red Russia.* London, 1932.

Selunskaia, V. M., ed. *Izmeneniia sotsial'noi struktury sovetskogo obshchestva. Oktiabr' 1917–1920.* Moscow, 1976.

———. *Izmeneniia sotsial'noi struktury sovetskogo obshchestva. 1921-seredina 30-kh godov.* Moscow, 1979.

Serge, Victor. *Memoirs of a Revolutionary 1901–1941.* London, 1967; reprint, 1975.

Shamurin, E. I. *Sovetskaia kniga za 15 let v tsifrakh.* Moscow, 1933.

Shapiro, D. *Kustarnaia promyshlennost' i narodnoe khoziaistvo SSSR.* Moscow-Leningrad, 1928.

Simis, Konstantin M. *USSR: The Corrupt Society.* New York, 1982.

Singleton, Seth. "The Tambov Revolt (1920–1921)." *Slavic Review* 25 (September 1966): 495–512.

Solzhenitsyn, Aleksandr I. *The Gulag Archipelago 1918–1956: An Experiment in Literary Investigation.* 3 vols. New York, 1974–78.

Sorokin, Pitirim A. *Hunger as a Factor in Human Affairs.* Gainesville, Fla., 1975.

———. *Leaves from a Russian Diary—and Thirty Years After.* Boston, 1950.

Spektator [Miron Isaakovich Nachimson]. *Russkii "Termidor."* Kharbin, 1927.

Spulber, Nicholas, ed. *Foundations of Soviet Strategy for Economic Growth: Selected Soviet Essays, 1924–1930.* Bloomington, 1964.

————. *Soviet Strategy for Economic Growth.* Bloomington, 1964.

Strong, Anna Louise. *The First Time in History.* New York, 1924.

Sutton, Anthony C. *Western Technology and Soviet Economic Development 1917 to 1930.* Stanford, 1968.

Tchernavin, Vladimir V. *I Speak for the Silent.* Boston–New York, 1935.

Thompson, Dorothy. *The New Russia.* New York, 1928.

Trifonov, I. Ia. *Klassy i klassovaia bor'ba v SSSR v nachale nepa.* Vol. 2, *Podgotovka ekonomicheskogo nastupleniia na novuiu burzhuaziiu.* Leningrad, 1969.

————. *Likvidatsiia ekspluatatorskikh klassov v SSSR.* Moscow, 1975.

————. *Ocherki istorii klassovoi bor'by v SSSR v gody NEPa (1921–1937).* Moscow, 1960.

Tsybul'skii, V. A. "Tovaroobmen mezhdu gorodom i derevnei v pervye mesiatsy nepa." *Istoriia SSSR,* 1968, No. 4, pp. 31–41.

Tucker, Robert C. *Stalin as Revolutionary, 1879–1929.* New York, 1974.

Utley, Freda. *The Dream We Lost.* New York, 1940.

Valentinov, N. *Doktrina pravogo kommunizma, 1924–1926 gody v istorii sovetskogo gosudarstva.* Munich, 1962.

Vasil'kov. *Chastnyi kapital v khoziaistve orlovskoi gubernii. (Issledovatel'skaia rabota Gubplana pod rukovodstvom i redaktsiei Vasil'kova).* Orel, 1928.

Viollis, Andrée. *A Girl in Soviet Russia.* New York, 1929.

*Vnutrenniaia torgovlia soiuza SSR za X let.* Moscow, 1928.

White, William C. *These Russians.* New York, 1931.

Wicksteed, Alexander. *Life Under the Soviets.* London, 1928.

Williams, Albert Rhys. *The Russian Land.* New York, 1927.

Winter, Ella. *Red Virtue: Human Relationships in the New Russia.* New York, 1933.

Zagorskii, S. O. *K sotsializmu ili k kapitalizmu?* Paris, 1927.

Zaleski, Eugène. *Planning for Economic Growth in the Soviet Union, 1918–1932.* Chapel Hill, 1971.

Zalkind, A., ed. *Chastnaia torgovlia Soiuza SSR.* Moscow, 1927.

Zelitch, Judah. *Soviet Administration of Criminal Law.* Philadelphia, 1931.

Zhirmunskii, M. M. *Chastnyi kapital v tovarooborote.* Moscow, 1924.

————. *Chastnyi torgovyi kapital v narodnom khoziaistve SSSR.* Moscow, 1927.

Zlobin, A. *Gosudarstvennyi, kooperativnyi i chastnyi kapital v tovarooborote sibirskogo kraia.* Novosibirsk, 1927.

Zolotarev, A. *Regulirovanie tovarooborota.* Khar'kov, 1926.

# Index

|            |                            |
|-----------:|----------------------------|
| Designer:  | Betty Gee                  |
| Compositor:| G & S Typesetters, Inc.    |
| Text:      | 10/13 Sabon                |
| Display:   | Sabon                      |
| Printer:   | Maple-Vail Book Mfg. Group |
| Binder:    | Maple-Vail Book Mfg. Group |